Who's the Boss?

Who's the Boss?

How to Regain and Maintain Your Parental Authority When Kids Rule the Roost

ALETA KOMAN, M.ED., with EDWARD MYERS

A PERIGEE BOOK

A Perigee Book
Published by The Berkley Publishing Group
A division of Penguin Putnam Inc.
375 Hudson Street
New York, New York 10014

First edition: September 2002

Visit our website at www.penguinputnam.com

Library of Congress Cataloging-in-Publication Data

Koman, Aleta.
    Who's the boss : how to regain and maintain your parental authority when kids rule
the roost / Aleta Koman with Edward Myers.
        p.   cm.
    Includes index.
    ISBN 0-399-52812-1
    1. Parent and child.   2. Parenting.   3. Authority.   I. Myers, Edward, 1950–
II. Title.

HQ755.85 .K65   2002
649'.1—dc21

                                                                                2002025129

Printed in the United States of America

10   9   8   7   6   5   4   3   2   1

To my beloved husband, Woody,
and our children, Jason, Adam, and Jessica,
with much love always!

A.K.

In memory of my parents,
Francis M. Myers and Estela M. Myers,
great friends and guiding lights.

E.M.

CONTENTS

Acknowledgments   ix

A Note Regarding Usage   xi

Introduction
   Timid Parents, Unruly Kids   1

Chapter 1
   The Growing Dilemma of Parental Authority   9

Chapter 2
   How Parenting Style Influences Authority   24

Chapter 3
   Discipline and Conflicts   48

Chapter 4
   The Influences of Temperament and Gender   78

Chapter 5
   The Burdens and Blessings of the Past   96

Chapter 6
   Values and Family Communication   110

Chapter 7
The Superparent Syndrome 136

Chapter 8
The Importance of Civility 152

Chapter 9
Solving the Latchkey Dilemma 169

Chapter 10
Coping with the Side Effects of Divorce 181

Chapter 11
Dealing with Mass Media 202

Conclusion
The Compass of Parental Authority 217

Appendix A
Child Development and Age-Appropriate Behavior 225

Appendix B
Resource Guide 239

Notes 265

Index 269

ACKNOWLEDGMENTS

Unfortunately, time and space limit my ability to thank all the wonderful people who have contributed so much time, energy, and love to my growth and development. However, I'd like to acknowledge a few very special people who have contributed to the creation of this book.

I am especially grateful to my co-author and friend, Ed Myers, who has put an enormous amount of time, energy, and literary expertise into this project. Ed carried much of the ball this past year, during which we were writing *Who's the Boss?*, as I was pregnant with my second child, Jessica. Ed's enthusiasm and support were the driving force during the process of creating and writing this book. Without his dedication and hard work, this book wouldn't have been possible. This is our third completed book together; as always, it was a pure delight to work with him.

For the second time around we've been fortunate to benefit from the skilled guidance of our editor, Sheila Curry Oakes. Sheila's belief in us and in this project have helped to make the writing process smooth and joyful. Thank you, Sheila, for being there from start to finish with your insights and clarity while also respecting our need to create a text that's authentically ours.

I am also indebted and grateful to my literary agent and friend, Faith Hamlin. Without Faith's guidance and support from the proposal stage onward, this book wouldn't have been published. Faith's dedication, support, and nurturance of my career as a writer and on-air expert over the past eight years has surpassed what most agents are willing to do. I'll be forever grateful.

Words can't express the gratitude I feel for my parents and my family for all they've given me over the years. They are people I love and admire more deeply with each passing year.

My husband, Woody, has been a constant source of love, peace, and contentment. I thank him for all his support and for our wonderful life together. He has given me a secure base camp that has enabled me to climb many mountains. Finally, I want to thank our three children—Jason, Adam, and Jessica—who are a constant source of great joy and delight.

I thank all of these people, as well as all the children and families that I've been so fortunate to work with over the years. Thanks for sharing your insights, and thanks also for reminding me that being in a family is a complex, joyful, and rich journey. Your enthusiasm and courage to take on and master the challenges of family life have been a constant inspiration.

A NOTE REGARDING USAGE

I am well aware that the English language is predisposed toward several kinds of linguistic gender bias, including use of the generic "he": "Listen to your child without interrupting what he's saying." However, many efforts to remedy this situation have been stylistically awkward or ridiculous (such as "Listen to your child without interrupting what he or she is saying"). As a result, I have opted simply to refer to "the child" as male in some chapters and as female in others.

Introduction

TIMID PARENTS, UNRULY KIDS

What's wrong with this picture?

- A young mother, waiting at an airport check-in gate with her two children, learns from the airline's agent that the flight has been canceled. The agent offers the woman several alternatives: a reservation on a later flight, a reservation with another airline, or an overnight stay at a local hotel. The mother checks with her children, who are about five and three years old, regarding their preferences. "Shall we go see Daddy tonight," she asks them, "or shall we stay at a nice hotel and go home in the morning?" The kids are exhausted and confused; they whine but can't make up their minds. After several minutes of dithering, the mom tells the agent, "I don't know what to do! My kids can't decide!" The agent, growing more and more exasperated with her customer, says, "Ma'am, what I need to know is what *you* want to do."

- On a rainy Saturday morning, a middle-aged father has taken his two school-age daughters and his toddler to the children's room at the local public library. The daughters busy themselves finding books to read. The two-year-old boy is too young to entertain himself, yet the dad ignores him and starts leafing through magazines nearby. Within a few minutes the toddler begins rearranging the furniture, taking books off the shelves, and removing CDs from their boxes. The father observes his son at play but only reluctantly intervenes. Any efforts to restrain the boy's activities trigger almost immediate tantrums. Rather than entertain or distract the child, however, the dad merely gives up. The toddler proceeds to make a mess of the library. When a staff member asks the man to pay attention to the child's mayhem, he grows irate: "Well, for crying out loud—this is the kids' area, isn't it?"

- A couple learns that their fourteen-year-old wants to attend the eighth-grade dance at her middle school. As part of her grandiose vision of this event, she wants to buy a fancy dress, have dinner before the dance at a local gourmet restaurant, and be chauffeured to and from the school in a hired limo. The parents protest; the plan is too extravagant for eighth grade. "This is fancier than what I did when I went my high school prom," the mother notes. "It's just too expensive," the father tells the girl. But she insists. Accusing them of being heartless and cheap, the daughter demands to have what she wants. The parents quickly agree and end up spending almost $800 on their daughter's attire, dinner, and transportation.

- A mother sits with her three school-age boys in a movie theater. The lights haven't dimmed yet; everyone is restless for the feature to begin. The boys, roughly seven, nine, and eleven years old, grow fidgety. Rather than entertain her children or encourage them to entertain themselves, the mom zones out and, filing her fingernails, ignores them altogether. Soon the oldest boy tosses a piece of popcorn at his mother. "Stop that!" she says. He tosses another piece, then another. "Stop that!" she insists after each bombardment, but she makes no other response. Soon the other

boys join the fun, each of them flicking popcorn at the belea-
guered mom. Her only response: "Stop! Stop that! *Stop!*" Even
when other moviegoers are struck by bits of popcorn, the mother
isn't willing to take action and curtail her sons' misbehavior.

Are these snapshots aberrations? Sad, comical misjudgments perpe-
trated by a few weak-kneed parents? I wish that were so. Unfortunately, what I'm describing isn't at all unusual; I witness similar
scenes almost every day. Perhaps you do, too. Look around almost
anywhere these days—at any grocery store, playground, mall, restaurant, or school—and you're likely to see demanding, unruly kids and
overly compliant parents. Perhaps you watch similar scenarios
unfold in your own family.

If so, you're not alone. And despite my dismay at the situation I'm
describing, I don't mean to sound "above it all." I wrestle with issues
of my kids' behavior, too. As a mother, a teacher, and a psychotherapist, however, I'm troubled by what I perceive as a growing crisis in
parent–child interactions and the behaviors that result.

I wrote *Who's the Boss? How to Regain and Maintain Authority
When Kids Rule the Roost* for two reasons.

First, I want to address the general issue of parental authority.
American parents' confusion over issues of authority is, I believe,
creating a country full of insecure, selfish, restless, unruly children.
This trend bodes ill for the nation's well-being; in addition, it contributes to some children being unhappy, frustrated, and frequently
in conflict with the people around them. *Who's the Boss?* explains
this situation and recommends specific ways in which mothers and
fathers can regain their authority and help their children grow
toward self-confidence, self-discipline, and consideration of others.

Second, I want to offer specific ideas and resources that can help
individual parents cope with issues of parental authority. If you're
like most mothers and fathers, you find that parental authority is a
tricky business—not just because children innately and appropriately test the limits and boundaries that their parents set, but also

because contemporary American culture is tending to create tension between parents and kids. Your family life may be fundamentally healthy and happy, but you may be coping with complex issues of parental authority regardless.

Who's the Boss? offers a sequence of practical discussions on many aspects of this subject. I believe that if parents are to regain and maintain their authority, they must thoughtfully address a series of issues that concern their children's best interests. This book offers detailed discussions of these issues.

The crisis in parental authority has come to my attention as a result of three kinds of interactions I have with families: as a parent, as a therapist, and as a teacher.

First of all, I've become concerned about issues of authority over the years because of situations I've observed as a mother. I've come into contact with all kinds of families while raising my son, Jason, who's currently a teenager. My daughter, Jessica, is much younger, so I'm interacting with families of young children as well. In both situations I meet many families I admire, families in which the parents have a calm sense of authority and the kids have a good balance of exuberance and age-appropriate responsibility. However, I also meet other families in which parents and kids alike seem stressed, frantic, self-centered, and mutually resentful. I've thought over the years about what makes the two groups different and what we all might learn from them.

In addition, I work with families in a clinical setting. I have a private clinical practice specializing in individual, marital, and family therapy. In much of my work, issues of parental authority arise either directly or indirectly—directly, when parents seek my help in dealing with behavioral issues; indirectly, when I see parent–child problems arising that the parents may not perceive or be willing to face. Many of these issues and problems concern how parents accept or reject their responsibility to make the decisions and take the consequences for what happens within their family.

Finally, I present parenting workshops and seminars in a variety of nonprofit and corporate settings. Some of these workshops and seminars occur in a small-group environment of just a half-dozen or a dozen participants. Others involve hundreds of attendees in a lecture setting. Regardless of the context, however, parent-participants often raise the same issues in the Q-and-A phase of my presentations. I hear a *lot* of questions about issues of behavior, discipline, and authority. Some parents are aware that their children are out of control, but they don't know how to deal with the situation. Their kids are fundamentally good kids yet often demanding, sassy, uncooperative, restless, and self-centered. Other parents complain about the difficulty of dealing with other families' children—children who pressure or coax their own kids into unpleasant or high-risk behavior. Still other participants are grandparents who worry that their own adult sons and daughters are spoiling their grandchildren. There are also questions about the disruptive, unruly behavior of kids in public. In any case, I often hear people express concerns that essentially focus on issues of parental authority.

While presenting a recent workshop to employees of a Head Start program, for instance, I interacted with a group of five hundred teachers, teachers' aides, and social workers. These are professionals who have devoted their careers to helping children; most are highly trained and experienced. An overwhelming percentage of them stated that weak parental authority is one of the most serious problems they face in their professional settings. The kids in their charge are often rude, restless, and unresponsive to anything other than their own momentary whims. The parents, meanwhile, make heavy demands about having their children's needs met, yet they rebuff or ignore the caregivers' needs for creative parental collaboration.

I found the Head Start staffers' complaints and laments discouraging. Is it possible that this situation is solely the result of Head Start's underresourced client base? I doubt it. I hear similar complaints from teachers, aides, and counselors in settings that range from private daycare centers to high-end public schools to the tiniest private academies.

I see other signs that this issue is widespread and troubling. A recent *Time* magazine cover story asked, "Do Kids Have Too Much Power?" The overall answer: yes. Based on results from a *Time*/CNN poll, this article states that when asked "Are children today more or less spoiled than children 10 or 15 years ago?" 80% of respondents answered "more." Even when asked "Are your own children spoiled or not spoiled?" a significant majority of respondents (fully 68%) answered that their kids are "very/somewhat spoiled." The article sums up its findings about contemporary kids:

> Go to the mall or a concert or a restaurant and you can find them in the wild, the kids who have never been told no, whose sense of power and entitlement leaves onlookers breathless, the sand-kicking, foot-stomping, arm-twisting, wheedling, whining despots whose parents presumably deserve the company of the monsters they, after all, created.

Discussions of similar issues have appeared in *Psychology Today*, including an article entitled "Why Our Kids Are Out of Control." Noting that "We seem to be in the midst of an epidemic" of out-of-control kids, the author, Jacob Azerrad, Ph.D., puts the situation in blunt, troubling terms:

> I have been a child psychologist for 35 years, and each year I see parents dealing with more and more severe problems. Their children are not just ill-mannered, they are whiny, selfish, arrogant, rude, defiant and violent. Most of them are also miserable, as are their parents.

Increasingly, I find similar statements online—both by psychologists and laypersons—in such venues as America Online's Parenting channel and Web sites such as FamilyEducation.com and Parentcenter.com. In short, the issue of parental authority—or lack thereof—is more and more visible on the public stage.

As you read *Who's the Boss?*, keep in mind that this book isn't a systematic program. I believe that every parent who's concerned with the issue of parental authority will find much that's useful here, but some chapters may not address your individual circumstances. I encourage you to pick and choose among the discussions I've included here.

I believe that if you can understand the nature of parental authority and how it influences child development and family life, you can parent your children more effectively and more confidently. My purpose in writing *Who's the Boss?* is to foster that understanding. I wish you well on the great adventure of parenthood!

Chapter 1

THE GROWING DILEMMA
OF PARENTAL AUTHORITY

More and more often, American parents refuse to act like parents. Instead, they're giving in to their kids on too many issues, they're giving up their right and obligation to be in charge, and they're allowing their children to assume that role. A French *au pair* employed in a large U.S. city a few years ago put the situation bluntly: "In France, the parents decide what must happen and the children obey. In America, the children decide and the parents obey."

Relinquishing parental authority can have a variety of results. In some cases, children make unreasonable demands for material goods or special privileges. In others, kids develop a tendency toward inconsiderate, rowdy, or chaotic behavior. In still others, kids make a habit of willful disruptiveness. In most instances, the result isn't malice or juvenile delinquency, but plain old bratty behavior. Many children don't know what's expected of them in different settings or circumstances. Often they lack an ability to regulate their own impulses; they're dependent on outside pressure (from parents, teachers, and other adults) to behave themselves. The result: children act out, annoy others, exhaust everyone around them, or make a nuisance of themselves despite being old enough to know better.

However, *I don't think children are to blame for this situation.* Yes, many American kids are self-indulgent, demanding, impatient, disruptive, and annoying. I'm often dismayed by how unpleasant so many children are these days. Are they intrinsically more obnoxious than kids in the past? No, they have *learned* to be self-indulgent, demanding, impatient, disruptive, and annoying. And they have learned these behaviors because their parents haven't taught them to be flexible, patient, and considerate toward others. In most instances, the misbehavior I witness day after day is simply what children have come to regard as acceptable.

These problems are cropping up so often because American parents are less and less often in charge of their families; instead, kids rule the roost. The result is a dramatic increase in selfish or antisocial behavior among children and between children and the rest of society. Generally speaking, this behavior takes fairly benign but irritating forms, such as unruly kids at shopping malls or increased tension within the family setting. This state of affairs is not healthy for parents or children. In more extreme instances, kids can fall into patterns of behavior that are hostile, purposefully annoying, manipulative, or destructive. Either way, parents need to deal with these situations more thoughtfully and forthrightly. It's fine to allow children some say in family matters—though the degree will vary according to their age and maturity—but parents should make decisions based on what they feel is best for their kids, *not* based on the kids' momentary whims or immature preferences. The truth is that children thrive on developmentally appropriate nurturance and limits, not on receiving *carte blanche* for whatever they happen to want to do or acquire at any given moment. Parents' abdication of responsibility is unfair and potentially destructive both to adults and to children; putting children in a position of premature authority exerts unneeded stress on adults at the same time that it harms kids' emotional and ethical development. To put it bluntly, many parents are refusing to be parents. Instead, they are placing the authority to make decisions about individual and family matters in their children's hands long before the kids are mature enough to assume such authority. This problem cuts across political, socioeconomic, ethnic, and regional lines.

WHY DOES PARENTAL AUTHORITY MATTER?

The issue of parental authority isn't just a social bellwether; I believe that this issue matters not just to society as a whole, but also family by family, parent by parent, child by child.

Children's Well-being

The erosion of parental authority isn't good for children. It may seem beneficial to give kids more freedom and responsibility, and it *is* beneficial if granted on an incremental basis as they grow and mature. But it can be detrimental if granted prematurely or excessively. There's a big difference between granting responsibility and relinquishing authority.

Here are two examples.

Let's say that your ten-year-old daughter is mature enough to walk home from school, let herself into the house, and spend a half-hour alone before the babysitter arrives. Given these circumstances, you can probably grant her the responsibility of looking after herself for a while. If you leave her home unattended all afternoon, however, you're not only risking her physical and emotional safety, you're relinquishing your authority as well.

On the other hand, suppose that your seven-year-old wants to stay up till ten each night. Few children that age can accurately monitor their own fatigue or make responsible decisions about when to go to bed. Yet many parents relent when their children object to an earlier bedtime. It's easy to give up the fight just to stop all the fussing, but it's not in your children's best interests, and giving up easily may undercut your authority. These and other situations highlight the risks of allowing kids too much control.

Aside from the potential for physical hazards (as in the "home alone" example above), there's the question of emotional well-being. Children thrive when provided with age-appropriate limits; a clear sense of what is and isn't acceptable allows them a deeper sense of security than vague or nonexistent limits do. (Clear limits also help them develop better self-control.) Yes, kids will challenge your authority. In many situations they'll resist you, protest your decisions, demand to have their own way, or throw tantrums. Retaining your authority is a long-term, labor-intensive effort. Still, it's crucial that you do so. The bottom line: you're not only in charge, you're in charge for your children's best interests.

Your Own Sanity

If you relinquish your authority, family life will probably suffer. I'm not saying that your children will run amok, swing from the chandeliers, paint the cat green, or burn the house down. In many families where the kids have too much power, day-to-day life proceeds without major calamities. The parents still leave on time for work, the kids go off to school, and everyone gets fed and bathed. However, the stress level is usually higher in these families than it ought to be, and it's often intolerable. The children nag the parents, pressure them, refuse the parents' requests, negotiate endlessly, misbehave, and exhaust everyone around them. In addition to being hard on the kids themselves, this situation is tough on the mom and dad. Letting children call the shots may seem easier in the long run—after all, this strategy prevents short-term conflict—but doing so quickly grows counterproductive. Parents who relinquish their authority are, in my experience, more exhausted, more stressed out, and more demoralized than parents who retain an appropriate level of control.

Society's Benefit

There's another reason why it's crucial for parents to retain their authority: it's important for our whole society. A nation full of impatient, spoiled, excessively empowered kids is not a happy place. Demanding, unruly children make life stressful for each other and for everyone around them. If you feel that my opinion is extreme, ask almost any schoolteacher, camp counselor, sports coach, or merchant what he or she thinks of today's children. Likely as not you'll hear answers such as these:

- "They're good kids but overly indulged."

- "Nobody has taught them how to behave."

- "They have so much but they always want more."

- "They'd grow up just fine if someone told them *no* now and then."

- "I want to like them, but they're so difficult to deal with."

- "They think they're entitled to anything they want."

The upshot: children whose parents have relinquished their authority stress out not only their own moms and dads, but many other people as well.

THE ORIGINS OF A CRISIS

How have we ended up with so many families in which the kids rule the roost?

It's difficult to answer this question. I'm not a sociologist, and I haven't done systematic research to study the issues and identify their sources. From the viewpoints I've mentioned already, however—from my roles as a parent, professor, and therapist—I'd like to offer this anecdotal speculation.

Abdication of Authority

I believe that, first and foremost, many parents are simply refusing to be parents. I'm not sure why. Some social observers chalk up the problem to Baby Boomer narcissism: Boomer dads and moms have been self-indulgent in so many other ways, so why not in regard to parenthood? There may be some truth to this assessment. A remarkable number of parents I encounter—including many bright, well-educated, well-intentioned men and women—put themselves at the heart of their concerns, leaving children and other family members somewhere off-center. Both in my clinical practice and in my private life I see incidents in which moms and dads seem far more focused on their careers, social lives, and gym memberships than on the details of their children's upbringing. The result: many parents don't seem to grasp how urgently and constantly they need to stand up to their own kids. They aren't consistent in what they expect. They are underinvolved in their kids' daily lives. They pass the buck to other authority figures, most often teachers and childcare surrogates, who end up assuming the role that traditionally belongs to parents.

Stress

The notion of family life as a juggling act is now more than a cliché—it's a given. In most two-parent households, both parents work. Single parents head a growing number of families. Making ends meet, dealing with long commute times, and being available 24/7 leaves most moms and dads exhausted. Meanwhile, children have their own rat race to run. School, after-school programs, home-work, sports, and scheduled playdates leave little time for kids to kick back and simply enjoy childhood. As a consequence, all the pressures on parents combine until moms and dads can't resist disengaging. It's not that these parents are indifferent or incompetent; on the contrary, they love their children deeply. But they are often exhausted to the point of emotional paralysis.

Lack of Insights into Child Development

No matter how well intentioned, many parents simply don't understand what children need at different stages of their development. I see this time after time in my clinical practice. Otherwise bright, well-educated moms and dads often lack a basic sense of what's appropriate and what's inappropriate. They don't grasp that children need limits as well as freedom, and they don't know the basic principles of discipline. This is ironic, for many of the parents who relinquish their authority are highly educated people; many have advanced degrees, and some manage other adults in corporate or academic settings. In addition, some of these moms and dads purchase a lot of books—some substantial, some gimmicky—about parenting issues. Despite all their education, however, they just don't seem to understand what parenthood requires at different stages of child development.

How does this situation apply to the issue of parental authority? It's not too surprising that if you're way off-base on what you expect from your kids—if you expect a toddler to stay patient very long, or if you leave an eight-year-old home alone for extended periods of time—you'll jeopardize your authority, stress out your child, and complicate your family life.

Social/Parental Trends

During the 1940s and 1950s, most parents raised their children in a traditional, somewhat authoritarian mode. The classic image of this era is the *Father Knows Best* style of parenting: Dad (and, to a lesser degree, Mom) proclaimed the law: the kids obeyed. This image oversimplifies the situation, of course, but it's not totally off the mark. By contrast, what we have now is a looser, more indulgent style of parenting. Many parents shape the kids' behavior less by "laying down the law" and more by making requests and suggestions. In theory, the current style of parenting is more democratic, less autocratic. In practice, the situation varies considerably.

Some observers have decried the trend away from the traditional, relatively authoritarian mode of parenting. For example, Dr. Laura Schlessinger, a well-known conservative radio talk-show host, has stated,

> Today's unsafe, unstable and unsatisfactory situation for children is, I believe, a direct result of the moral laxity that has infected American society since the 1960s. Absolutes, right and wrong, sacrifice and obligation have been abandoned in the name of personal freedom and "rights."

Some conservative critics of what they call "permissive parenting" feel that only when mothers and fathers exert their authority in a hierarchical manner, with the parents completely in charge and the children completely submissive, can kids develop properly. In fairness to these observers, I should add that there's considerable diversity in their opinions. In any case, the trend toward a looser, more permissive mode of parental authority has inspired considerable criticism.

I share some of these reservations. However, I believe that it's crucial to perceive the big picture. The more permissive mode of parenting of the past three or four decades was a backlash against earlier eras of rigidity. The pendulum of beliefs about parenting swings back and forth, just like other pendulums. This swing is understandable, and to some extent it provides a means for making necessary corrections. However, I believe that the correction has gone too far. Neither extreme makes much sense.

Once we had dictatorial parents. Now we have dictatorial kids. We haven't really eliminated the pathology of the earlier era; we've only reversed the polarity, thus continuing a cycle of troubled interaction.

Lack of Common Sense

As I mentioned earlier, some of what some contemporary parents lack is a subtle knowledge of child development. How children think and behave isn't always as obvious as it looks. An example: kids in late childhood (ages eight to twelve) often speak with such verbal facility and confidence that it's easy to assume they possess greater sophistication than they really do. Many parents take their kids' comments at face value. I know lots of moms and dads, for instance, who will ask their preteens if they feel comfortable staying home alone for extended periods of time. Most of the kids tell the parents that they're fine about it. In therapeutic sessions, however, and in other settings—such as the call-in radio show I co-hosted for children—some of these kids will express fears of being alone and resentment toward their parents for leaving them at home. Why do parents assume that everything's okay? To some extent it's wishful thinking, because many parents are in a bind for childcare. To some degree it's a lack of knowledge about child development. There's something else at work here, too: lack of common sense. Many parents today just don't quite "get it" when dealing with a number of issues they face.

Among the most problematic issues are these:

- *Overintellectualization.* Many parents can rattle on about various psychological issues, quoting from this expert or that, but they lack any basic horse sense of what their kids need.

- *Overindulgence.* Especially among professional-class parents, there's a tendency to give children too much of what they *want* and too little of what they really *need*. We're all prey to the pressures of consumerism, and kids learn early how to coax their parents into buying lots of goodies. It's a difficult dilemma. Still, many parents go overboard.

- *Unwillingness to set sensible, age-appropriate limits.* Many parents wimp out when confronted with kids' demands and misbehavior. Children often have an amazing knack for coaxing and cajoling parents into giving them what they want. However, kids thrive and develop best when provided with thoughtful boundaries and limits. Neglecting or refusing to do so can be directly damaging to kids and indirectly so for the whole family.

- *Inability to assess temperamental issues.* Each kid is different. It's hard to know exactly what a child needs in response to his or her own individual needs. Figuring out the specifics is unquestionably one of the hardest tasks in parenthood. Unfortunately, many parents these days are too stressed or confused to take the necessary steps.

- *Inability to assess the "fit" between parent and child.* Similarly, there's the issue of how each individual child's personality and temperament affect the parents, and in turn how the parents' personalities and temperaments affect the child. These are tricky issues. Dealing with them effectively requires patience, insight, and effort, but many contemporary parents aren't willing to go the extra mile.

On these and other issues, parents need to exercise common sense as well as acquire detailed knowledge of child development.

"Affluenza"

At the time of my writing this book, the United States has entered a recession. Unemployment is up, consumer confidence is down, and we face a long-term international crisis. Yet compared to most people throughout history and, for that matter, in most of the contemporary world, we still live in relatively prosperous times. America remains the richest, most powerful country on earth. Good news? Mostly. But affluence has its downside. I certainly don't wish to see a further slump into economic hardship, but I believe that the great wealth we possess as a nation can be a burden as well as a blessing. We have attained such extreme affluence that we risk spoiling our children.

The risk is that we often define ourselves by what we purchase— our homes, cars, vacations, electronic gear, fancy sports equipment, and so forth. By modeling this acquisitiveness, we inspire our children to do the same. Today's kids crave consumer goods, too, and many parents indulge them heavily.

A related risk is a side effect: parents work so hard to *acquire* all this stuff. What's wrong with working hard? Well, nothing—up to a point. But when parents put in fifty-, sixty-, and eighty-hour weeks pursuing their careers, there's less time with kids, which in turn frustrates the kids and leads the parents to use more *things* as a way of compensating children for their absence, busyness, and high stress levels. When children have whatever they want, they don't gain awareness of which goods are necessities and which are luxuries.

In addition, I believe that building a life based on endless acquisition of goods is fundamentally unsatisfying; stuff can't substitute for rich relationships, a sense of common endeavor, or personal competence and self-discipline. Affluence thus tends to become a source of frustration and anxiety rather than a relief from worry. It's possible to catch what some observers have called "affluenza"—affluence as an existential malady. Ironically, one of the responses that people make to this state of unease is to relieve the internal "ache" by acquiring yet more stuff. As applied to parenting, this tendency takes the shape of appeasing or buying off kids with yet more consumer goods, more high-tech gadgets, and more expensive outings.

Perfectionism

Many contemporary parents are weak in authority, yet, ironically, they are perfectionistic about what they want. They are demanding in many ways. Some of this demanding attitude is a reflection of a consumerism: "I want what I want and I want it *now*." The resulting attitude may include a perception of children partly (or even essentially) as consumer goods—the ultimate accoutrements to an affluent lifestyle. But for this to be satisfying, kids must be high-quality, high-end "products." They must look good, wear the right clothes, go to the right schools, have the right friends, own the right gadgets, and so forth. They must be *perfect*.

This attitude is a big mistake. Like adults, children aren't perfect—they are wonderfully, delightfully *im*perfect. Children are always works-in-progress. They're constantly changing, exploring the world in complex and often messy ways, and making necessary mistakes as part of learning what they need to learn. What complicates the situation is that many contemporary parents have high standards for kids, but, as a result of their work-intensive, affluent lifestyles, they aren't really available to interact with the children when the kids need it—a situation guaranteed to create tensions within the family and likely to undermine parental authority.

Cultural Issues

Contemporary American culture includes elements that erode or even assault parental authority. Examples include movies, TV shows, computer games, and popular music. Even when not directly undermining parental authority, popular culture is a major influence on kids. Some aspects of this situation, such as computer technology, leave children in a position of having greater (often far greater) knowledge than their parents possess. These cultural issues aren't going to go away. It isn't possible simply to turn our backs on American culture and its more frustrating components; we have no choice but to deal with them. However, the ways in which many families deal with this situation compound their problems.

One issue is that parents often wash their hands of the situation. For instance, I know some moms and dads who have decided that instead of learning more about the Internet, they'll simply let their kids explore it according to their own whims. This approach is risky in several ways. First, it's risky because of hazardous aspects of the Net, such as the presence of pornographic and hate-oriented Web sites. It's also risky because parents who back away from a gatekeeping role demonstrate indifference about their children's well-being or an unwillingness to exert themselves in dealing with it.

Another cultural issue concerns use of the media, including TV, movies, and videos. I'm constantly amazed by how many parents allow their kids free rein to watch whatever they want whenever they want it. Once again I'm aware that it's time-consuming to assess the media and make decisions about what's appropriate. I've struggled with this issue myself. There's not only the problem of screening TV shows and movies for content; there's also the added factor of dealing with kids' peer pressure. Still, many parents do far too little to consider how the media affects their children. In this sense, as in others, it appears that many American moms and dads are comfortable, even eager, to relinquish their authority and appoint the media as de facto parent-surrogate.

Role Isolation

Many American parents are relatively isolated. I say "relatively" in comparison to parents in other cultures, where they (usually the mothers) are often surrounded by a complex network of relatives. Children in most parts of the world grow up in a web of uncles, aunts, grandparents, cousins, and other kin, some of whom have a supportive role as co-parents. By contrast, parents in the United States may have fewer relatives in the geographic area; they may have less-close relationships with members of an extended family; and they may have less frequent contact even with relatives they're close to. The result: parents carry a greater burden of work and responsibility in raising any given child. This kind of isolation doesn't by itself jeopardize parental authority; however, it can lead to fatigue and frustration that can reduce a parent's effectiveness, thus undercutting parental authority in the long run.

Divorce

Many divorced mothers and fathers are highly competent, effective, authoritative parents. Whether in a custodial or noncustodial role, these moms and dads maintain their authority with their children and attend to the kids' needs without major problems. Other divorced parents, however, face significant stress following a divorce, which can damage their authority. Some divorced parents also find themselves undercut by their ex-spouse as a result of rivalries and resentments; this situation can severely damage a parent's credibility in the children's eyes.

WHERE DOES THIS LEAVE US?

Throughout this chapter, I've tried to sketch a portrait of what I perceive to be a growing problem in American families: a tendency for mothers and fathers to relinquish their authority and let their kids make too many decisions about daily life.

What follows throughout Who's the Boss? is my best effort at responding to these issues. I can't cover all possible relevant topics; rather, I've attempted to treat those that arise most often and cause most parents the greatest difficulty. Not all topics will apply to your own situation, so feel free to browse among them, finding those that are most appropriate while ignoring the rest.

A Tenuous Balance

I'd like to quote a passage from Ellen Galinsky's *The Six Stages of Parenthood*, one of the books that every parent should read. (For a guide to books and other resources I recommend, see Appendix B of this book.) One of the major tasks of parenthood, Galinsky writes, is to become an authority. In turn, one of the related tasks is to determine the scope of parental authority.

> [Scope] means that parents are deciding what they are in charge of and what their child is in charge of . . . In handling issues of authority, most parents feel alternating desires. They know they need to set limits, yet they want to give the child latitude; they want to provide an atmosphere of order and respect, and yet they don't want to squash the child's spirit . . . It seems like a tenuous balance to achieve, and parents, particularly first-time parents, wonder, "Am I coming down too hard or not hard enough?"

I would never wish to understate the complexity and importance of this task. Parents rightly wonder, even worry, about whether they are achieving this tenuous balance and, in so doing, serving their children well. But there are ways to address these issues, and that's what I hope to do throughout *Who's the Boss?*

Chapter 2

HOW PARENTING STYLE INFLUENCES AUTHORITY

I spend a lot of time speaking with people about issues of parenthood. I also observe mothers and fathers on a day-to-day basis as they interact with their children. As a psychotherapist, as a teacher of parenting skills seminars, and as a mother, I think about what makes some parents effective and creative and what makes other parents less so. I'd even say that this subject is the heart of my professional life.

Given all the time and effort I spend thinking, talking, and reading about parenthood, I'd like nothing better than to offer some sort of easy answers—the Seven Steps to Good Parenting—that would resolve all the quandaries of raising children. The truth is, I haven't found it yet. I'm not even sure that such a thing exists. Parenthood and all the complex skills involved don't lend themselves to tidy solutions. At the same time, I do feel that a few issues are especially central and important as we consider the question of parental authority.

One of these issues is parenting style—the manner in which mothers and fathers go about the tasks of parenthood, especially the relatively greater or lesser degree of authority with which they interact with their children.

MORE SNAPSHOTS OF PARENTS IN ACTION

Consider these families as they go about their business:

- Mandy and Derek want the best for their children. Mandy is intent that the couple's daughter, Taylor, age twelve, and their son, Ned, age ten, should not suffer the kinds of material privation that she endured as a child. Derek is protective in a somewhat different way: his mother and father were rigid, emotionally cold parents, so he wants to insulate his own kids in a cocoon of affection and freedom to do as they please. As a result, both Mandy and Derek give their children enormous leeway to do as they please, indulge them in the purchase of many toys and gadgets, and take them on frequent special outings. Taylor and Ned are good kids and close to their parents in many ways. What surprises Derek and Mandy, however, is how demanding and irritable the children seem much of the time, frequently complaining about the boredom of family life. The parents respond to their kids' complaints by giving Taylor and Ned more say in decisions, such as what schools to attend and what vacations to take, and by deferring to their preferences about meals, playtime, bedtime, shopping trips, and other aspects of family life.

- Joseph has custody of his daughter, Arielle, who is fourteen. Although he fought hard to become the custodial parent following his divorce, Joseph finds parenthood perplexing and exhausting. He knows that Arielle misses her mother and resents both parents for divorcing, but he isn't sure how to communicate with the teenager; he argues with her frequently and he resents her increasingly distant, dismissive behavior toward him. Perhaps this situation is just what happens between par ents and teenagers, he tells himself. Unsure what else to do, Joseph has essentially withdrawn from his daughter's life and allows her to do pretty much whatever she wants as long as she doesn't cause him or anyone else any trouble.

- Barbara sees contemporary life as so chaotic that she makes all decisions for her eleven-year-old twin daughters, Jessie and Karen. She won't let them walk to school; instead, she drops them off and picks them up. She questions them about their friends, their school activities, and their social lives to make sure that the girls aren't doing anything dangerous. She avoids any situation that might put her kids at risk. "It's not that I don't trust *them*," she told me recently. "It's that I don't trust what's going on *out there*. I mean, life is so hazardous these days. I don't want to be a control freak—I'm just keeping things under control for the girls' own good."

- Rob and Tina consider life risky, too. Their attitude, however, is that their children (two boys and a girl, currently ages twelve, eleven, and nine) have to face the world little by little and learn to cope with its risks. They are protective of their kids yet also willing to let them experiment as their own abilities and skills develop. For this reason, Tina and Rob include the children in family discussions; they allow them to make decisions that seem appropriate to their ages and levels of responsibility; and they help them understand the situations they're dealing with. This approach to parenthood is by no means a blank check. On the contrary, these parents are comfortable being in charge, and they have no problem telling their kids exactly what has to be done if either external circumstances or the kids' own behavior warrants it.

Observing these and many other families, I'm often struck by the most consistent feature of parents' actions and attitudes: they love their kids. I see very few mothers and fathers who don't make their best efforts on behalf of their children. Why, then, are parents often ineffective — even counterproductive — as they make their day-to-day choices? Why are some parents more creative in dealing with the large and small decisions that make up family life? In particular, why do some parents manage the issue of parental authority more skillfully than others?

A partial answer to these questions is that some mothers and fathers have a more thoughtful, effective parenting style than others. (As I mentioned earlier, I'm using the term *parenting style* to mean the manner in which mothers and fathers go about the tasks of parenthood, especially regarding the greater or lesser degree of authority with which they interact with their children.) Some parents simply exert their authority in ways that accomplish what needs to be done with admirable creativity, sensitivity, insight, and even humor. Others make decisions that are less creative and that somehow antagonize kids, fail to enlist their cooperation, or simply don't get the task done as easily.

The Mysteries of Parenting Style

Why do these differences exist? I suspect that parenting styles are a combination of culture, family influences, and personal idiosyncracies.

A (Very) Short History of Parenting Style

One of the few things I'm sure about is that in many cultures and throughout most eras of history, the behaviors and attitudes that I'm calling parenting style didn't make a pretty picture. Most were strict, even severe. The father's role as parent was often distinct from, or even diametrically opposed to, the mother's. Writing about parenthood in his time, for instance, the first-century Roman philosopher Seneca stated that "parents subject the still malleable characters of their children to what will do them good . . . [W]e instill liberal culture by means of terror if they refuse to learn." A French historian, Paul Veyne, notes that in ancient Rome, "severity was part of the father's role; the mother pleaded for leniency . . ." For fathers, "tenderness was misplaced."

Much of Western history has reflected a similar severity. Throughout the Middle Ages and the Renaissance, parental authority remained almost absolute. Medieval European family structure continued the ancient pattern of the husband/father as monarch enthroned in his own little kingdom; the family patriarch had almost absolute authority, and mothers had little or none. Even the liberalization of society during the Enlightenment did little to soften this rigidity. Arlette Farge writes that the government of late-eighteenth-century France, for instance, granted fathers such power that they had "the right to imprison a child of twelve" (though "a constable must give his authorization for the imprisonment of a child over sixteen"). She goes on to state that even by the mid-nineteenth century, men still possessed "the right to punish those who were the source of domestic woe . . . The family was an authoritarian realm within which women's rights were nonexistent."

Fathers continued to hold sway in Europe throughout the nineteenth century and much of the twentieth. Of the transition into the early modern era, Michelle Perrot and Anne Martin-Fugier write, "Figurehead of the family as well as of civil society, the father dominates the history of private life in the nineteenth century . . . The father's omnipotence extended to the children. Greater sensitivity to childhood had by no means reduced the family's authority or the father's power . . ." In short, the father's word was law. Women retained a degree of practical control, however, because mothers continued to have more day-to-day contact with their children. The level of mothers' authority varied in accordance with local customs. "Everyday relations between parents and children varied enormously from town to country. In rural areas displays of affection were discouraged. Different conceptions of authority . . . influenced the individual's choice of words and gestures . . . Children were corrected for mistakes or for bad posture; they were told to sit straight, eat properly, and so on. On the other hand, exchanges of affection between parents and children were tolerated and even desired, at least in bourgeois families." Mothers as well as fathers could be strict, however, even harsh. As quoted by Michelle Perrot and Anne Martin-Fugier, the French writer Stendahl recalled his mother in these words: "[She] says that children must not be spoiled, and she whips me every morning. When she has no time in the morning, the whipping is put off till noon, rarely later than four o'clock."

I offer these dreary snapshots not to indulge in a sense of historical superiority but simply to note that throughout most of Western history, what we'd now term "parenting style" was highly authoritarian, and that most of the power resided in the father. Non-Western cultures have addressed the issue of parental authority in other ways. Among the Na of China, for example, fathers have almost no contact at all with their children—thus no role, no duties, and no authority. Similarly, the native peoples of Amazonia, such as the Yanomami, most often delegate parenting tasks to the mothers, though fathers take responsibility for boys' education from about the time of puberty. Are these customs preferable to classic Western patriarchy? Maybe, maybe not. Here again, the nature of these specific arrangements isn't my point. Rather, I'm just emphasizing that parental authority and parenting style vary considerably throughout the world's cultures. There's no single pattern of how parents raise and teach their children.

Trends within a Culture

For our purposes, what's most interesting and important is that even within American culture over the past one hundred years, parenting style has changed in many ways. Parenthood during the early twentieth century remained largely authoritarian, with fathers officially in command and mothers doing most of the day-to-day childcare. The 1920s witnessed a surge of interest in psychology, however, with John B. Watson and others founding a new school of thought called Behaviorism, which emphasized the study of observable phenomena rather than speculation about thoughts and feelings. Watson performed research on children and, in 1928, published his insights and recommendations in *Psychological Care of Infant and Child*. This book had tremendous influence throughout the '30s and '40s, with advice for a mode of parenting suggested by this passage:

> Never hug and kiss them, never let them sit on your lap. If you must, kiss them once on the forehead when they say good night. Shake hands with them in the morning. Give them a pat on the head if they have made an extraordinarily good job of a difficult task. Try it out. In a week's time you will find how easy it is to be perfectly objective with your child and at the same time kindly. You will be utterly ashamed of the mawkish, sentimental way you have been handling it.

This era intensified an already widespread interest in what scientific research revealed about childhood and parenthood. We might even call it the Medical Era of parenting. Many publishers issued books on these topics—some with an academic bent, such as Arnold Gesell and Frances Ilg's *Infant and Child in the Culture of Today* (1943), others more popular in nature, such as Emily Post's *Children Are People, and Ideal Parents Are Comrades* (1940). The stiffness and formality of these books' recommendations are what made Benjamin Spock's *Common Sense Book of Baby and Child Care* so revolutionary when it first appeared in 1946. Starting with his first two sentences—"Trust yourself. You know more than you think you do"—Dr. Spock removed parenting from the laboratory and returned it to mothers and fathers themselves. *Baby and Child Care* eventually sold 50 million copies and started a trend in child-oriented parenting books that continues to this day.

Since then, the issue of parenting style has varied within the

United States, though the basic trend has been tolerant and accepting rather than the authoritarian mode that preceded World War II. Many observers have felt that parents have been *too* tolerant and accepting. From the 1960s on, social critics, politicians, educators, and parents themselves have often commented that the pendulum of parental authority had swung too far toward permissiveness. Dr. Spock himself took much of the blame—though Spock actually advocated far less permissive attitudes than what his critics claim. (What inspired conservatives' wrath against Spock was, in fact, his vocal, influential opposition to the war in Vietnam.) Yet even parenting experts who exonerated Benjamin Spock sometimes felt that many parents had grown too permissive. Fitzhugh Dodson, for instance, writing in the mid-1970s, stated that "a minority [of parents] . . . are desperately trying to keep control over their children, but are not succeeding."

We now live in an era of multiple, contradictory voices. Just as you can enter a supermarket and find sixty kinds of salad dressing, each concocted to please a different palate, so, too, can you enter a chain bookstore and find sixty different books on parenting, each with a different angle, audience, and set of recommendations. This welter of advice isn't necessarily a bad thing, but the multiplicity of voices can be confusing.

Personal Experience

The expectations and customs of our culture will certainly influence you, but so will aspects of your temperament, your marriage, your upbringing, and your child's temperament. Here are some of the influences that I consider most important.

Your Temperament

Are you generally relaxed or anxious? Shy or confident? Intense or calm? Active or passive? These and other aspects of your temperament will invariably affect your parenting style. These attributes aren't good or bad in their own right; they do, however, make a difference in how you perceive and respond to parenthood.

Your Spouse's Temperament (and the Synergy between You)

The same holds true for your spouse. He or she will cope with parenting tasks partly based on his or her own temperament; in addition, the combination of your own and your spouse's temperament will affect your parenting style. Here's an example: an intense father and a calm mother. A couple of this sort may find that they "divvy up" certain aspects of parenthood partly on the basis of their temperaments. They may find, for instance, that the father reacts too intensely to their child (such as when a toddler throws a tantrum) and that the mother then works to calm everyone in this situation. In short, there's a kind of action/reaction, even a kind of synergy, as the parents react to one another.

Your Child's Temperament

Similarly, there's the issue—and a major issue at that—of your child's own temperament. This is the issue of "fit" between the parents' temperament and the child's. If you and your spouse are basically quiet, easy-going people, for instance, and if you have a boisterous, emotionally intense child, the difference between your child's temperament and your own will probably create some tensions for all parties. The same would hold true if you and your spouse are gregarious, emotionally expressive people, while your child is shy and subdued. I'm not saying that disparities of this sort are necessarily problematic; on the contrary, many families find that part of the delight of living together stems from the variety of members' temperaments. It's common, however, for parents to find children more perplexing, even challenging, when they are temperamentally dissimilar from the mother and father. And I believe it's safe to say that your parenting style will differ depending on whether your child's temperament is like or unlike your own.

The Side Effects of Your Upbringing

Parents are your first role models; it's impossible for you *not* to be influenced by what they did or didn't do when you were a child. In addition to influencing you in many other ways, your parents will also influence how you perceive aspects of parenting. This influence may be relatively straightforward or relatively complex. If your parents were nurturing and supportive, you may tend to be nurturing and supportive toward your own children. If, on the other hand, you had an ambivalent relationship with your parents, you may tend to feel more ambivalent toward your own role as a parent. (It's also possible that you'll react against the ambivalence you felt toward your parents and strive to be especially nurturing toward your own children. The daughter of inflexible parents, for example, may swear that she'll never boss her own kids around, thus becoming a more permissive parent.) One way or another, it's safe to say that whatever your experience of family life—including your mother's and father's parenting styles—that experience will probably influence your own attitudes and actions as a parent.

DIFFERENT PARENTING STYLES

Here's what I think is most important. Despite the huge variety of attitudes and behaviors among parents, I see four fundamental parenting styles: flexible, inflexible, permissive, and disengaged.

Flexible

The flexible parent is warm, affectionate, reasonable, capable of good listening, and neither neglectful nor too indulgent. Although confident of his or her authority, this kind of parent isn't strident or rigid. The flexible parent encourages the child's positive self-esteem, includes the child in negotiations about behavior and activities, fosters collaboration in problem-solving, and is open-minded but not overly permissive. Though flexible, this kind of parent is willing to make clear decisions and guide the child toward age-appropriate behavior. In short, the flexible parent is *authoritative* but not *authoritarian*.

Among my favorite examples of flexible parents are Petra and Jared. This couple has a complex task before them: parenting fraternal triplets (two girls and a boy, currently nine years old) and a five-year-old daughter. Petra is a biologist by training and currently a full-time homemaker. Jared works a demanding job as a business consultant but is heavily involved with family matters when he's at home. What impresses me about this couple is that despite the pressures they face, and despite the varied and complex demands that their children place on them, they consistently find the right balance in coping with day-to-day and long-term issues. I'm constantly amazed by Petra's ability to stay cool and focused on her children's needs. (How she has maintained this degree of composure while dealing with triplets is beyond me.) She is attentive to each child yet able to convince them that she can't attend to everyone at once. She jokes about being impatient, but she's more even-tempered than almost any other parent I know. She manages to sort out issues with her kids while making it clear that she and Jared are the final authority on what happens within the family.

In short, Petra and Jared have discovered a way—either through innate ability, trial and error, or both—to walk the fine line between being too lenient and being too strict. I don't want to make this couple sound like a pair of saints; they have good days and bad days like everyone else. Petra states that she knows she falls short some of the time, and that she and Jared have many, many years to go before their parental tasks are finished. I'm pleased to say, too, that I know lots of other couples who have achieved this happy medium in their parental styles. My point is simply that Petra and Jared are the sort of parents I admire most because they allow their children room to grow, change, and explore while simultaneously offering clear, age-appropriate limits that keep the kids safe and focused on what they ought to be doing.

What's the effect of the flexible parenting style? It's hard to generalize, because so many other factors affect children within each family. Overall, however, researchers have found that children of flexible parents have high self-esteem, are good problem-solvers, are achievement-oriented, are often leaders and excellent students, and tend to be cooperative, creative, basically happy kids. I believe that these positive outcomes are a result of combined freedom and security: freedom, because flexible parents allow their children room to grow emotionally and intellectually; security, because flexible parents who are authoritative in ways that provide good limits and boundaries that help kids feel safe and confident.

Inflexible

By contrast, the inflexible parent is controlling, rigid, strict, and overly concerned with maintaining control over children. The inflexible parent doesn't allow children to make mistakes; he or she expects perfectionism and has inappropriate expectations about children's abilities at various developmental stages. The inflexible parent can't adjust his or her parenting style to the child's changing abilities and emotional needs. These parents tend to have precise (and often inaccurate) images of what kids should be like. Many inflexible parents are domineering; their rule of thumb is "It's my way or the highway."

Inflexible parents aren't as rare as you might think. Although the *Father Knows Best* type of parent may seem as extinct as the dodo, plenty of rigid moms and dads are alive and well. What seems to have changed is their appearance. I don't know a single parent who holds sway over his family in the style of the old-time patriarch or matriarch, but I'm aware of plenty who are demanding and rigid in their expectations.

One such parent is Judy. Assistant director of a regional HMO,

Judy and her husband, Ken, have two sons, Jake and Alan. Ken travels a lot, so Judy handles most family matters. She enjoys her work and relishes parenthood. As with all the parents I'm describing, she clearly loves her children, so I have no criticism of her intentions or her commitment. What concerns me is that Judy doesn't allow her sons—particularly the elder child, Jake—enough emotional "wiggle room." She holds high expectations, which can be fine in principle, but she's rigid in expressing them. She also tends to focus too much on external appearances. For instance, she has stated outright that she expects both boys to earn straight As, and she grounds them or punishes them in other ways if they fall short of this edict. She refuses to consider that a lower grade might simply indicate a need for improvement, a sign of stress, or something other than abject failure. Judy also demands that her sons maintain perfect formal etiquette not just at the dinner table but also at more casual occasions, such as picnics and backyard suppers. Jake and Alan submit to these demands but seem to suffer emotional stress as a result. A child I know told me that Jake, on receiving a 94% grade on a math test, panicked and shouted, "My mother's gonna kill me!"

I fear that Judy's rigid parenting style will undermine rather than promote her sons' confidence and emotional growth. My perception is that the children of inflexible parents tend more often to be moody, anxious, fearful of their parents' reactions, and characterized by lower self-esteem than are kids of flexible parents. They can be well behaved, but they are basically followers rather than leaders, and they tend to be inconsistent in their academic performance, as they often worry more about external measures of success (such as grades) rather than the intrinsic value of learning.

Permissive

Another basic parenting style is that of the permissive parent—the indulgent dad or mom who allows his or her children an excess of control and decision-making power. These are anything-goes, nondemanding parents who don't set limits or guide their children adequately. Because of issues stemming from their own childhood, they may be afraid to set limits, and they may feel an inordinate need to be loved.

Annette and Jason provide good examples of the permissive mothers and fathers I see in abundant numbers nowadays. Far from being the self-indulgent, amoral parents that some observers decry, Jason and Annette are earnest, hard-working, and devoted to their son, Will, age five. In fact, I'd say that Jason and Annette are devoted to a fault. It's not just that they provide Will with an excess of toys, electronic games, videos and DVDs, and other expensive playthings, or that they "reward" him with excursions, shopping trips, meals at fancy restaurants, and frequent vacations. The problem goes far beyond the specifics of overindulgence.

What I find most disturbing is that Annette and Jason consult with their son on many matters that are well beyond the boy's ability to understand, and they defer to him on decisions that they themselves should be making outright. For instance, both parents allow Will to determine what he eats at most meals; they offer long lists of options, as if they were waiters at a restaurant; they make special trips to the grocery store to purchase foods that Will has specified. A more troubling example of their deference concerns Annette and Jason's choice of a kindergarten. After touring three different schools, the parents offered their son *carte blanche* to select whichever of the three he wanted. Will decided that he didn't like any of them, at which point Jason and Annette scrapped the first three options, renewed their search, and struggled to come up with an alternative that met their child's specifications. (The defining factor turned out to be the size of the playground.)

Ironically, Jason and Annette consider themselves to be highly disciplined go-getters. Annette works as an account executive at an advertising firm; Jason is a bond trader. By excelling in these competitive fields, they perceive themselves as rigorous and well-versed in the real world. Why, then, are they so indulgent toward their son?

Why are they so permissive of his progressively more demanding behavior? These are tough questions to answer—questions that this book will consider in other chapters.

What are the results of the permissive parenting style? The offspring of these parents tend to be whiny, egocentric, self-centered children with relatively low self-esteem. They can also be grandiose, which is often the flip side of low self-esteem. They may not achieve their full potential and may tend to be followers more often than leaders, or else bossy leaders.

Disengaged

The disengaged, uninvolved parent is emotionally detached. Disengaged parents don't set sufficient limits and may be less available, whether emotionally or in terms of practical, day-to-day involvement with their children. The cause of their lack of engagement is rarely that these mothers and fathers don't love their kids; rather, some other factor (or factors) creates this parenting style, whether it's a result of a passive temperament, physical or emotional illness (such as clinical depression), or a tendency to avoid interacting with other people.

Martin is a pretty typical disengaged parent. His wife, Alice, is a systems analyst for a large consulting firm. Because of Alice's heavy travel schedule, Martin has assumed the predominant parental role within his family. The couple's three kids are currently eleven, eight, and six. Martin runs a small business out of his home, an arrangement that has allowed for a high degree of flexibility and convenience. So far so good. What concerns me, however, is this father's laissez-faire attitude. It's all well and good that he grants his oldest child a fair amount of autonomy, and Martin is available to all three kids if they need him. But Martin often isn't truly *present*. He goes about his business; the children go about theirs; he intervenes now and then. Otherwise, it's as if the kids and the adult inhabit different worlds even within the same house. "Can't you see I'm busy?"

is Martin's standard response to most of his children's comments and questions to him.

I sense that the kids feel hurt by their father's rebuffs, but they've learned to insulate themselves and to go about their business. Kids are generally adaptable, and Martin and Alice's have certainly learned to adapt. The situation isn't all bad. These children are pretty skilled at looking after themselves, and to some degree they've compensated for parental disengagement by being more engaged with each other. The catch, however, is a degree of wistfulness that's obvious whenever I visit this family. The two younger children, especially, often watch their dad expectantly, almost eagerly, as if hoping that he'll notice them, respond to them, and provide them with some of the sustenance that kids need from caring adults. I'm sure they know their father loves them. They just want more day-to-day interaction, guidance, information, and playfulness.

The effect of the disengaged parenting style is that the kids tend to be needier, less secure, and sometimes more aggressive or rebellious. Lacking a sense of warm, consistent interaction with their parents, these children often suffer from low self-esteem. Some have a tendency to get in trouble, either at school or in the wider world. Some act in ways that seem emotionally hungry, with expressions of eager, whiny, or demanding behavior. Others simply develop a diffident attitude toward other people, as if to insulate themselves from further hurt.

Why the Flexible Style Is Best

It's not hard to see why many experts on child development feel that the flexible style of parenting is the best.

It Helps a Child Gain Confidence

If you can maintain a flexible style of parenting, you're basically telling your child "I believe in you." Allowing him an age-appropriate degree of autonomy gives him room to grow, allows him a sense of security, and boosts his trust in his own abilities. Instead of ordering him around or leaving him solely to his own devices, you're simultaneously providing guidance but also showing that you believe in his growing capacity to make decisions. The issues may be as simple as helping to select clothes to wear at school or deciding when to clean up the playroom, but the effects go far beyond these simple tasks. The flexible style is the style that best helps a child develop at a comfortable, individual pace.

It Fosters Growth

The flexible style offers the greatest opportunities for the child to grow. By saying "We can work this through together," or "I can give you some suggestions, but you need to be part of the decision," you are challenging your child to use his best judgment, to be resourceful, to be responsible, and to come up with some ideas. This process requires great patience—it's often easier to make the decisions yourself—but involving your child in these ways will pay off in the long run.

It Diminishes Stress

Children, like adults, resent being ordered around; it's frustrating to be told constantly what to do. At the same time, children feel anxious having little or no structure in activities; they need guidance. The flexible parent is more likely than the inflexible, the permissive, or the detached parent to find a happy medium between bossiness and a hands-off attitude. The result: a greater likelihood that your child will proceed through the various developmental stages without unnecessary stress. (A detailed discussion of children's developmental stages is beyond the scope of Who's the Boss?, but you can find information of several kinds listed in this book's Resource Guide, Appendix B.)

It Teaches Negotiation and Compromise

The flexible style also helps children to learn important social skills, including negotiation and compromise. By being flexible, you're not saying "You're out there all alone"; at the same time, you're not saying "Do it my way or else." Instead, your flexibility stresses the need for family life to be a collaborative effort. You're essentially saying "Let's talk about all the options here, let's sort out our feelings, and let's work together." The skills your child acquires in sorting things out will serve him well throughout his lifetime.

THE GOAL OF A GOOD PARENTING STYLE

Ultimately, the goal of a good parenting style is to attend to your children's needs as effectively, creatively, and flexibly as possible. Respond to your child's individuality. Help him by setting good limits *and* by giving him the freedom to grow. Try to find a good balance. Don't feel that you must either imitate or reject everything your parents or anyone else recommends. Consider various courses of action and choose carefully. How? By learning from thoughtful friends, siblings, and others who can show you what to do (or to avoid doing) as you tackle this most difficult of tasks. As much as possible, trust your instincts. When you feel unsure or uneasy about the situations you're dealing with, read books about parenting. Take parenting courses that offer new ideas about raising kids. (See this book's Resource Guide for suggestions.) Above all, be flexible and patient. Don't expect perfection from yourself or from your kids. Precisely because parenthood is a process, you'll cause yourself a lot of needless grief if you expect to master all the necessary skills at once.

Be a Good Listener

One of the keys to flexibility is staying alert and open to your child's needs. Among other things, this state of mind means listening closely—without interrupting or passing judgment—to what your kids are telling you. In addition, however, it means listening to their tone of voice and, at times, to their silence. What do you detect about your child's mood—about his anxieties and uncertainties? What do you see in his body language? What is he too young to express by any means? If you can "read" your child thoughtfully, you'll have more information to work from, thus more opportunities to respond flexibly to what he needs.

Be Empathic

Try to understand and validate your child's feelings. Being a kid is often stressful. Although you're in charge of your family, you should attempt to imagine what your child is experiencing and empathize with him even when your decisions take a course he doesn't like. Voicing empathy for his emotions may go a long way toward reassuring him, despite the need to take actions he finds unappealing.

Communicate Honestly and Openly

Linked to empathy is honesty and openness. Depending on your child's age, you may find it appropriate to explain your own feelings about situations you face as a parent. Such explanations won't be beneficial for young children, who may feel confused or frightened by excessive information; however, older children may benefit from more context about what you're thinking or feeling. You might say, for instance, "I need your help straightening up your room—we need to work together." Open, honest communication is, in fact, one of the foundations of flexible parenting. Try to foster a mood of warm, accepting, mutually respectful communication.

Keep Your Mind Open

Parenthood is one surprise after another. Few children develop precisely as we anticipate. If you can listen attentively to your child's thoughts, emotions, hopes, and worries, you'll gain a degree of flexibility that will help your kid unfold to his fullest. Try to avoid prejudging, negating, or diminishing what your child expresses about his thoughts or feelings. Take the long view; parenthood is a long, complex process, and focusing only on the crises of the moment can limit your ability to anticipate what matters most in the long run.

Avoid Reactivity

Children are intensely emotional. Their intensity will test your patience and stamina, especially when they willfully attempt to bait or aggravate you. If possible, avoid reacting to every stimulus. This is a difficult task, especially when you're already exhausted from other responsibilities. But try to stay calm, assess what's really at work in each situation, and think a few steps ahead. Let's say your child is whiny and uncooperative each evening. Rather than overreacting (or, for that matter, rather than just ignoring the situation), attempt to size up the situation. Is he simply tired? Hypoglycemic? Stressed out by his own day at school? Try to diagnosis the situation and respond in ways that look beyond the immediate problem. Look at the big picture. Consider what other factors may be prompting your child's fussiness or difficult behavior.

Solve Problems in an Age-Appropriate Way

Kids are moving targets in more than one sense. By the time you feel you've figured out your child, he'll grow, change, and enter a whole new developmental stage. Being a flexible parent means adapting to these constant changes and dealing with situations in ways that meet your child's needs. Among other things, this flexibility means not only sizing up problems but also responding to them as your child grows intellectually and emotionally. How can you decide on the appropriate response? To some extent you'll have to learn through trial and error. That said, you'll benefit—and you'll help your child greatly—if you speak to more experienced parents you trust and respect, read books about child development, and attend a few parenting courses or workshops. See your local community college or adult education center for suggestions.

Set Age-Appropriate Rules

Similarly, the rules you set will vary as your child grows and changes. Experimenting with what works is inevitable, because each kid is different. The key to flexible parenting in this regard is, again, to keep an open mind, to watch carefully, and to obtain outside insights whenever possible, especially if you feel frustrated, anxious, angry, or stumped.

What is age-appropriate at each stage of childhood? This question has complex answers, which have prompted child psychologists to write entire books. For an overview of these books, see Appendix B, Resource Guide, for suggestions. I especially recommend the books by Erik Erikson, Selma Fraiberg, and Jean Piaget. In addition, I've summarized major developmental milestones in Appendix A.

Use Positive Reinforcement

When enforcing the rules you've set, emphasize positive reinforcement—praise, rewards, humor, and affection—rather than criticism or punishment. Positive reinforcement is more effective than negative reinforcement, and it leads to a better mood within the family. It also allows you more flexibility as a parent. That said, you may have to use punishment at times. If so, do not spank or use other forms of physical punishment; they are demoralizing, damaging to your child's self-esteem, and ineffective in the long run. Time out is acceptable but shouldn't be overused, and its usefulness diminishes as children reach age five or six.

Admit When You're Wrong

The goal of parenthood isn't perfection. All parents make mistakes. Being a flexible parent means that when you're wrong, you're capable of saying so. This willingness is especially important between spouses; your willingness to apologize will help foster good will and a sense of common purpose. When interacting with your children, too, admitting fallibility won't undermine your authority; on the contrary, it makes you more human and more approachable to your children, which is likely to help them feel comfortable with the decisions you make. (It also gives *them* permission to make mistakes and be human.) At the same time, it's important to stress that you remain the ultimate decision-maker within the family.

Encourage Creativity

A rigid attitude toward family life—"my way or the highway"—creates stress and resentment. It also tends to limit family members' willingness to collaborate in solving problems and dealing with issues creatively. A more flexible attitude is open to each member's capacities for insight, sensitivity, and humor, each of which is a form of creativity that can make family life easier and more enjoyable. Do whatever you can to foster your children's creativity in dealing with everyday ups and downs. Stay open to your own creativity, too. Surprise yourself; don't insist on doing something the same way just because that's how you've always done it. One of the great delights of family life is the novelty and unpredictability that children offer—and that they inspire in parents as well.

Counteract Your Stress

Despite all its pleasures, family life is stressful. Raising kids requires constant attention, patience, imagination, and stamina. It's easy to let day-to-day events grind you down and deplete your sense of humor. How should you respond? There's no simple answer to that question, but you should counteract the stress you face. In two-parent families, the mother and father can take turns dealing with their children's issues so that neither parent carries the whole burden. The task is more difficult in single-parent families, but a parent should still attempt to find a respite from parental duties by asking for help from relatives and friends. Responsibly planned "bail-out" time away from your kids will refresh you and leave you rested — which means you'll be more responsive to your children's needs.

Encourage Independence

Children have an innate drive toward independence. One of the problems I see among some contemporary parents, however, is a tendency to be too protective in ways that thwart (or at least diminish) kids' efforts to learn self-sufficiency. Such parents are well meaning, but their protective impulses can be damaging regardless. Instead, parents should foster age-appropriate independence. Reinforce your children's abilities and self-esteem by encouraging new skills, as well as a general tendency toward resourcefulness, responsibility, and reliability. If you model flexibility yourself, you'll inspire your children to emulate it, which will boost both their independence and their willingness to collaborate with other members of the family for the common good.

THE QUEST (STRUGGLE?!) FOR FLEXIBILITY

Parenting is such a complex, often stressful endeavor that many mothers and fathers struggle to stay flexible in meeting their children's needs. It's tempting either to lay down the law or simply go with the flow. Unfortunately, both authoritarian and permissive approaches, though easy in the short run, can cause difficulties for parents and kids alike in the longer term. My advice is to strive for a flexible parenting style. Be authoritative, not authoritarian. Take charge—and take responsibility—but allow your children age-appropriate levels of independence as they grow and develop. The quest for flexibility isn't a simple task. You'll have to redefine it continuously throughout the parenting years. But striving for it will pay off handsomely for your entire family.

Chapter 3

DISCIPLINE AND CONFLICTS

- Alyssa, age thirty, is a full-time mother of three young children, currently ages six, five, and three. She enjoys parenthood but finds it wearisome, especially late each day. Although she's aware that many parents find afternoons and evenings difficult, she isn't sure how to remedy the situation. She finds dinnertime especially stressful, because each of her children prefers different meals. The two younger kids, especially, often throw tantrums if their food isn't exactly what they've specified. When I suggested that she might simply serve dinner and let the children learn to adapt, Alyssa asked me, in amazement, "What am I supposed to do, let my own kids starve to death?"

- Zoë is close to her thirteen-year-old daughter, Adele. Over the past year, however, the girl seems more distant, at times even defiant, and she sometimes makes choices that appear provocative to this attentive mother. "I know teens flex their muscles," Zoë admits, "and that's what they need to do. Still, I find it frustrating." What Zoë finds most difficult is that although Adele used to follow her mother's preferences no matter what they were, the daughter now demands complex explanations for every request. Zoë says, "We spend long hours discussing everything. Adele used to be content with what I told her; now she wants to know *why*. Sometimes we talk every issue half to death." She contents herself with this reassurance, however: at least her daughter still listens to her, and Adele knows that her mother will always listen in turn.

- A forty-something father, Zachary, sits with his middle school–age boys at the dinner table. His wife is away on a business trip; the dad is attempting to catch up on work during suppertime. Responding to e-mail, Zachary ignores his sons throughout the meal. The boys grow restless, then rowdy, resenting his inattention. They tease one another, steal food from one another's plates, and flick bits of bread across the table. At last Zachary snaps, "You guys are impossible! Can't anyone get any work done around here!"

- Sam and Cathy came to me for family counseling. The couple's four children were doing well enough individually, they explained, but the kids couldn't seem to get along with each other. "The tension is so thick," Cathy told me, "you can just about cut it with a knife." Sam huffed at his wife's description: "That's so trite—can't you think of a better way to explain your own family?" As our interview proceeded, both parents sniped at one another almost nonstop. A home visit confirmed what I expected; much of the infighting among the children simply emulated their parents' cold and testy interactions.

I could offer many similar snapshots of family life. Even happy families experience conflicts, and all parents struggle with issues of discipline. Conflicts and discipline aren't issues that any of us can sidestep; they are intricately woven into the fabric of our days. It's true, however, that issues of discipline and conflict are challenging, frustrating, and exhausting.

But I believe that, like parenting style, discipline is one of the most crucial, central aspects of parental authority. Discipline is both an expression of authority—that is, a way in which you show your children that you're in charge—and also a source of authority. In addition, discipline has a close relationship to how you cope with family conflict.

DISCIPLINE

The word *discipline* has acquired a bad reputation. People tend to associate it with the notion of punishment or of *making* children do what the parents want them to do. However, developmental psychologists now perceive the situation differently: discipline is—or ought to be—a way of helping children to develop social skills, a conscience, impulse control, values, self-esteem, and a capacity for moral judgment and responsibility. The goal of discipline is ultimately *self-discipline*. In this sense, discipline involves a crucial and beneficial element of choice: the child learns to choose behavior that serves a good purpose both for himself and for others.

The truth is that even happy, well-adjusted kids sometimes act out, hunker down, or grow defiant. The causes of these difficult or frustrating behaviors are numerous and varied. Your child may feel challenged by some aspect of his life. He may be testing the limits you've set. He may be exploring new options for autonomy. He may be trying to get your attention. He may be feeling unsafe or anxious. He may be feeling stressed out or tired. For one reason or another, he behaves in ways that are unacceptable. How should you cope with your child at such times?

What's the Real Issue?

If your child misbehaves, you should attempt to determine the real issue before taking action. It's easy to move fast, only to discover that you've jumped to the wrong conclusion. For example, let's say that your eight-year-old son is aggressively teasing his younger brother. This behavior is unacceptable. You'll need to state that you won't permit this kind of teasing, and you'll need to discipline the older boy. As you take action, however, try to figure out the root cause of what's happening. Here are some possibilities to investigate:

- Did your son have a bad day at school?

- Did someone hurt his feelings?

- Was he feeling pressured by a teacher or another child?

- Is he feeling depressed because he didn't do well on a test?

- Is he overwhelmed by the demands he's facing?

- Is he feeling overscheduled?

- Is he struggling with sibling rivalry?

- Is he signaling that you aren't setting enough limits or giving him enough positive attention?

- Is one of his siblings provoking him?

- Is he reacting to something you did or said that might have upset him or made him angry?

Your son's aggressive behavior may be symptomatic of an experience that's far more complex than it first appears. Jealousy, rivalry, tension, and anxiety frequently signal more complex issues hidden within more obvious behaviors. Understanding the deeper issues doesn't mean that you won't discipline your child; you'll need to stress that your son's frustration doesn't justify his behaving obnoxiously toward his brother. He'll have to take the consequences for his behavior. But if you can identify the root causes of this incident, you'll gain a sense of perspective about what's happening and how to respond.

In addition, keep in mind that "misbehavior" or "acting out" may indicate a positive event in your child's development. For instance, a toddler may throw a tantrum because he feels torn between a desire to express his burgeoning abilities and a desire for structure and limits—in short, between dependence and independence. Similarly, a teenager may express defiance not so much out of negativity but as a way of exploring the new aspects of personal identity. Disruptive, annoying, or frustrating behavior may signal normal developmental processes. In acknowledging these situations, I don't mean to say that developmental changes allow your child to do as he pleases. On the contrary, children need to learn civility, self-control, and respect for other people. There's no reason to tolerate aggressive or obnoxious behavior. However, don't overreact—or react to the wrong issue. Do what you can to identify the real problem; then determine what will help your child cope with the situation facing him, and help him learn age-appropriate self-discipline.

Discipline and the Developmental Stages

Each stage of your child's development involves specific issues that will affect how you approach the subject of discipline. The more you understand about child development, the better you'll be able to choose the right ways to shape your child's behavior. For an overview of developmental milestones and appropriate behavior, see Appendix A.

Discipline for Kids Aged Eighteen Months to Three Years

Babies are too young to grasp the notion of "good" or "bad" behavior, so discipline is a non-issue until the age of about eighteen months. As the parent of a baby, your goal is simply to make sure that your child is safe and feels loved, accepted, and cherished. Intervene directly to keep him away from danger (household hazards, traffic, and so forth). When your child is about a year and a half old, however, you can start to help him deal with his frustrations and impulses.

Coax and Collaborate

One of the most effective steps you can take is to collaborate with your child to help him deal with situations he finds frustrating. Toddlers are just beginning to grasp what's acceptable and what's unacceptable; they need your guidance. If you can coax your toddler into joining forces with you, you'll get much farther than if you prod or coerce him. Positive reinforcement works more effectively than punishment. Seeing you as an ally in coping with frustration will encourage his future cooperation far better than ordering him around will.

Encourage Your Child to Feel a Sense of Control

Convincing a toddler that he's partially in control of a situation can go a long way toward easing his anxieties and avoiding parent–child conflict. Be attentive to your toddler by mirroring his behavior and staying close by. If your toddler is acting out of control, distract him and offer something constructive to play with.

Use Stories to Provide Guidance

One method for reassuring and guiding children is to tell them stories—either stories you make up yourself or stories you read from books. Judith Viorst's *Alexander and the Terrible, Horrible, No Good,*

Very Bad Day and Maurice Sendak's *Where the Wild Things Are* appeal to children because they allow them a vicarious way to vent their aggression. The result is beneficial in two ways: first, because your child can ease his tensions harmlessly; second, because he can grasp that he's not "bad" for feeling angry or aggressive emotions. Some books (the *Berenstain Bears* series) also provide problem-solving techniques that children can emulate. (See Appendix B, Resource Guide, for other suggestions.)

Vent Frustrations

All toddlers feel intense emotions that they aren't yet able to understand or verbalize. Such tumultuous feelings will probably be manifested as wild energy and aggressive impulses. Adults often feel uncomfortable with such normal releases of energy; in response, they may abdicate their authority by becoming passive or else respond in ways that are too punitive. Instead of these reactions, you should encourage (and *monitor*) physical activities that let young children release their energy and strong feelings. Let them knead bread dough, pound clay, or hammer wooden pegs. Physical projects vent tension and energy creatively, and some of these activities also help children learn a skill. Allow your child to draw an angry picture, punch a punching bag, tear up pieces of paper, or throw soft cloth balls at bowling pins.

Encourage Kids to Identify Their Feelings

Your child gains an important measure of control by labeling his emotions. Help him put words to his experiences: "Boy, that must have made you feel disappointed (frustrated, sad, angry)." His growing skills with language can be a positive vehicle for discharging tension, frustration, and anxiety. As he gains more verbal skills and can express his feelings more fully, his anger may dissipate.

Discipline for Preschoolers

If you can consistently and patiently communicate your expectations to your preschool-age child, you can build a foundation for good behavior and cooperation that will serve you both in the short and long terms.

Be Empathic

Adults often forget that childhood can be stressful. You face your own pressures and demands, but so does your child. Push beyond your concerns and empathize with your child's difficulties. Try to put yourself in your child's shoes as he faces the frustrations of his own activities. What may seem trivial or even comical—such as a concern that his lunch box isn't "cool"—may be a source of concern or even anguish. Ask questions about what's happening. Find out about his day, his interests, his worries. Listen for hidden messages. Ask for more details: "So you're saying the teacher was in a bad mood?" or "So Martin tried to hit you? Can you tell me more about that?" Support him verbally: "I know you're having a tough time today," or "You seem worried [or frustrated] about what happened." A parent's empathy is often so reassuring that it eliminates the need for any other interventions.

Look for Root Causes

Even seemingly "pointless" misbehavior has an underlying cause or message. Listen closely to what your child is telling you. Is he hungry? Tired? Scared? Feeling ignored? Wanting more independence? Finding the root cause of your child's behavior often solves the problem far more effectively than attempting to suppress the behavior itself. Ask questions about what's happening. Doing so offers both empathy and a source of information.

Paraphrase Your Child's Statements and Emotions

Your child may not even be aware of what he's feeling. If he says, "You're a dope," avoid taking this "insult" personally; instead, help him understand the situation by paraphrasing his emotional state. ("It seems like you're angry because I wouldn't give you more ice cream.") Help him learn to understand his own emotions. Teach him the words that help him express his feelings clearly and directly without having to act them out.

Solve Problems Together

Try to find a solution together. Children generally want to please their parents; if you can work out a mutually acceptable way of dealing with behavioral expectations, your child is more likely to go along with the program. For younger preschool-age kids, direct their aggressive impulses with specific directions: "Sand stays in the sandbox—it's not for throwing," or "Teeth are for chewing, not for biting your friends." Ask older preschoolers to collaborate with you by means of age-appropriate questions: "How can we solve this problem together?" or "How can we be a team in solving this problem?" Request his input and *value* it.

You can also help him to take control of his impulses by having him tell his body what needs to be done: "Tell your feet to walk," or "Tell your hands to be patient." This technique is simple, but it empowers your child to be the boss over his own body, which in turn helps him to develop internal controls and strength.

Give Advance Warning

Discipline is most effective when you specify the consequences in advance. Give warnings; if the misbehavior persists, follow through with the consequences. Make sure that cause–effect relationships between infractions and punishment are clear: "If you can't get ready for bed more quickly, you'll miss your extra reading time." Don't spring new disciplinary measures on your child out of nowhere. Most importantly, don't give warnings but *fail* to deliver the consequences, which will severely undercut your parental authority.

Even if you specify the rules and cause–effect relationships, you may confuse your child if you waffle about your expectations and the consequences. Give your child advance notice if possible: "It'll be bedtime once your game is done." If he isn't responsive, follow through—and be consistent.

Make Sure That Consequences Fit the Problem

Your efforts at discipline will be self-defeating if they're either too severe or too lenient. Moreover, discipline must be age appropriate. When you specify limits and rewards, make sure that they're clear and concise before the child acts out. Both over- and underreacting will damage your parental authority and risk demoralizing your child.

Use "I"-Statements

Communicate how you feel about your child's behavior without demeaning or humiliating him. If your child has a messy room, for instance, saying "You're such a messy kid" or "This room looks like a pigpen" may come across as severely judgmental. He may wonder whether, if he's living like a pig, you mean that you feel *he's* a pig. Instead, try to phrase your complaint in "I"-statements—words that state how you feel without passing judgment on your child's personality or being. For example, you could state "When you won't help me pick up the toys, I feel frustrated." This approach gets the necessary message across without the risk of hurting your child's feelings.

Don't Berate Your Child or Preach at Him

Most children detest being lectured, nagged, or harangued; if you barrage them with too many words, they'll just tune you out. Explain your perceptions of the situation or make your request (or demand) about what has to happen, but leave it at that. Rattling on will aggra-

vate the problem and dilute the effectiveness of your statements. In
the long run, haranguing or preaching to your child will damage
your parental authority.

Be Consistent
Some situations justify making exceptions; overall, however, consistency will benefit both you and your child. He'll know that you
mean what you say, and he'll be more likely to respond accordingly.
Consistency is, in fact, one of the most important variables in establishing and maintaining your parental authority. This doesn't mean
that you have to be entirely rigid; exceptions will occur, and you
need to be flexible when circumstances warrant. But your child
must understand that when you make a request, he needs to
respond.

Consider Using Time Out
When used thoughtfully and sparingly, this popular method for
disciplining children offers several clear benefits.

- It's a safe way to express your disapproval as a parent.

- It provides an opportunity for your child to see the connection
  between his behavior and your disapproval.

- It allows you to role-model calm self-control rather than anger
  and lack of control.

- It allows your child a chance to calm down and to avoid
  "revving up" or spinning out of control.

- Just as important, it offers *you* a chance to calm down and to
  reduce the risk of protracted or no-win conflicts.

For these reasons, the time-out method of discipline can offer you
some real advantages as you cope with issues of discipline and maintain your parental authority.

Parents sometimes overuse or even misuse time out, however. Consider these other aspects of the situation:

Age. Time out is appropriate for preschoolers and kids in the early elementary school years—depending on your child's maturity—but it's less effective or counterproductive for older children. You can start using time out when your child is around three years old. Phase out its use when he's in kindergarten or perhaps first grade. I don't recommend using time out past second grade. (Possible exceptions: if your child is developmentally delayed or socially immature—and even then only with great care, and perhaps with professional guidance.)

Location. Pick a safe, neutral spot that allows you to monitor your child yet keep him "out of the action." Ideal spots include a corner of the living room or dining room. Never confine him in a closet, utility room, or other closed space. Avoid using his bedroom or bed as a place of punishment, because you want him to associate his room with safety and comfort, not with punishment and separation.

Frequency. If time out doesn't seem effective, you may be dealing with an issue other than routine misbehavior. The problem may be fairly minor, such as hunger or fatigue, or it may be more substantial, such as hyperactivity. Either way, look beyond the immediate situation. Consider the possibility of a developmental issue or an issue of family dynamics. If you're concerned about the situation, seek help from a counselor, family therapist, or other professional clinician.

If All Else Fails, Be Categorical

You are the parent; you're in charge. Some aspects of family life aren't negotiable. If your child doesn't respond to rational persuasion, gently but firmly exert your authority and indicate what must be done.

Discipline for School-Age Children

The recommendations outlined above, once adjusted for age, generally apply to school-age children as well. (One exception: time out, which isn't usually appropriate for this age group.) The specific situations will have changed over time, and the nature of parent–child interactions will have become more complex, but the same approaches that are creative for five-year-olds should be effective for ten-year-olds, including:

- Being empathetic

- Looking for root causes of behavior

- Solving problems together

- Clarifying situations

- Negotiating clear limits together

- Being consistent in following through.

My general recommendation is to "stay the course." Here are a few additional suggestions.

Keep Developmental Issues in Mind

As the years pass, children alternate periods of organized behavior with periods of disorganized or regressive behavior. Many difficulties and conflicts result from changes in your child's emotional, social, motor, intellectual, and linguistic development, or from disparities among these various aspects. You need to expect age-appropriate behavior from your child; at the same time, you need to be flexible. Your child's development won't be consistent. He may seem mature and well-behaved at certain times but surprisingly immature and "difficult" at others. These inconsistencies are normal, so you should be ready for many ups and downs. Children don't develop in a steady, clear-cut progression of stages. To complicate matters, each child is different from all other children, so you can't assume that his development will necessarily follow the sequence you see in his siblings or in friends' or relatives' kids. (See Appendix A for details.)

Be Prepared for Regression

A corollary to the above: even the most verbal, accomplished, sophisticated children can regress to earlier developmental stages. In addition, children often "hold themselves together" while at school or elsewhere, then regress once they're back home. Precisely because you're the parent, your child sees you as safe; he can risk being immature, disorganized, outrageous, silly, and babyish in your company. As frustrating as this situation may feel, it's a good sign, for it shows that your child can hold himself together elsewhere, then let loose when he's in an environment he fully trusts. Stay patient with these regressions; they're simply part of your child's gradual process of maturation.

Stress *Preventive* Attention Rather Than *Reactive* Attention

Giving your child attention and TLC when he's behaving well is more effective than responding only when he misbehaves. Close, caring time together will, in fact, reinforce his good behavior, while reactive attention inadvertently gives the message that he must misbehave for you to notice him.

Monitor the Limits You've Set

What works at one developmental stage may be ineffective or counterproductive a few months later, so be ready to change your expectations for your child's behavior. Don't expect to coast for long—if at all. Go with the ups and downs of your child's development.

Take Advantage of Older Kids' More Sophisticated Skills

Some of the challenges you'll face may now seem more complex than before, but dealing with the challenges may grow easier. School-age children can often explain more clearly what's bothering them. If you can encourage and cultivate your child's verbal sophistication, you'll have an easier task now than when he was less articulate. Foster and reward good-faith efforts at negotiation; stay calm as you deal with situations; take advantage of opportunities to solve problems together.

Discipline for Teens

The teen years present numerous and often difficult challenges regarding discipline and parental authority. As they mature, adolescents grow more and more independent; at the same time, they can be inconsistent, willfully provocative, and capable of major lapses of judgment. The result is that most parents face a tricky series of decisions about what constitutes acceptable behavior and what should be the consequences for infractions.

Many of the basic principles we've already discussed regarding discipline and younger children also apply (with some necessary modifications) to teenagers as well. For children of any age, I suggest these precepts:

- Look for the root causes of misbehavior.

- Communicate openly and calmly.

- Set clear limits.

- Be consistent.

- Collaborate on solving problems.

- Emphasize positive rather than negative reinforcement.

- Avoid any kind of physical punishment.

In addition, you should pay special attention to setting and maintaining age-appropriate limits, as this issue will have an inordinate effect on your parental authority and its effectiveness in shaping your teen's behavior.

Many parents struggle with adolescents' growing independence. Teens are notoriously social creatures, and peers are central to their lives. A gradually increasing level of freedom is crucial to teenagers' happiness and development. What, though, is the proper level? The answer to that question depends on their age and maturity. You'll need to assess the situation based on the nature of your community, your teen's age, his overall behavior, and other factors. In general, though, it's important for you to remain fully involved in deciding the nature and timing of your child's activities. It's true that teens will generally demand more rather than less autonomy; they will "push the envelope." That said, you are still the parent; you are still in charge. You should use your authority with care, but it's also important that you not let teens' assumptions about what's acceptable erode your authority as a parent.

In response to this situation, you should set clear limits on what is and isn't acceptable, both in terms of activities and the timing of those activities. Here are my suggestions:

- Don't set limits according to what your child tells you about other families' rules. If you wish, check with other parents about their expectations and activities, but make your own decisions.

- As your teen earns your trust, you can extend the limits you've set—limits for what he can do, how long he can be out, and so forth.

- Insist on having a phone number where you can reach your child. If necessary, call other parents to verify that the activities are what you assume they are and that adult supervision will be present.

- Don't feel intimidated by your child's claims that "You're the only parent who calls," or similar objections. He may complain about your rules, but he'll know you care and will appreciate your concern, at least in the long run.

- Explain the background for why you're setting limits. "We trust you and care about you, but we do worry about outside influences, and we want you to be safe." The message throughout is respect, love, and concern.

- Major violations of the limits should warrant grounding or other appropriate consequences, with the severity of the consequences dependent on the severity of the problem. Try not to over- or underreact. Sometimes giving your teen the benefit of the doubt is effective; just pointing out the problem will remind him of what you expect or identify the natural consequences of his behavior. This strategy may prompt his compliance in the future.

- When setting limits, stand firm. Follow through on consequences; don't threaten, then back off. Waffling and inconsistency will erode your authority faster and more severely than almost anything else you do or don't do.

- It's easier to set firm limits initially, then ease up as your child grows and matures; if you set vague limits and only later attempt to tighten the rules, you'll have a far more difficult task.

The Do's and Don'ts of Discipline

Although discipline is a complex set of issues in any family, here are some suggestions that summarize issues of discipline at most developmental stages:

- Stay in the present; focus on what's affecting your child *now* rather than what you experienced during your own childhood.

- Teach your child discipline through role-modeling and love rather than through domination and punishment.

- Have high but not extreme standards.

- Make the rules reasonable, clear, and consistent.

- Don't be judgmental; whenever possible, comment on your child's behavior, not on his being or essence. For example, say, "I love you, but I don't like your behavior right now."

- Avoid anger—be curious, not furious.

- Avoid sarcasm, ridicule, or other indirect, ineffective forms of communication.

- Don't scream, nag, moralize, or resort to name-calling.

- Don't humiliate—validate; give your kid lots of positive reinforcement.

- Teach internal self-control rather than resorting to external pressure.

- Negotiate, helping your child to compromise on age-appropriate issues.

- Help your child learn to express his feelings verbally rather than by lashing out physically.

- Give your child plenty of one-on-one attention so he doesn't have to act out negatively to gain the spotlight.

- Don't overschedule your child, because lack of "downtime" can stress out kids and lead to aggression.

- Don't spank your child, as physical punishment humiliates children, shames them, and teaches them to express frustration through aggressive behavior.

- Choose your battles; rather than responding to every negative behavior or saying no all the time, find ways to reframe your child's behavior in a positive manner.

CONFLICT

Conflict is inevitable in family life. No matter how thoughtful you are and no matter how well your children behave, disagreements and misunderstandings will occur. You will have to insist on behavior that your child resents. You will annoy or aggravate your child at times; he will annoy or aggravate you in turn. This situation isn't altogether pleasant, but anger, frustration, and irritability are potentially normal, healthy emotions within the context of family life. What's important is to be open to your feelings, open to your child's feelings as well, and willing to deal with the give-and-take of solving problems together. If you can respond in these ways, conflicts are generally manageable and potentially creative. After all, family life is the first (and often ideal) place in which children master the intricate task of getting along with other people.

At the same time, it's true that managing conflict requires time, attention, and sensitivity. Dealing with conflict creatively makes the difference between a pleasant, relatively low-stress family life and an unpleasant, stressful family life. In addition, coping successfully with conflict will bolster your parental authority, which in turn will facilitate dealing with conflicts in the future.

Here are some suggestions for coping with family conflicts.

Validate Your Child's Feelings

When your child has acquired enough language skills to speak about his feelings, one of your tasks will be to validate his emotions verbally. By "validate" I don't mean that you necessarily accept or agree with what he's saying or doing; rather, you're giving him a kind of mirror in which he can see his emotions and clarify the situation. He may not even *understand* what he feels, but mirroring his emotions will help him learn to perceive his own state of mind. Some typical validations:

- "You seem frustrated with what your teacher said."

- "It must be hard to have a new baby in the house."

- "It seems like you're very angry with me today."

- "You must feel annoyed to throw the toy down on the floor like that."

By validating your child's feelings, you allow him to express all sides of himself, including expressions of normal aggression and anger. You are also showing your respect for his emotions. This accepting, nonjudgmental attitude helps him identify his feelings and have more control over them in the future.

Your effort to mirror his emotions shouldn't be limited to "negative" feelings; you can also comment on your child's pride in a job well done, his kindness or generosity toward others, his delight in pleasant experiences, and so forth. This process is especially constructive among younger children, who respond warmly to parents' acknowledgment of good behavior. Helping your child become aware of his positive states of mind—and to feel good about them—will limit his need to act negatively as a way of getting your attention.

Be Supportive and Nonjudgmental

You should also help your child understand that feelings aren't right or wrong; they just *are*. Some emotions may feel unpleasant, but the feelings themselves won't hurt your child or anyone else. Although feelings are complex and often intense, they are usually normal. Reassure him, too, that he can feel simultaneously happy and sad; he can even feel love, annoyance, longing, and anger all at once.

These are normal emotions for people to feel in a close relationship. If you can reassure your child that his feelings aren't bad, your reassurance can help him accept himself, which in turn can ease feelings of wariness or hostility toward others. Emotional awareness of this sort will also help him understand what others are feeling and doing. If another kid acts in negative ways, your child will be less likely to take the offense so personally. By being empathic—and by modeling empathic behavior—you will also help your child develop empathy. All of these efforts will reinforce your parental authority by strengthening the parent–child bond through love, understanding, and mutual respect.

Look for Root Causes

Root causes generally lie beneath every misbehavior or misconduct. Your child may feel jealous of a newborn brother or sister; he may resent you for working long hours; he may feel stressed by an impending move. Try to consider not just the outwardly visible situation—a fussy, angry, or uncooperative child—but also whatever is going on *within* the child or his environment. Go beyond the behavior to consider the source of these problems. To the degree that you can figure out the larger picture, you'll make better sense of why your child acts or feels as he does.

Allow Choice—Or the Illusion of Choice

Many conflicts occur when children can't decide how to respond to a situation. They feel uncertain about what's going to happen, or they want both of two contradictory options, such as going to the movies *and* staying home to play. How can you respond to these situations? To some degree, the answer depends on your child's age.

If your child is under six or seven, you should respond by offering only limited choices:

- "I'll fix you either a sandwich or some pizza."

- "You can either play with Matthew or come with me to the park."

- "Here are two outfits you can wear, so pick the one you prefer."

- "You can have either a movie or a zoo outing for your birthday party."

Limited choices allow your child a measure of independence but avoid overwhelming him with too many options, which children often find confusing or anxiety producing.

Older children need more flexibility. Eight- to twelve-year-olds will want a variety of options about what they can or can't do; teenagers should have opportunities for even greater input. Don't grant free rein; as the parent, you still have a right to make the final decisions. However, it's appropriate to allow children greater responsibility as they grow and develop. Your role includes compromise and negotiation. At the same time, you should stress that family life requires compromise and accommodation by all parties, your child included.

Choose Your Battles

Don't make every disagreement or misbehavior into a battle, as you and your child will both become frustrated and exhausted. Avoid reacting to every challenge, taunt, provocation, or incident that family life presents; there just isn't enough time in the day to struggle with your child every time he disagrees with you. More to the point, it's not healthy for anyone in the family if every issue becomes contentious. So when your child confronts you with frustrating challenges, how should you respond?

Stress Cooperation and Negotiation

Some families are so competitive that every conflict leads to a "winner" and a "loser." In many cases, children imitate the parents' contentious, high-stress behavior. I find this situation unfortunate. In my opinion, allowing or encouraging this sort of competition depletes family life of its potential for congenial, low-keyed satisfaction. My suggestion: stop trying to score points! Don't set up a divisive mood in the family or stress winning arguments and disagreements; focus instead on how family members should work together.

Let Your Child "Win" Some of the Time

Children feel frustrated and anxious when they believe that adults have all the power. In fact, adults really *ought* to be in control of most situations. Obviously this situation changes as kids grow up and mature; however, the bedrock of family life should be that adults are in charge. How, then, should you deal with your child's need to feel a sense of participation and mastery?

For starters, let him feel a degree of control some of the time. This response can vary according to the situation and your child's age. In playing sports, it's appropriate to let younger kids believe they're capable of gaining the upper hand—scoring the goal, hitting the homer—some of the time. The same holds true for board games, quiz games, and so forth. Older kids must learn to face the reality of their skill levels, however, and not be indulged into believing that they're competent beyond their true abilities. Most kids also benefit from an element of limited choice, such as having some input on selection of foods. That's also valid for selection of clothes to wear. The key throughout is to find a happy medium—some choice, but not too much.

Reassure Your Child about Your Presence

Some conflicts occur because children are simply trying to get your attention. Instead of waiting for their anxieties to promote attention-getting misbehavior, give them as much comforting reassurance as possible, and do so *before* they feel a need to behave in negative ways to gain your attention. Parents of young children need to get down to their level, provide eye contact, and speak face to face, especially when giving directions. Your tone of voice should be firm, direct, and warm, not loud, angry, or hostile. For older children, reassurance has more to do with your availability after school and each evening, when kids need parents to be around for discussions of the school day, help with homework, and so forth.

Be Aware of Developmental Leaps

At certain stages of development—the most obvious being the toddler years—children change and develop with dramatic speed. These surges can lead to conflicts over certain issues, because your child may be acquiring a need for greater independence, autonomy, or responsibility. If you insist on adhering to long-standing assumptions about what's appropriate or inappropriate for your child, you may end up in needless conflict. There's no easy answer to this dilemma. An awareness of child development issues, however, can prepare you for dealing with the situation. Parenting books, videos, and magazines can be helpful. Parenting groups are a common and useful resource as well. (See Appendix A, Child Development, and Appendix B, Resource Guide, for suggestions.)

Express Empathy

Empathy is one of the keys to resolving conflicts. Try to recall how you felt at your child's age. Read books on child development to keep your perspective. Validate your child's feelings. Offer praise rather than criticism. Set age-appropriate limits. Use your sense of humor to defuse tensions. Open your child's mind to alternatives. Never attack your child's character; instead, focus on his behavior.

Model Appropriate Behavior

As we've discussed, your child will tend to model his behavior after your own. If you're tense, he's more likely to be tense; if you're bossy, he's more likely to be bossy; if you're accusatory, he's more likely to be, too. The same holds true if you deal with conflict by shouting, throwing tantrums, or resorting to the "silent treatment." He will, in short, tend to act as you do. For this reason, I urge you to be consistent, not only regarding your child's behavior but your own as well. Demanding that he work through conflicts rationally and peacefully simply won't pay off if your own behavior is irrational or belligerent.

When Necessary, Exert Your Authority

Inevitably there will be times when your child's behavior is relentless, chaotic, disruptive, or risky to himself or others. There will be times when nothing you say or do seems to resolve the situation. Under these circumstances, you have no alternative but to exert your authority. Your child may resent your intervention, and you may feel hesitant about doing so, but it has to be done. You are the parent—and you have both the legal right and the moral responsibility to do what's in your child's best interests.

What you do, of course, will vary in accordance with your child's developmental stage. The situation is relatively simple with a toddler or preschooler: you take a stand, act decisively, and do what needs to be done. The situation is more complex with an older child. Still, taking action is part of your parental role. Although the words may sound trite, there will be times during the parenting years when you simply have to say "This is how it's going to be," "Because I'm your mother," or "Because I say so." I urge you to use these categorical statements *as a last resort*; if you rely on them too frequently, you'll reduce their effectiveness and damage your parental authority. That said, you should draw the line when it's necessary.

Track the Sources of Your Own Response

Conflict isn't always what it seems. Let's say you react to your child's behavior in an especially intense way, or else you can't shake a negative response to what's happening. In such cases, consider what other issues may be influencing you. It's possible, for instance, that certain aspects of your own past—memories of your own upbringing, perhaps, or conflicts with your parents—are influencing what you're saying and doing in the present. You may resist this notion, but it isn't farfetched. All of us have learned much of what we know about parent–child interactions from our own families; the past retains a powerful grip even decades later.

How can you deal with these issues? First of all, it's unlikely that you'll be able to resolve the situation in the midst of a heated conflict with your child. Instead, it's best to step back, cope as well as possible under the circumstances, and face the wider issues later. This usually means a parent–child discussion after the conflict has subsided. In cases of severe or recurrent conflicts, it may involve working with a counselor or therapist. See chapter 4 of this book for further discussions of these issues.

Read Your Child for Signs of Stress

The conflict you're coping with may be nothing more than what it seems to be. However, many parent–child conflicts aren't evident on the surface, and many also become supercharged by stress (including stress that isn't even relevant to the main problem). For this reason, it's important to keep an eye on your child's stress level.

Like adults, children often show signs that indicate stress reactions. These reactions aren't necessarily problematic in their own right; however, they can indicate that your child is under pressure and needs more empathy, affection, guidance, or support than usual. How can you tell? Tip-offs include biting or chewing of nails, picking at skin, clearing the throat, sucking fingers, verbal tics or stuttering, facial twitching, erratic appetite, protracted moodiness, or sleep disturbances. Trying to find the root cause of these behaviors is crucial; scolding or shaming your child won't help and may aggravate the situation. If you notice your child exhibiting one or more of these signs, obtain further input from your child's teacher, the school guidance counselor, or your pediatrician.

Let Your Child Vent His Frustration

All children feel aggressive impulses, frustration, anger, and other "negative" emotions. If you force your child to ignore, deny, or repress these feelings, the effort may backfire and cause further difficulties. That said, your child needs to learn appropriate ways to express what he's feeling and to avoid disturbing other people. Acquiring the verbal skills to put frustrations into perspective is one such way. In addition, your child needs outlets that will let him vent frustration and release tension.

One channel is physical activity: running, jumping, playing at a playground, or taking part in age-appropriate sports. Other channels involve punching pillows, hitting a punching bag, or releasing energy in other harmless ways. Less physically active children can let off steam by drawing pictures, playing with clay, kneading dough, or using puppets to act out aggression and frustration. Try to respond to these outpourings of emotion without taking them personally. Children need useful ways to learn self-control without denying the reality of their emotions.

Have Realistic Expectations

Rules and limits are important in every household, but make sure that they are realistic, because setting expectations too high or too low may frustrate your child and lead to conflict. If you expect a three-year-old to sit alone for an hour while assembling a puzzle, for instance, you're likely to encounter trouble; sitting with your child and helping him assemble the puzzle is far more appropriate. Another example: expecting a teenager to focus on family get-togethers to the exclusion of peer-group activities will often lead to conflict. To simplify the task of avoiding and resolving conflicts with children, know what's truly realistic at a given developmental stage and adapt your expectations appropriately to meet your child's developmental needs.

Monitor Dependence and Independence

At the root of many conflicts are issues of dependence and independence, which are complex and often contradictory. On the one hand, your child may resent you for allowing him too little freedom, which restricts his ability to grow and change; on the other hand, he may feel pressured to grow up too quickly. Every child must separate and individuate, but doing so successfully requires a strong sense of security—security in terms of both trusting himself and trusting the people around him. He also needs enough freedom to explore his abilities and develop new skills. If there's an imbalance between security and freedom, there may be an increase in parent–child tensions. If you can monitor these issues and find a balance between them, you'll be more responsive to what your child needs.

Bolster Self-Respect

A child who feels respected will respect others too, and he'll have higher standards for his own behavior. He'll have a strong sense of himself and a clearer sense of security. He'll be less inclined to whine, blame others for his difficulties, or act out. He'll be more capable of taking responsibility and standing up for himself. He will feel more complete as a human being, more accepting of himself.

By contrast, a child who doesn't feel respected will feel incomplete, restless, and insecure. He'll feel less sure of what he needs and less confident about getting his needs met, which can lead to demanding, fussy behavior. He may be less capable of controlling his impulses and more likely to lash out at others or demonstrate other compulsive behaviors, such as undereating or overeating, talking obsessively, or touching other children aggressively.

In general, children feel highly affected by how others treat them—and especially by how their parents treat them. As a result, I strongly urge parents to do whatever they can to reinforce their children's self-respect. Children who feel secure and good about themselves will be disinclined to conflicts with others. If your child feels confident of your love, there still will be conflicts because some conflict is inherent in family life. But the conflicts will be manageable and creative—part of the process of learning to get along with others and to compromise as you try to fulfill each others' needs.

DISCIPLINE AS GUIDANCE

When social scientists have asked parents which aspects of family life they find most stressful, discipline has often shown up at the top of the list. It's not hard to imagine why. The need for discipline arises during some of the most stressful parent–child interactions. Discipline often requires actions that the parent doesn't want to take and that the child doesn't want to tolerate. In addition, discipline isn't a one-time event; it occurs over the long haul, often with ambiguous results. Small wonder that parents feel uneasy about having to discipline their kids.

The key, I believe, is to view discipline as education. The connection between these two concepts is implicit in the Latin root *disciplina*: "instruction, teaching; training; order, way of living." I agree with Selma Fraiberg, who, writing in *The Magic Years: Understanding and Handling the Problems of Early Childhood*, stated that "I am in favor of restoring the word 'discipline' to its ancient and honorable sense . . . [W]hen employed for child-rearing it should have the significance of education of character." Or, as Dr. Spock puts it more bluntly:

The everyday job of the parent is to keep the child on the right track by means of firmness and consistency. Though children do the major share in civilizing themselves, through love and imitation, it still leaves plenty for parents to do . . . [T]he child supplies the power but the parents have to do the steering.

As you cope with the issues of parental authority, I encourage you to embrace this notion of discipline as guidance.

Chapter 4

THE INFLUENCES OF TEMPERAMENT AND GENDER

Marissa and David Jesperson are experienced parents. During her late twenties, Marissa gave birth to two daughters, Sadie and Jacqueline. Both parents have been heavily involved in raising the girls. By the time the new arrival was born, Sadie and Jacqueline were six and four, and David and Marissa felt they knew the ropes. "We were ready for anything," Marissa explains. "We'd been through the early childhood stages not once but twice. Would it be so difficult to raise a third child? Well—it was. Nothing about raising the girls prepared us for Damien's arrival on the scene."

The new baby was totally unlike his sisters. Sadie and Jacqueline had been different from one another in many ways: Sadie was quieter, while Jacqueline was more rambunctious. Still, Damien had a personality altogether different from his sisters. He was fussy, restless, and demanding. His toddler years strained the whole family's patience as Damien tested limits, threw tantrums, and took the lion's share of his parents' attention. As he entered elementary school, Damien acted more self-centered, less cooperative, more manipulative, and in all ways more challenging than the other two children. Both Marissa and David often felt as if they'd needed to acquire a whole new set of parenting skills to cope with their son.

"The hardest part for me was not knowing what would work," David says. "I prided myself on being a good father. I wanted to do the right thing for Damien, just as I'd tried to do the right thing for the girls. But I didn't know anymore what the right thing *was*."

Marissa concurs but adds, "Dealing with him would have been easier if we'd understood what accounted for his behavior. He's been this huge puzzle from the start. He is so unlike his sisters! But we've never really understood why—whether it's a boy–girl thing, or maybe birth order, or just the nature of his personality. Maybe Damien is difficult just because he's Damien."

In a sense, Marissa and David's parenting tasks would be similar regardless of the cause of their son's behavior. They'd need to feed and protect the new baby during his first two years; they'd need to continue nurturing him while simultaneously allowing him to explore the world during his toddler years; and they'd need to provide age-appropriate opportunities and limits as their son grew. These tasks have a lot in common regardless of the individual child's specific attributes. That said, it's true that almost all parents try to make sense of their children's personalities, and many (perhaps most) attempt to figure out why their children behave as they do. Ascribing attitudes and behaviors to factors such as temperament, gender, and personality are among the ways that mothers and fathers try to understand their kids and determine how better to attend to their needs.

THE PUZZLE OF INDIVIDUALITY

Speak to anyone who's the parent of two or more children and you'll probably hear him or her remark at some point on the puzzle of individuality. "I can't believe how *different* they are," people say, or "It's amazing that such different children can have the same biological origin," or "They're so unlike each other." Underlying all these exclamations is a fundamental question: How is it possible that kids who share the same parents and the same family environment can be such remarkably distinct people?

No one has definitively answered this question. On the contrary, a debate has raged for generations regarding what's often summed up as Nature versus Nurture. Is the personality determined more by the roll of the DNA "dice," or is it affected more by environment, including such issues as birth order, the effects of the parents' personalities, sibling relationships, the presence of surrogate caregivers, and so forth? The short answer seems to be that both genetics and outside influences matter greatly. Genetics unquestionably provide the raw materials that constitute a human being, but outside influences, including the parents, have a vast ability to shape those materials.

How Does Individuality Affect Parental Authority?

For parents, one of the most vexing aspects of children's individuality is how it affects parental authority. Kids are anything but generic. Even as newborns, when children's needs are relatively uniform, babies can be strikingly specific about what they like and don't like. Toddlers are notoriously opinionated about what they'll accept and what they'll reject. During later years, preschoolers and school-age children are idiosyncratic as well. During these developmental stages, some parental approaches are highly productive while others seem ineffective, pointless, or even counterproductive. Although it's true that some patterns of parenting work well and others don't, all children benefit from parental consistency. All need affection, affirmation, and support. At the same time, individual children have their own needs and preferences, and these needs and preferences influence what parents find useful in helping kids grow, learn, and mature.

To complicate matters, parents themselves are unique individuals. Each mother or father comes to the task of raising children with a complex mix of skills, shortcomings, personal attributes, cultural expectations, fears, hopes, and memories. Parents' own personalities influence how they perceive and exert their authority. Each dad's or mom's parental choices are influenced by his or her own temperament, assumptions about gender roles, and past personal experiences.

It's challenging to deal with issues of parental authority while taking your child's (and your own) individuality into account. Unfortunately, there are no easy answers to the complex interplay between parents and children. However, I believe that examining certain aspects of individuality can be useful. You can benefit from insights into what makes your children who they are. You can also benefit from understanding influences on your own personality. Regarding parental authority, the most important among these insights are those concerning *temperament, gender*, and *the past*.

TEMPERAMENT

One of the most remarkable things about babies is how different they are from each other. Even as newborns, babies are anything but the "blank slates" that some people tend to consider them. Some are serene, some nervous, some alert; some are easily reassured when uncomfortable, some difficult to calm; some are eager to be held, some less comfortable with human contact. Older infants, too, have distinct personality attributes. Studying hundreds of children as part of a long-term study, psychologists Stella Chess, Alexander Thomas, and Herbert G. Birch analyzed and described some of the characteristics that are generally called *temperament*, the individual's specific inborn characteristics. Chess and her colleagues ultimately listed nine features of temperament:

- Activity level
- Regularity (in eating, sleeping, and elimination)

- Approach or withdrawal in response to new situations

- Adaptability to changes in routine

- Level of sensitivity to sensory thresholds

- Positive or negative mood

- Intensity of response (that is, in energy expended)

- Distractibility (that is, ability to concentrate or tendency to lose concentration)

- Persistence and attention span.

Intermixed, these nine features combined to form a great variety of personalities—the aggregates of response to experience. As babies grow and develop, temperament can undergo changes as a result of outside influences. A child with a high degree of sensitivity to sensory stimulation (what we might call a "jumpy" child) who's also inclined to withdraw from new situations (what we might call "shy") may, over time, respond favorably to a calm, reassuring parent. By contrast, a jumpy, shy child might tend to become more sensitive to stimulation and more inclined to withdraw in a family situation where the parents aren't willing or able to offer reassurance. Does this mean that the child's temperament has changed in either situation? Probably not. However, what I'm describing touches on an issue that we discussed earlier: the interplay between nature and nurture. Parenting has the potential to diminish or intensify at least the expression of inborn temperament. The child adapts to the parents as much as the parent adapts to the child.

There's another important aspect to this situation. Temperament doesn't exist in isolation. The parent–child relationship is interactive, and temperament plays a major role in that interaction. Just as the parent's moods and behaviors influence the child, the child's moods and behaviors in turn influence the parent. Ellen Galinsky eloquently describes this mutual interaction in *The Six Stages of Parenthood*:

> In the first weeks of life, parents begin discovering what pleases and what distresses the baby . . . Parents learn the skill of paying attention, of being empathetic with and responding to the baby's cues and clues. This is the way that parents answer their own questions, reduce their anxieties, sort through their images . . . and strengthen their relationship with their newborn. This skill, one which often has to be learned and relearned, underlies the entire course of parenthood.

Part of what all mothers and fathers must do is assess how their own temperaments interact with the child's temperament, combining to create a relationship that's complex and—to complicate matters further—constantly changing. For instance, sedate parents with a high-energy child may tend to regard that child as too active—perhaps even as clinically hyperactive—simply because of the disparity between their own energy level and the child's. There may be nothing *wrong* with either the parents or the child; there's simply an awkward "fit" between them. The same lack of "fit" can occur when energetic parents are caring for a quiet or withdrawn child. Either way, the disparity between temperaments may create unease, frustration, or resentment.

Here's an example. I know a Midwestern couple who are raising a large family—four sons and a daughter. The oldest three children are boys, currently fourteen, twelve, and eleven years old; the fourth child is a girl, age nine; and the youngest child is a boy, age seven. The first three boys have all been energetic, loud, and gregarious from the start. They gravitated toward sports and outdoor activities, and they are all high-spirited and group-oriented. Meg and Drew, the mother and father, have experienced the normal ups and downs throughout the years of raising these boys, but they adjusted well to their sons' intensity, as both parents are active, physical people themselves. It never really troubled the parents that their sons would bomb into the house, whooping and hollering, or that their favorite activities all involved aggressive sports.

What mystified them, however, was their daughter, Sue, born two years after the third son. Sue was an altogether different creature. Though physically strong, she gravitated toward quieter pursuits, especially science and math. She always seemed uneasy with her brothers' intensity and leery of their activities. Was it a consequence of gender, Drew and Meg wondered, that Sue preferred less "boyish" pursuits? Both parents—Meg especially—resisted this notion. They had tried from the start to avoid stereotyping their kids along gender lines, and Meg herself had always been a tomboy, so they wanted to avoid pegging Sue as subdued by virtue of her femininity. What concerned them more than classifying Sue was simply dealing with her. They found her dislike of sports baffling, they worried that she was too withdrawn, and they wished they could draw her out of her shell.

Interestingly, they faced a similar dilemma upon the birth of their fifth child. Jared was a boy, yet he acted at least as quiet as Sue, often more so. Unlike Sue, who expressed occasional interest in noncompetitive sports, Jared expressed an almost total aversion to physical activities. He appeared to be artistically gifted, especially in music and the visual arts, and he felt happiest when left to play by himself. Drew and Meg now faced a second challenge: first, how to explain their youngest child's attitudes and behaviors when gender clearly played no part in determining them; second, how to respond imaginatively to the practical tasks of parenting such different children.

The issue of parental authority can be daunting in this sort of situation. Meg and Drew found, as many parents do, that exerting their authority meant different things with different children. "With the older boys," Meg explains, "we had to shape their behavior in the same way we did everything else with them—with lots of energy! If they did what they were supposed to, we rewarded them with lots of hugs and affectionate rough-housing. If they misbehaved as toddlers, we had to restrain them during their tantrums or they'd have knocked the house down. Later, as they grew older, we'd punish any misbehavior by depriving them of physical activities they wanted, such as sports or camping trips. There's no way a technique like time out would've worked with them—they'd've just run away." The situation with the two younger kids was far different. "Sue and Jared were something else. I could just look at them and they'd shape up. They were *so* responsive to approval and disapproval. Time out was very effective." Because the older two children and the younger three children were temperamentally different, Meg and Drew needed two different styles of authority—one more outgoing and direct, the other more restrained and subtle.

Coping with Issues of Temperament

To cope with temperament and its affects on parental authority, I have the following suggestions:

- *Keep in mind that temperament is a "given."* Just as your child is born with certain inherent physical characteristics, he has certain inherent temperamental tendencies, too. Temperament can't be totally changed; you can't *make* a shy child be more forthright by force of will. That said, temperament isn't entirely unchanging either. You can reassure and nurture a shy child, for instance, in ways that may build confidence and strengthen emotional stability.

- *Don't take your child's temperament personally.* If you find aspects of his behavior exhausting or frustrating, that's fair enough. But keep in mind that your child isn't behaving in those ways on purpose any more than he's making his hair black on purpose. Try to stay steady in such situations; your emotional stability and nonjudgmental tone will do far more to ease tensions than resisting your child.

- *Take the long view.* Whatever else, children develop and change. A jumpy, restless child may grow more relaxed over time. A shy child may become more confident. Consistent, patient expressions of your authority will help both you and your child over the long haul.

GENDER

The second issue that frequently affects how parents view and express their authority is gender.

- Mariella describes the tasks she faces in getting her eight-year-old daughter and seven-year-old son to cooperate: "If I explain what needs to be done, Noël gets the picture at once and helps me out. Jason may or may not understand, but in any case I have to nag and nag to get him on board."

- By contrast, Jeannine and Jeff have three sons, each of whom responds differently to parental requests and demands. "Our sons are all such 'typical boys'—they love sports, rough-housing, and kidding around. But they're so different in how they respond to us as parents. Mike, the oldest, has always been a real trouper and helps us out in any way he can. Billie, the middle child, is quiet but incredibly stubborn. Jackson is the youngest and definitely tenderhearted, yet he can cause twice the trouble of the other two combined."

- Sally and Pete face an even more complex situation with their kids: fraternal triplets, two boys and a girl, currently all ten years old; and a younger daughter, age six. Of the boys, one is shy and quiet-spoken, while the other is more demanding, even aggressive. The older daughter is rather brash, perhaps out of necessity, given two brothers exactly her age. The younger daughter is often subdued, even withdrawn, in the company of her siblings.

Asked outright about gender differences, most parents tend to state that boys and girls behave differently in some respects. Many mothers and fathers assert that such differences exist even at a very early age. Some even believe that they can see the differences from the time of their children's birth. "Boys and girls are so *different*," many parents have told me. A friend describes her daughter and son in all-or-nothing terms: "Brenda is 100% girl and Rick is 100% boy."

How valid are these claims? The data on innate male–female differences is still accumulating, and much of it is subtle and ambiguous. To complicate matters, every culture—ours included—holds some prejudices about the "nature" of males and the "nature" of females. As a result, our society expects at least slightly different behavior from girls and boys; we respond differently to boys' and girls' behavior, and our expectations in turn affect how our sons and daughters respond to us. The jumble of all these influences complicates the task of determining the effects of gender on personality and behavior, which in turn complicates the tasks that parents face in defining their authority within the family and responding creatively to their kids.

Innate Male–Female Differences

In addition to having slightly different genetic makeups and different reproductive and urinary anatomy, boys and girls differ in a number of subtle or striking ways.

- The endocrine system, including the composition and levels of hormones at various developmental stages, differs markedly in males and females.

- Brain structure, as well as other aspects of neuroanatomy and neurophysiology, differs in males and females. Most notably, the corpus callosum—the bundle of nerve fibers that connects the two brain hemispheres—is larger in females than in males.

The two hemispheres of the brain also develop at different rates in the two sexes.

- Girls are hardier and physiologically more resilient than boys. From birth on, boys suffer from more health problems than girls do, including significantly greater risks for asthma, intellectual disabilities, and sudden infant death syndrome.

- Baby boys and male toddlers appear to be more emotionally vulnerable than girls; changes of routine, intense stimuli, or even tones of voice upset young boys more than girls. Baby boys and male toddlers cry more, become upset more easily, and remain upset longer than girls do.

- Girls are more physically mature than boys even in utero, and girls mature faster than boys in most respects following birth.

- Even very young boys have higher levels of testosterone than girls do; in addition, researchers know that boys have lower levels of serotonin, a neurotransmitter that inhibits aggression and impulsivity.

I should offer several caveats, however.

First, these differences apply to boys *as a group* and to girls *as a group*. Individual boys and girls may manifest individual characteristics that overrule the generalities.

Second, these differences are only now beginning to be identified and understood; it's easy to jump to conclusions about them or to use them to justify gender bias. (I'm dismayed by how many parents still stereotype their kids according to rigid assumptions about boys and girls.)

Third, these anatomic and physiological differences are *only one aspect* of what makes boys different from girls. Many social issues, such as gender stereotypes and parental responses to boys and girls, influence the situation at least as much as innate characteristics do.

Nurture as Well as Nature

Not just nature, but also nurture shapes children. Parents, siblings, teachers, and society all affect kids and their development—how they learn to behave, how they perceive themselves and others, and how they acquire the values they consider important. The elements of nurture are at least as complex as the elements of nature. Among other things, children are influenced by expectations about sex roles, which heavily affect kids' perceptions of how they should interact with others. There's no question that how parents perceive and treat their children will influence the kids' development. Susan Gilbert sums up this situation in *A Field Guide to Boys and Girls*:

> [Boys and girls] are treated differently, and the ways that parents . . . respond to them can amplify or mute their biological tendencies. Baby girls may get the language centers of their brains up and running before boys do, but parents and other adults also spend more time talking to girls. So, both nature and nurture help give them an edge verbally. We can't change nature, but tinkering with the nurture part of the equation can influence whether gender differences in language and other areas are great or small.

The Risks of Gender Bias

As a parent, your attitudes and actions about gender differences help to form your child's sense of self, self-esteem, and confidence. You want to help your child become the best person that he or she can be. Your expectations can influence how far your child will go in reaching his or her greatest potential. Either high or low expectations can be self-perpetuating. Low expectations can lead to indifference, discouragement, and limited success or endeavors. High expectations can lead to confidence, pride, and greater success. (That said, high-pressure or unreasonable expectations can be as harmful as low expectations.) If you have certain preconceived ideas of what constitutes a boy and what constitutes a girl—that is, if you have a predefined sense of what interests are appropriate and what behaviors are permissible for each sex—then you risk limiting your child. You aren't really looking at the child as a whole person, but rather are imposing our own gender biases onto the child. This attitude can create a vicious cycle that alters your child's self-image.

One of the trickiest issues affected by gender differences is parental authority. My specific concern is that if you view your child too thoroughly through the lens of gender, you risk distorting your perceptions of your son or daughter. This distortion can, in turn, damage your parental authority. I'm not saying that you should attempt to see your child as "gender neutral"; on the contrary, it's important to cherish your son as a boy and your daughter as a girl. But cherishing your son's masculinity and your daughter's femininity doesn't mean following societal stereotypes for male and female behavior. I urge you to take a wide view of "maleness" and "femaleness" as you parent your child. Doing so will help you see gender as a complex *range* of behaviors and attitudes rather than as a narrow *wedge* of preconceived and predefined behaviors and attitudes. Your flexibility will bolster your child's self-confidence, and in turn reinforce his or her trust in your authority.

Bret and Olga are raising a son and a daughter. Both children are thoughtful and artistic. Judith, fourteen, loves ballet, modern dance, and classical music. Ben, twelve, is a gifted singer who also enjoys painting and other visual arts. The parents admire the kids' achievements although—or because—neither the mom or the dad has any talents in these areas. Bret feels concerned, however, that his son has become too preoccupied with his musical pursuits. He's fine about Ben delving into the arts, but he wishes that the boy would "balance" his interests with more traditionally male avocations such as sports. It bothers Bret that Ben couldn't care less about sports. Ben has even told his dad to "get off my back," which Bret finds deeply hurtful. As a result, the father tends to nag his son about these issues, which heightens tension between him and the boy. My hope is that

Bret will ease off somewhat and allow Ben simply to explore his interests unobstructed; nothing in Bret's efforts to sway Ben will be likely to change the boy's artistic bent, and recurrent nagging will undercut Bret's authority and Ben's responsiveness to his father.

Given these and similar issues, you can help your son or daughter to develop without complicating his or her tasks with gender bias.

Look at Your Own Roles, Relationships, and Behavior

Consider your values and beliefs about gender roles. Ask yourself these questions:

- What did your parents and other relatives believe about gender roles?

- How did your parents and other relatives treat you that may have influenced or shaped your perceptions of gender roles?

- How polarized is your sense of masculine and feminine "nature"?

- How traditional are your views of male and female abilities and interests?

- How open-minded are you regarding what both boys and girls can achieve and become?

- What are your expectations and attitudes about boys and girls?

- In what ways do you treat them differently?

- In what ways do you treat them the same?

Be Flexible about Gender Roles and Behaviors

Allow your son—in fact, encourage him—to be empathic. Let him engage in care-giving roles. By all means encourage his interests in traditionally "masculine" pursuits (math, science, sports, etc.)

but support his interests in literature, art, music, drama, and other pursuits that our culture tends to label as "feminine."

Likewise, encourage your daughter's interests in all studies, disciplines, and activities. Give her strong reinforcement as she studies math and science. Encourage her interests in sports, travel, and so forth.

Be Patient

These tasks will be especially difficult during the middle school years, when social pressures to conform are especially intense. My experience, however, is that after those early teen years—once children have gone through puberty and have established a clearer sense of identity—they don't have to adhere to such exaggerated images of male and female. Be patient. This phase, like all others, will pass.

Don't Be Alarmed by Experimentation

Children who have manifested traditional gender norms—the all-American boy, for instance, who loves sports and rough play—may eventually start to explore other roles and activities. Such shifts in focus are potentially promising, as they suggest a willingness to consider a range of what life has to offer. Encourage exploration by being supportive and open-minded about new interests. On the other hand, some independent-minded kids may suddenly grow more conventional. One example is the practical, no-nonsense girl who suddenly becomes obsessed with hair, nails, and makeup. This may strike some parents as backsliding, but here again you should be patient. She's probably just trying out new ideas and roles. At some point her behavior will probably stabilize. The same holds true if your son, who has been kind and affectionate, suddenly pulls back emotionally.

Children can, in fact, become extremely conservative, even small-minded, and sometimes act out stereotypical male/female behaviors. They'll imitate these stereotypes despite what they know about reality. When I was head teacher in the nursery school at the Duke University Lab Pre-School, one of the little girls, Darla, insisted that girls couldn't be doctors, only nurses. "It's wonderful to be a nurse, but your mommy is a doctor," I told her. "No, no, no," Darla insisted, "mommies can only be nurses!" Such is the power of sexual stereotypes that during certain developmental phases, children will rigidly adhere to certain criteria for what is feminine and what is masculine. Fortunately, this rigidity often diminishes as children begin to feel more comfortable within their own gender identification.

Take Action

Do what you can to overcome gender bias directly.

- Encourage girls in technological studies and pursuits. Do science, math, and computer activities with your daughter.

- Teach girls practical skills—carpentry, house painting, car repair, or any other skills you possess. Encourage interests in a full range of disciplines, sports, trades, and professions.

- Sign your daughter up for a science lab or a computer course.

- Encourage boys to express themselves verbally.

- Encourage boys to be open to their own feelings. What disappoints them? What makes them feel vulnerable? What scares them?

- Give boys the vocabulary and communication skills to verbalize and identify what they're feeling. And let them know that is a strength, not a weakness.

- Stress to both boys and girls that every person has the right to express his or her own personality.

- Reassure your daughter that girls have the right to express anger, to speak out on issues, to have opinions, to stand up for themselves, to be assertive, and to be counted on and valued.

- Give boys ample opportunities to take care of others, to nurture others, and to be caretakers.

- When boys act in egocentric or noncommunicative ways, encourage them to "get out of themselves" and get involved with people and relationships.

- Express affection through hugs, praise, and supportive statements to both boys and girls.

- Stress to boys that it's okay to get mad, but help them develop ways of expressing themselves in nonphysical ways. Create opportunities that help boys to communicate.

The Importance of Emotional Literacy

One of the biggest tasks involved in overcoming gender bias is emotional literacy. Gender bias in our culture limits the ways in which both boys and girls learn to express themselves. To some degree, emotions are parceled out as relatively masculine or relatively feminine. Certain feelings are allowed or disallowed to members of each sex. Traditional biases suggest that anger is fine for boys but unseemly for girls to feel and express, and that hurt or sadness are acceptable for girls but pathetic or contemptible in boys. This dividing up of the emotional spectrum is a loss for everyone. As a parent, you should do what you can to allow your children—boys and girls alike—to feel the entire range of emotions.

The situation may be especially restrictive for boys. On an emotional level, boys often struggle with the desire to be close to people and to have warmth, affection, and intimacy. At the same time, they often pull away from intimacy because they're socialized to believe that interpersonal warmth isn't manly—that boys and men should be strong, tough, and independent. American culture often gives the message that boys should suppress their feelings. Another message is that the only socially acceptable emotion for boys and men is anger, and that assertiveness and aggression are the best ways to get things accomplished. There are obviously individual differences. Each boy has his own inborn temperament, and each family will influence each child within it. But regarding the culture at large, these are some of the messages that boys hear loud and clear. Not only families, but peer pressure and socialization as well exert a great deal of pressure over each child's gender development.

A final suggestion: don't pull away from your children physically. Children need demonstrative affection. They sometimes bellyache about it, protest, or holler "Yuck!" Still, they often need to be hugged, kissed, and patted. Physical affection is important for long-term development of intimate relationships—for the ability for men to stay involved and connected in an intimate relationship and for women to trust men. They need to have healthy, strong, nonconflictual, trusting relationships with their parents of the other sex to help set the stage for intimacy down the road. Remember that the more your child feels accepted and understood for who he is—not for who you want him to be—the healthier and closer he'll feel to you. This closeness will ultimately lead to mutual respect, which is the foundation of healthy, creative parental authority.

Chapter 5

THE BURDENS AND BLESSINGS OF THE PAST

Adele, thirty-eight, is close to her fifteen-year-old daughter, Patricia, yet she finds herself increasingly at odds with the teenager. Adele knows that mother–daughter tensions often run high during the teen years, and she's able to cope well enough with the ups and downs of raising an adolescent. During a recent crisis, however, Adele found herself so furious toward Patricia that her anger exceeded anything she'd experienced before. "Patricia went to the sophomore dance," Adele explains, "and she promised to be back by midnight. She wasn't—and not by one or two, either. When she got home around 3 A.M., I just exploded. I yelled, screamed, and made all sorts of accusations. I practically attacked her." Eventually the situation calmed down, but Adele felt shaken by her wild reaction to her daughter's misbehavior.

What startled and frightened Adele wasn't just her anger—after all, Patricia had violated her curfew—but rather her own excessive verbal assault on her daughter. "I really blasted her. I accused her of all kinds of things she probably hadn't done. But you know what spooked me most of all? I sounded just like my mother did when *she* blasted *me* as a teenager."

This kind of interaction isn't uncommon, but it's unfortunate, for it can diminish your parental authority. Why? Because your child will feel vulnerable, and she'll have less respect for you, which in turn can prompt rebellion rather than cooperation. Adele's reaction also showed poor role modeling, which can prompt a child to engage in hostile, undisciplined behavior.

THE BURDENS OF THE PAST

Despite your best efforts, you may sometimes act less generously than you intend, say things you don't mean, do things you've preferred to avoid, or sabotage your own good-heartedness. Why? A common reason is that forces beyond your awareness may be influencing your actions as a parent.

Why do otherwise well-intentioned parents sometimes act selfishly, thoughtlessly, clumsily, even cruelly, or else jeopardize their authority through excessive or insufficient actions? One of the reasons is ordinary fallibility. We fall short simply because we're imperfect human beings. But there's another reason for our missteps as parents, one that can be hard to face but crucial to understand: the influences of the past.

No matter what you believe, you've learned much of what you know about parenting from your own family of origin. It's true that raising children involves some innate abilities—what we tend to call maternal or paternal instinct—but most of what takes place during parenthood *isn't* instinctual. It's learned. Because your first and most powerful relationships were those between you and your parents, you acquired your image of parenthood from your mother and father. The same holds true about many of the specific beliefs you hold about parenthood and the skills you use in raising your children. In short, your own parents have modeled behaviors that have powerfully shaped your assumptions about parenthood. The impact of those early relationships will linger within you for the rest of your life. Your image of family life, your expectations about interpersonal communication, your notions of trust, and your feelings about love originate in your own experience of family life.

That said, your early experiences won't fully *determine* your beliefs and behavior as a parent. Your temperament, your state of health, your beliefs and values, your strength of character, your ability to make rational decisions, and your education will all combine with aspects of your past to shape your responses to parenthood. In short, the past will *influence* your response. This influence may be relatively great or relatively slight, but to some extent the influence is inevitable.

Some of these influences are:

- Expectations about what it means to be a mother or a father

- Expectations about the nature of family life—is it happy or sad, collaborative or divisive, harmonious or fractious?

- Experiences during your own childhood of feeling loved or unloved; accepted or rejected; nurtured, tolerated, or thwarted

- Expectations about what constitutes good or bad behavior

- Experiences of sibling rivalry or closeness

- Experiences of family life—whether your family members supported or thwarted each other

- Experiences of your parents' age (that is, whether they were relatively young or relatively more mature when they had children)

- Experiences of your parents' relative satisfaction or dissatisfaction with parenthood

- Experiences of your family's economic well-being or hardship

- Experiences of being rewarded or punished.

Given these influences, the past may erupt into your present-day efforts as a parent in many ways:

- You may fall "into a rut" of certain behaviors—irritability, depression, scolding, punitiveness—despite your efforts to behave in a different way.

- You may say "just what Mom and Dad used to say" when speaking with your child.

- You may feel hurt or lose your temper in response to your child's seemingly trivial comments, gestures, or other actions.

- You may feel depressed or "blue" at certain times of year, or during certain kid-related events such as holidays, birthdays, the start of school, family trips, vacation times, and so forth.

- You may act out of control when scolding or punishing your child.

- You may feel that you're letting your child down despite your fundamentally competent, well-meaning actions as a parent.

If you have experiences of these sorts, the past may be welling up into the present and influencing your actions as a parent. In some situations, you may find yourself doing or saying things that reflect your experiences as a child; in other situations, what happens is more subtle. The experience can be unnerving either way. You may treat your child in ways that contradict your preferences; you may hurt your child's feelings; or you may simply feel as if you've violated your beliefs and preferences. In any case, what's happening is that some experience in your past—one that you may not even remember clearly—is influencing your actions in the present. The result may or may not do major damage.

Influences of this sort can limit your control over the choices you make as a parent; until you understand the nature of the past and its power over you, you will lack some degree of freedom in your thoughts and actions. You will be less capable of perceiving your children clearly. You will be less able to be emotionally available, responsive, and empathic to them. These influences may limit or damage your parental authority.

THE BLESSINGS OF THE PAST

My comments so far may suggest that most people feel only haunted by the past—by their parents' shortcomings, by experiences of loss or deprivation, or by regrets and resentments. That negative portrait isn't what I wish to convey. In fact, most people recall the past in positive as well as negative ways. The negative ways can, of course, linger with great intensity. But the past isn't just a burden; it's also a blessing. Many of your childhood memories may be suffused with great warmth and sweetness. These memories, too, will influence your feelings toward yourself, toward parenthood, and toward your children. And here again, understanding your past can illuminate the present and allow you a greater degree of choice over the decisions you make and the actions you take.

Here's an example.

Janelle, thirty-two, is the mother of eight-year-old twins. She enjoys most aspects of motherhood and feels close to her daughters. In general, parent–child interactions in Janelle's household are congenial. Janelle sometimes struggles with depression, however, and worries that she's not as good a mother as her daughters deserve. She tries to do more for them—fixing special meals, buying extra clothes, and arranging elaborate playdates. The girls seem indifferent to these efforts, at times even contemptuous of what Janelle is doing for them. To some degree the mother's intense efforts tend to undercut rather than strengthen her parental authority.

Janelle has reached some insights, however, that have clarified the situation. Through a combination of psychotherapy and independent introspection, she has started to understand the connections between her own past and her obsessive attention toward her daughters. Janelle's mother, Patricia, had always felt obliged to be the perfect mother. She tolerated no lapses in domestic perfection: she kept the family home perfectly clean, cooked perfect meals, and threw perfect parties. While growing up, Janelle resented her mother's obsessiveness and vowed that she would never succumb to the same excesses. It's hard to resist an internalized image of what parenthood should be, however, and so Janelle finds herself influenced against her will. Her recent insights have helped. Janelle attained a greater degree of freedom in making decisions about parenting, which prompts her to ease the pressure on her daughters, which in turn bolsters her authority.

Understanding the past can help bestow insights that are potentially beneficial and creative:

- The nature of parenthood is to be fallible.

- Much of what your parents did wasn't always a consequence of choices they made, but simply a result of their best efforts to muddle through.

- Your childhood was more complex (and maybe more or less problematic?) than you recall.

- Some of your negative experiences (getting grounded, losing a contest, feeling embarrassed, and so on) may not have been as bad as you felt at the time.

- Your own efforts as a parent are as fallible as your own parents' efforts were.

- Your own children will probably feel some hurt and resentment too, despite your own best efforts to muddle through — and what they feel is probably inevitable and normal.

- Family life is by nature a state of imperfection, and it's fine to accept your own imperfect decisions and actions.

The more you understand your past, the less likely it is that you'll transfer or project unresolved conflicts onto your children. If you can resolve these old conflicts—if you can understand some of the root causes and their influence on the present—you'll have a much greater chance of gaining control over the situation. In so doing, you'll be less likely to:

- Live primarily through your children

- Expect them to meet your emotional needs

- Pressure them into being other than who they really are

- Love them for their accomplishments rather than for their being or soul

- Attempt to control them rather than let them unfold as individuals

- Treat them as possessions rather than as beings

- Manipulate them for your own needs

- Subject them to anger, envy, or unreasonable criticism

- Experience conflicts with your spouse, friends, and other adults.

If you can understand both the positive and negative aspects of your past, you may be able to gain a degree of freedom you'll otherwise lack, and this freedom may help you reach better insights and make better decisions about the tasks of parenthood, including tasks relevant to parental authority. These insights and decisions may include:

- Having expectations about your kids that are age-appropriate

- Setting limits that are age-appropriate

- Establishing realistic, fair, and balanced consequences for unacceptable behavior

- Following those guidelines for behavior consistently

- Learning what things you can change about children's behavior and what things you can't change (and seeing the difference between them)

- Having reasonable, age-appropriate expectations about family activities, including chores

- Communicating directly, openly, and authoritatively, when appropriate.

HOW TO COPE WITH THE PAST

Here are some specific practical methods to consider as you work to understand and cope with the past.

Psychotherapy

Most people benefit from having a guide to help them understand their personal and family past. A trained psychotherapist or counselor can ask you questions, help you see patterns, and clarify events that occurred during your childhood or are occurring now. In the midst of family life, it may be difficult for you to make those connections. It's difficult to be objective about your own life, and examining these issues can prompt strong emotional responses. A skilled psychotherapist, however, can facilitate insights partly because of his or her greater objectivity. In addition, a therapist can reassure you about difficult aspects of this task that may be confusing or upsetting as you encounter them.

Psychotherapy can also offer another advantage: a second chance at being "parented" by someone who is consistent, nonjudgmental, and perhaps more understanding than your own parents were. Individual therapists' skills vary; however, a good psychotherapist can provide you with the chance to perceive your life in new ways. Suppose that you tend to form problematically dependent relationships. You have needs for other people that exceed what they're willing to provide you, or that exceed what they ought to provide you. A psychotherapist can help you understand your intense needs and help you attain different, less dependent forms of human intimacy. By this means, therapy can help you learn more nurturing, more loving, less dependent interactions within your own family.

There are several ways to locate a psychotherapist. One option is to ask your primary-care physician for a referral. Your priest, minister, rabbi, or pastoral counselor may also have suggestions. Many cities and counties also maintain a referral service or hotline for mental health services; see your community's phone listings or Web site for details.

The main drawback to psychotherapy is its cost. Especially in this era of HMOs, many insurance plans offer only limited benefits for psychotherapy, so size up the situation carefully before you start treatment. In addition, I should state outright that therapy is almost always hard work. Exploring your past, delving into long-past events, and making sense of confusing emotions takes great effort and courage. As a result of these two "costs"—financial and emotional— many people resist the notion of psychotherapy. That's each person's decision to make. I believe, however, that the financial and emotional costs of therapy are often far lower than the cost of ignoring the past and its influence on the present.

Journals

Another way to explore the past is to keep a journal of your thoughts, feelings, memories, and experiences. You might say that journal keeping is a kind of private psychotherapy: both methods involve digging into the past and bringing half-understood experiences to light.

In order to use a journal for this purpose, you can proceed in just about any way you wish. What's most important is not to censor what you write. Write by free association, noting whatever thoughts or feelings you experience. Try not to inhibit what you think or feel. Write as honestly and as clearly as possible, without feeling that you have to hide anything, or that your emotions are embarrassing or shameful. Note any thoughts or feelings of rage, anger, desire, or destructive impulses. Anything that you feel you *don't* want to write is probably something you need to write about! Don't censor anything, especially events and feelings that make you feel uncomfortable.

Keeping an uncensored, uninhibited journal is a good way to release your most intimate emotions in a nonthreatening, safe, non-destructive way. Precisely because the topics you describe are so inti-mate, however, you should make provisions in advance to maintain your privacy. Put the journal in a place where no one else can find it. Find somewhere that's safe enough that you don't have to worry about discovery. Once you've written your entries, you may have a cathartic experience that crystallizes your insights; later, you may decide to destroy or discard the journal. That's fine, too. You don't have to consider the journal a permanent fixture in your life. Think of it as a *process*, not a *product*.

Tape Recorders

An alternative to using a journal is recording your thoughts with a tape recorder. This method appeals to people who are more com-fortable talking than writing. In addition, tape recorders provide the advantage of letting you hear your tone of voice, which can reveal inflections of fear, longing, or anxiety, which in turn can disclose a lot about your state of mind. The experience of speaking into a tape recorder can accomplish many of the same goals as using a journal: creating a window into your experiences, helping you remember half-recalled events, and assisting you in understanding aspects of your past.

Letters

An additional method of delving into the past involves writing letters. You may or may not have any intention of sending these letters;
in fact, writing but *not* sending these letters is, ironically, often especially useful. The goal isn't necessarily to make a statement to the
person you're addressing, but rather to release thoughts and feelings
about your own past.

To use this method, you write a letter to a specific person (your
mother, father, siblings, or whomever) and say whatever you may
have left unsaid. The words you write can express disappointment,
anger, frustration, grief—whatever you're feeling. It doesn't matter
how hostile or hurtful your words, because the "recipient" of your
letter will never receive it anyway. In fact, the recipient doesn't even
need to be still alive. (This exercise can be especially powerful
regarding someone long deceased.) The point is simply to vent what
you're feeling—to get it off your chest. In doing so, the anxiety, fear,
and anger you've experienced can surge outward rather than remain
submerged, which can help you move on and find more energy to
devote to the present. You may need to write more than one letter to
a specific person before you purge your angry feelings and begin to
feel relief. This, too, is a cathartic expression. (Destroying the letter
at a later date may also feel cathartic.)

The Risks Involved

I need to alert you to a few risks, however, that these various methods
entail.

First of all, think carefully before proceeding with any of these
alternatives. They may seem easy and harmless, but they can trigger
surprisingly intense reactions. Writing a letter in which you blast
your long-dead mother, for instance, may unleash far more powerful
emotions than you anticipate. That's possible, too, if you write
entries in a journal or dictate remarks into a tape recorder. Step care-

fully. Above all, maintain your privacy; the words you write may be harmless if you succeed in keeping them private but profoundly destructive if they fall into the wrong hands.

Second, consider combining the journal/recorder/letter approach with psychotherapy. Any of these methods can be productive when pursued alone, but the experience will be less stressful and lonely if you have a guide along the way.

Third, keep an eye on depression. Precisely because parenthood is so stressful and demanding, some people respond to its rigors by becoming depressed. This response is surprisingly common. Parenthood is hard work, and our society gives little more than lip service to its importance. If you feel that the demands of parenthood create any feelings of depression, do *not* ignore those feelings or simply shove them under the carpet. Depression takes many forms. Some are short-term reactions to finite problems—job stress, family difficulties, contradictory expectations, marital disagreements—but they still need attention. Others are long-term, often biochemically based problems that warrant immediate attention. It's common, too, that earnest efforts to deal with the past can trigger feelings of confusion, sadness, or depression. In each of these situations, it's important to seek outside help. A psychotherapist's helpful guidance may help you gain control of what you're feeling. In some cases, antidepressant medication is helpful, too. The most common signs of depression are:

- A marked sense of low energy or fatigue

- A protracted, constant feeling of profound sadness

- The loss of a sense of who you are, what you need, what you want, and what you're feeling

- Protracted irritability or feelings that you can't cope with everyday stresses

- Inability to function in normal ways

- A deep sense of shame, insecurity, and guilt

- A sense of emptiness, loneliness, or worthlessness

- A feeling of being overwhelmed by life

- An inability to get up in the morning and cope with everyday life

- Suicidal thoughts or actions.

If you find yourself struggling with one or more of these signs and symptoms of depression, seek help from your physician or mental health provider as soon as possible.

In Search of Healing, Not Perfection

By its very nature, parenthood means making mistakes. Your parents made plenty; you will, too. Welcome to the human race.

It's true, however, that some of the mistakes your parents made may have hurt you, and that the resulting pain can linger. This is true for seemingly trivial childhood wounds—the thoughtless words spoken, the wrong gift, the forgotten recital—and it's certainly true for the more willful, angry, cruel wounds that parents sometimes inflict on their children.

But the truth remains: wounds can heal. Even some of the oldest, deepest, most painful wounds can stop festering and cease to hurt. How? By bringing the pain to the surface. In dealing with the past, hidden wounds do the most damage, while those that we expose to the light usually (though sometimes gradually) can cease to trouble us as deeply as before. Is this process foolproof? No. Can you accomplish it without effort? Almost certainly not. Still, coming to terms with your own past is one of the best ways to soothe the pain that's an inevitable part of being human.

It's not easy. It's not always pleasant. The process of dealing with the past will shed light on your attitudes and feelings toward issues of parental authority. In addition, facing the past will help you to understand yourself better and thus open yourself more fully to your children. If you can accept the complexity of your own past, you'll see your kids with open eyes, new respect, deeper understanding, and empathy for what they feel, experience, and hope for. You'll perceive your children not as extensions of yourself, but as separate from yourself—a realization which, ironically, will allow you to embrace them and love them even more deeply than before.

Chapter 6

VALUES AND FAMILY COMMUNICATION

No matter what certain cultural observers may claim, there's no single set of values that will foster strong parental authority. To assume that only certain values are substantive and noble seems arrogant and unpersuasive. That said, I'm skeptical about moral relativity, too, in which every value is considered equally valid. Some values serve us better than others.

I can't answer the question of how values affect parenthood and parental authority in a way that will suit all readers' needs, but I encourage you to clarify your values within the context of your own cultural and religious traditions. This task won't necessarily be easy. It may require you to examine your own personal assumptions, behaviors, and goals. However, clarifying your values is a crucial step if you wish to understand the tasks of parenthood and to reinforce your parental authority.

There's a related issue as well: the way in which you *communicate* your values to your children will powerfully influence your parental authority. A common problem of this sort is the classic disparity between parents' statements and their actions—for instance, when a father argues that all drug use is bad yet smokes and drinks to excess. Another problem frequently arises from a disparity between one parent's values and the other's, such as when a mother encourages a son's intellectual pursuits while the father presses the boy "not to waste your time on egghead stuff." In these and other instances, parents should examine their values, discuss important issues together on a regular basis, make decisions based on their children's best interests, and communicate clearly with one another and with their children.

Some parents also run into trouble as a result of their communication style. They may have a clear sense of their values and priorities but fail to communicate clearly or effectively. One such problem is an unempathic or "chilly" manner of communicating; another is indirect or vague statements that leave kids feeling confused about parents' expectations; still another is a tendency to avoid communication altogether.

THE IMPORTANCE OF VALUES

The process of imparting values is chiefly a matter of consistency. By this statement I mean two things.

First, your values must be *consistent in relation to each other*. If you wish to impart the values of nonviolent conflict resolution, for instance, you need to resolve conflicts consistently through verbal rather than physical means. You can't tell your son not to hit other children, then punish him for doing so by spanking him.

Second, your values must be *consistent over time*. You can't spank your child some of the time, forego spanking at other times, and then claim that you don't believe in corporal punishment.

As in so many other ways, parental authority depends on establishing a clear pattern of what you expect. A lack of parental authority is often the consequence of an unclear pattern of expectations.

The Role of Conscience

Values are simultaneously the source and the effect of conscience. Employing the standard definition of conscience—"restraint or exercise over one's impulses, emotions, or desires"—I'd say that a child's conscience often emerges from her experience of what her parents expect of her and how consistently they express those expectations. Conscience in turn makes these behaviors and attitudes more likely in the future.

Here are some standard consequences of a well-developed conscience:

- Developing patience

- Learning to tame anger

- Accepting responsibility to follow the rules at home and at school

- Manifesting socially acceptable behavior

- Tolerating frustration

- Knowing how to delay gratification.

Children inevitably experience many primitive drives and impulses. They express anger, affection, and other emotions spontaneously and freely. They want what they want. Over the years, kids learn to control their impulses and, through the process of socialization, learn right from wrong. Parents and teachers provide external incentives to foster this process—most often by expressing approval or disapproval. As your child grows and matures, she'll be less dependent on you to "shape" her behavior, and she'll begin to develop her own internal controls. When a sense of conscience does emerge, it's an important milestone. However, her conscience won't be completely self-directed until the last phase of adolescence, as she moves into young adulthood.

The ways in which parents set limits in the early years actually set the stage for later aspects of self-control. Self-control is crucial, and children who lack it risk a number of personal and social difficulties, among them:

- Lack of self-discipline

- Minimal self-control (which can lead to external controls— warnings, punishments, and so forth)

- Trouble in developing intimate relationships

- Conflicts with parents and teachers

- Difficulties with academic achievement

- Difficulties in building a successful career.

In addition, a child's lack of self-control can strain parental authority, because the parents need to intervene more often, and perhaps more aggressively, to foster appropriate behavior.

Fostering Values in Young Children

If you can encourage your child to develop a conscience and strong values, you'll make parenthood easier for yourself, and the process of growing up will be easier for your child. Following are age-appropriate issues to consider for children ages two through five.

Love Your Child Unconditionally

Loving your child regardless of her behavior is the foundation on which you should base all values. If your child truly grasps how much you love her, she'll respond more readily to your expectations and preferences. Separate your child's behavior from her being (soul, nature). If you're in conflict, tell her, "I love you, but at the moment I don't like your behavior." Young children want to please their parents; they want love and approval. For this reason, your approval is a powerful tool. I don't mean to suggest that you should withdraw your love and affection, but you can temporarily withhold your approval. (Doing so can include time out, denying specific privileges, and withholding praise. The choice of these means will depend on your child's age, level of maturity, temperament, and patterns of behavior.)

Keep Rules Simple

Young children don't benefit from complex rules and alternatives. It's easy to confuse them by offering too many options. Rather, you should provide a few simple rules that preschoolers can grasp. Reinforce the rule in a positive way. Stress compliance by means of simple, gentle, consistent statements:

- "I know it's hard to wait your turn, but you have to. Can you sing a song while we wait? Then it'll be your turn."

- "Tell your feet to walk, not run, when we're indoors."

- "Use your indoor voice."

- "I know you're angry because Sasha took the toy, but I'm not going to let you hit her. Use your words instead."

Arrange the Environment to Redirect or Substitute Activities

Suppose your four-year-old daughter hits her younger sister. This behavior is unacceptable, yet simply saying *no* may not solve the problem. Children have aggressive impulses that won't necessarily go away on command. Though hitting other children is unacceptable, the larger issue may be excess energy rather than hostility. One of the ways that your daughter can learn the value of impulse control

is to vent her pent-up energy in nonaggressive ways. Hitting her sister isn't tolerable; by contrast, though, hitting a punching bag or a
pillow is acceptable. Channel aggression in positive ways. Let kids
vent their steam by tearing old newspaper, knocking down blocks in
a safe way, or running around outdoors.

Use Guilt Selectively

To develop your child's self-control and sense of right and wrong,
you may need to appeal selectively to her sense of guilt. Don't
overdo it, but don't consider guilt out of bounds when used carefully. For example, your four-year-old daughter has taken a neighbor's toy. Appropriate questions to ask a preschooler include: "How
would you feel if Johnny took *your* toy?" and "How do you think
Johnny feels right now?" In the long run, a mild experience of guilt
can help a child develop empathy and a conscience. It can also reinforce the kinds of behaviors and values that you want to instill in
your child—kindness, sharing, patience, and self-control.

Delay Gratification and Develop Patience

One of the problems that often contributes to familial tensions
and conflict is kids' short attention spans. This issue is common
among adults too, but rampant among children. Brought up on fast-
paced TV programs and rapid-fire computer games, many kids have
few opportunities to develop patience in response to daily life. One
result of this situation is children's annoyance when parents make
requests about homework, chores, and family activities. My suggestion: help your child learn early on to delay gratification and
develop patience. Spend time with your child by doing activities
that can increase her attention span. I suggest slower-paced, process-
oriented pastimes such as reading books, building with Legos, doing
art projects, and so forth. Helping a child see a project through from
beginning to end can help foster a stick-to-it mentality.

Fostering Values in Older Children

The suggestions I've made so far can be modified for school-age kids, but children past seven to eleven years of age need their own guidelines. Here are some tips for developing a conscience in school-age children.

Assign Age-Appropriate Chores and Responsibilities

I believe that almost all children should have specific chores, tasks, or responsibilities that fit their developmental stages. Far too many American parents wait hand-and-foot on their kids, which deprives children of opportunities to acquire skills, learn teamwork, and enjoy the delights of common endeavor. For this reason, I feel that you shouldn't perform tasks that your child can accomplish on her own. A seven- or eight-year-old can help you keep her room clean, help clear the table after meals, and help sort laundry. Be consistent in your requests; follow through on your expectations. Instill a sense of group responsibility—doing what needs to be done as part of being a family. The results will include a growing sense of pride in working together. Your child's cooperation will help her in many ways but will also reinforce your parental authority.

Stick to a Consistent Schedule

Your children may benefit from a daily schedule of homework, chores, and other tasks. Don't be rigid with younger school-age children. On the other hand, a flexible, kid-friendly schedule can be helpful for children from ages eight to twelve. Don't make a "to-do" list into a form of punishment; emphasize that being organized is a natural part of daily family life. Try to make the process fun. Working together can be far more fun than pursuing separate tasks. Using a calendar and bright stickers can also appeal to some kids.

Listen Attentively

Your child will listen more attentively to you if you listen attentively to her as well. (We'll discuss these issues in more detail shortly, under "Communication." My point here is simply that school-age children often thrive on close parental attention.) If you show that your child's thoughts and feelings matter to you, she'll be more likely to absorb the value of concern about others. Validate your child's feelings. Figure out what's bothering her. Praise her and reinforce her behavior whenever she's patient, kind, thoughtful, and persistent.

Use Role Playing to Foster Insights

Children generally don't reason abstractly until about age eight, and rational thinking doesn't develop fully until the teens. As a result, your child may have difficulty grasping certain aspects of values. One solution: use role playing. Help your child understand her behavior and how it affects other people, including siblings, friends, and teachers. "How would you feel if you sat quietly and waited to be called on but another child called out first?" Role playing can help her develop a conscience and empathy. Assist her effort to become more aware of other people's feelings, desires, and needs.

Negotiate to Resolve Conflicts

At times, parental authority means simply that you state what needs to occur and then make sure that everyone gets with the program. At other times, parental authority doesn't mean imposing your will on your child; rather, you need to *lead* your family toward a decision or action. If your child can take part in evaluating her behavior, she'll be much more likely to follow through when trying to cooperate. For this reason, two of the most important values to teach are negotiation and conflict resolution.

Let's say that your child has repeatedly neglected to turn in her homework assignments. Rather than punishing her, ask, "What do you think will get you focused on your schoolwork?" or "What do you think the consequences should be if you don't do your assignments?" Include your child in the process of dealing with conflicts; give her a chance to respond and to offer solutions. If she has misbehaved, don't be too quick to punish her, but don't be too permissive, either. Find the middle ground. A balanced approach is important in developing your child's values.

Teach Persistence and Responsibility

Help your child to understand the importance of commitment and responsibility. If your child agrees to do something, insist that she follow through. Emphasize the need to fulfill commitments unless there's an unavoidable disruption, such as illness. It's possible that she'll have to turn down an invitation because of a prior commitment—homework, for instance. A situation of this sort may cause some frustration, but it's important for you not to let your child off the hook without good cause. Teach her that she must honor her obligations.

Be a Good Role Model

The words are ancient but worth repeating: practice what you preach. If you urge your child to be nonjudgmental at the same time that you constantly pass judgment on others, she'll notice what you do and will model her behavior accordingly. If you're impatient, inconsistent, unreliable, or disrespectful of others, your child will emulate your behavior. If you demand truthfulness yet speak dishonestly yourself, she'll ignore your words and follow your actions.

Fostering Values in Teenagers

Your child's adolescence will present you with a mix of crises and opportunities. Among other things, teenagers are famous (infamous?) for experimenting with values, and the adolescent quest for personal identity leads many teens to redefine what they believe and what they're willing to do. This situation often presents a crisis because parents find themselves living with children whose values regarding behavior, language, friends, family, food, and almost everything else are in flux, often in ways that the parents find confusing, alarming, or simply unacceptable. On the other hand, the situation is also an opportunity because parents can—if they step carefully—guide their teens toward insight and maturity. That said, I'd be quick to add that this situation is complex and often stressful for parents and teenagers alike.

Precisely because the issues are so complex and volatile, this book can only touch on a few of the ways you can foster values in teens. Here are a few general suggestions, though, that may be helpful. (See Appendix B, Resource Guide, for other options.)

Set a Good Example

During your child's teen years, you must practice what you preach. Teenagers have built-in, shockproof hypocrisy detectors, so they'll spot any inconsistencies between what you say and what you do. It's true that many teenagers (perhaps most) will dismiss their parents as hopelessly uncool. At the same time, I believe that even the teenagers who most loudly protest their parents' lack of coolness really do take their mom and dad's actions to heart. Teens have deep concerns about loyalty, justice, and the meaning of life. Major discrepancies between your stated beliefs and your actions will significantly undermine your authority.

One example is Jenna and her father, Bill. As the manager of a large grocery store, Bill has often boasted about his attention to his employees' well-being. When his daughter Jenna learned that Bill had been engaging in unfair labor practices, however, she expressed outrage at her father's exploitative treatment of the workers. Other situations may not be as extreme, but they hit home easily and often. For example, many parents have felt the sting of their teens' disapproval for insufficient concern about the environment, social justice, race relations, and other complex ethical and practical issues.

Avoid Lecturing, Preaching, Berating, and Nagging

A corollary to the above: don't hassle your teen with sermons, diatribes, or repetitive requests. Preachiness will only backfire, alienating your adolescent child and driving her away. I don't mean to imply that you should allow her to do anything she pleases; rather, you need to shape her values by less strident and repetitive means. Options include open-ended (and open-minded) discussion; indirect or understated reminders; and, if necessary, agreed-upon contracts that state your expectations and specify your teen's necessary response.

Set Clear, Consistent Limits

Although adolescence is a time when children often move rapidly into new areas of competence, teens still need clear limits to help shape their values and actions. Set these limits clearly in advance to avoid misunderstandings. Be flexible but firm. Emphasize that everyone in the family needs to compromise.

Stress the Need for Civility

Teenagers are notorious for engaging in abrasive or irritating behavior. Some of these behaviors are merely self-centered or thoughtless; others are more willfully obnoxious. To some degree, putting up with these annoyances is part of your fate as the parent of an adolescent. However, you shouldn't tolerate every annoyance just because your teen happens to be in a bad mood. You're a person too, and you have a right to be treated with normal civility. Be firm with your teenager. Don't allow yourself to be verbally or physically abused.

If you find yourself dealing with constant sassy language, or if your teen is constantly abrasive, press the point that such behavior is unacceptable. Try to assess your own contribution to the problem as well. Have you been a good enough role model in this regard? How do you speak to your teenager, spouse, other family members, and friends? Try to understand the dynamics between you and your teen. Have you provoked any of this behavior by using an abrasive communication style yourself, by paying insufficient attention to your kids, or by ignoring (or not validating) your teen's feelings? Attending to these issues may clarify the situation for you. In extreme cases—such as when the family dynamic becomes chronically stressful—consider seeking the insights of an objective counselor. For further discussions of civility, see chapter 8 in this book.

Punish Thoughtfully

Make the consequences clear if your teen violates the rules you've set. Make sure that the punishment fits the infraction. Being either too harsh or too lenient may jeopardize your parental authority. If necessary, make exceptions to the rules. There's nothing wrong with admitting that you, too, have made mistakes. Try to be compassionate about the challenges that your teen faces during adolescence.

Help Your Teen Cope with Peer Pressure

One of the hallmarks of adolescence is the power that peers have in influencing teenagers' values. To some degree, this situation is inevitable; your teen's allegiances will almost inevitably shift from the family to a peer group. However, the *degree* of allegiance varies. Those with a limited sense of self-confidence may be vulnerable to peers' expectations; others, however—often those with a stronger core identity—respond to peer pressure as only one factor in making decisions, and they remain responsive to their parents' values. Research shows that a strong family support system, highly involved and emotionally aware parents, and high self-esteem provide the core elements that help teens resist peer pressure. By contrast, teens with rigid, authoritarian parents have generally had less practice making their own decisions while growing up and hence often feel less able to resist peer influences on behaviors and values.

Maintain Open Dialogue

Most parents realize that they can't force values on their teenagers. If you can keep the lines of communication open and maintain a dialogue, however, you'll have a far better chance of influencing your teens' values and decisions. This dialogue may not be easy, especially when you're discussing loaded subjects like sex, drugs, smoking, and violence. But if you can be available and fairly open-minded, your teen will be more likely to approach you without feeling that you'll overreact or respond in a judgmental way. You have more power than you realize. You may not believe that your teenager wants to please you, but she needs your approval and love as much as in the past, even though she may not demonstrate her need as openly.

Respect Your Teen's Privacy

Avoid intruding on your teen's private territory or snooping around in her belongings. Don't eavesdrop on her telephone calls. Don't spy on her by asking other parents or kids about her behavior or activities. Instead, talk to your teen directly if you perceive a problem. (One important exception to this rule: if you believe that your child is engaging in high-risk behavior such as use of illicit drugs. This is an exception because your teenager is demonstrating irresponsible, self-destructive behavior, which forfeits her right to privacy.) By showing respect for your teenager's rights and opinions, you'll bolster the chances that she'll respect your opinions too, which in turn will increase the chances of her accepting your values as her own.

COMMUNICATION BETWEEN SPOUSES

Of the two communications issues I want to discuss—communication between spouses and communication between parents and children—the first may seem off the subject. Communication between spouses, however, is the bedrock of parental authority in most families. How parents communicate with one another dramatically influences kids' responses to the parents as they grow and develop. Parents who respect one another and who communicate well are likely to have a relatively easy time maintaining parental authority. By contrast, parents who don't respect one another or who don't communicate well are more likely to struggle in their attempt to maintain authority.

Developing and maintaining good communication between partners isn't easy; disagreements are part of every close relationship. These disagreements often result simply from the normal give-and-take of marriage and parenthood, while at other times they may mask other problems. For instance, the superficial nature of a statement or question isn't always what it seems. The words you hear may be "Isn't this your third golf game this month?" when the real question is "Aren't I important to you any more?" Communication can reinforce a marriage, but it can undermine it, too.

Issues for Marital Communication

Why do some couples have trouble sorting out what they believe— including what they believe about parental issues? As a result of my work as a therapist, I believe that most marital problems stem directly or indirectly from difficulties in communication. Because all couples have disagreements, the core issue is often the partners' ability (or inability) to communicate effectively. This issue is, I admit, big and complex. Some loving couples struggle to communicate and, despite their best intentions, fail. Some less-close couples successfully overcome their obstacles through a capacity to learn effective communication skills. The truth is that almost all marriages can benefit from good marital communication. The payoffs include not only less stress between the spouses but also indirect but significant benefits to the children, because good communication reinforces parental authority.

Identify the Sources of Your Anger and Frustration

You may have good reason to feel frustrated with your spouse, but it's important for you to identify the specific issues. Don't assume that you understand what's on your spouse's mind; similarly, don't assume that your spouse knows what's on *your* mind. To the degree possible, clarify the issues. This task can be especially important regarding the tasks of parenthood. What are your expectations about child rearing? How do you feel about the division of labor in your family? What changes would improve the family situation? Identifying these and other issues can diminish both partners' anger and frustration.

Learn to Fight Fairly

Avoid unfair, harsh, and counterproductive ways of sorting out issues. When you argue, do so in a constructive, open-minded spirit. Sneak attacks, sarcasm, wild accusations, public humiliation, and other indirect "tactics" almost always backfire and complicate the situation. Time your discussions so that you're both calm, undistracted by other matters, and (if possible) relatively well rested. State your concerns directly, without exaggerating or attempting to score points. Allow your partner to respond in full.

Avoid Fighting in Front of the Kids

Just as *how* you fight is important, so is *when*. If possible, don't argue in front of your kids. You and your spouse may be well intentioned, but children often feel disturbed by parents' arguments. Kids don't understand the issues involved; they may overinterpret what's happening, or they may worry that they've caused the problem. Try to keep them off-scene when you sort out complex matters. In particular, avoid arguing loudly or shouting in front of the kids, as doing so will alarm most children and significantly undercut your parental authority.

An exception to this rule, however: children may actually benefit from seeing their parents solve problems together. "Solving problems" is, of course, potentially different from arguing. But because some discussions between a husband and a wife can become intense, kids may overhear or witness discussions that shift into arguments. This is a problem for young children. For school-age children and teens, however, it's not necessarily unacceptable. In addition, kids may learn from observing their parents sort through issues in a civil, constructive manner that spouses can disagree and still reach common ground. Parents who can model this sort of positive behavior may teach their kids important lessons about collaboration within the family.

Choose Your Battles Carefully

All marriages have friction points, and all spouses must work hard to resolve disagreements effectively. Attempting to tackle every single unresolved issue, however, may complicate your chances of resolving those that matter most. Don't insist on winning every fight. Instead, focus on the problems that cause the most difficulty, strain, or resentment. Ignore relatively trivial issues. Also, avoid "sniping" at your spouse, especially in the kids' presence, as this action, too, may damage both your individual authority and what you share as parents.

Level with One Another

Don't let resentments and animosities build up until they explode, or until your partner goes outside the relationship to find support and understanding. Be direct about what's on your mind. Prioritize the problems you wish to address. State your concerns openly, without rancor, and as clearly as possible. I don't mean to say that you should be unemotional; you have a right to feel what you're feeling. But if possible, communicate in a matter-of-fact way rather than by overwhelming your spouse with dramatics or accusations.

Model Healthy Relationships

Try to maintain mutual respect. Serious efforts at communication will pay off in ways that far transcend your marriage; your kids, too, will benefit from your efforts at solving problems and working together. First of all, your children will feel reassured by observing a cooperative process and constructive tone as you and your spouse communicate. In addition, your collaboration will reinforce rather than diminish your parental authority. Finally, this positive tone will teach your kids important lessons about communication, which will serve the whole family well as you interact with them over the years.

Find Time Together as a Couple

Many spouses don't have enough time together. Some resent not getting enough attention from one another, or else they feel that they're no longer their husband's or wife's top priority. Sometimes, too, communication breaks down under the stress of raising children. Hectic schedules often leave couples attempting to communicate late at night, early in the morning, or at other times when everyone feels depleted, unfocused, and irritable.

To counter these obstacles to communication, try to pick a more promising time to sort through issues and problems. If possible, schedule some good "private time" together—time to go out for an evening, to talk without interruptions, to be husband and wife without the stresses and burdens of being parents. Ironically, finding time away from the kids may allow you to regain your perspective and to recharge your batteries, thus giving you new energy for parenthood, which will in turn energize your parental authority.

Tackle Kid-Related Issues

Spouses often have different parenting styles. For cultural, individual, or gender-oriented reasons, spouses may also have different parenting *content*. By "content" I mean all the various expectations, rules, procedures, and habits that constitute a parent's attitudes and actions toward family life. Whether as a result of style or content, you may experience conflicts with your spouse over how to raise your children. These conflicts are stressful in their own right. To complicate matters, your kids may learn to play one parent against the other, which often creates further conflict. An example: you have insisted on an early bedtime, but your child says, "Daddy told me I could stay up till ten." How should you respond?

First, clarify the situation before you react. If your child comes to you with a request or demand, ask her, "Have you talked to your father [or mother] about this yet?" If the child says yes, find out what the answer was or say, "Wait a minute, we have to discuss this further." That way you empower both yourself and your spouse, and you avoid diminishing your (and your spouse's) authority. Together you can make a comfortable, unified response. At times you may have to go along with your spouse—at least for that particular incident—to prevent undercutting him or her. Later, you can reevaluate your decision and come up with a different solution, if necessary. In short, there are differences in parenting styles, personalities, and values, and such differences can cause conflict. Your goal isn't to *eliminate* all conflicts—that's not possible. Rather, your goal is to sort through conflicts open-mindedly and to resolve them through compromise and collaboration.

Do's and Don'ts for Communicating with Your Spouse

Here are some issues that deserve specific attention:

- Do confront problems in an assertive, honest way.

- Don't use unfair fighting tactics such as blaming, accusing, yelling, or name-calling.

- Do find a quiet, peaceful time and place to talk.

- Don't avoid conflict when something is bothering you; likewise, don't sulk quietly or express your frustrations in passive-aggressive ways.

- Do level with your spouse in a calm, collected manner.

- Don't try to communicate when you're tired, anxious, or stressed by outside demands.

- Do stick to the core problem rather than unnecessarily expanding it to other issues.

- Don't bring up old incidents that are irrelevant to what's at hand.

- Do listen to your spouse's response without interrupting, judging, or thwarting his or her own feelings and experiences.

- Do express how you're feeling without blame or accusation; if possible, use "I"-messages (such as "I feel hurt when you say that," "I feel overwhelmed when the house is so messy," and so forth, rather than "You make me feel bad when you say that" or "You make me feel terrible when you make such a mess").

- Don't try to repress your feelings of anger and resentment.

- Do empathize with and validate your partner's feelings whenever possible.

- Do focus on the issues, not on who's at fault.

- Don't blame your spouse for every problem; alternatively, don't try to accept all the blame.

- Do look at both sides of the issues you're facing.

- Do focus your communication on the process, not on winning the argument. Lead your discussion to a win–win outcome in which you and your spouse both feel heard and validated, and in which you find options for resolving your difficulties.

COMMUNICATION BETWEEN PARENTS AND CHILDREN

The other major communication issue we should examine concerns what occurs between parents and children. This issue is important in its own right but also has an enormous influence (for better or worse) on parental authority.

Communication is the heart of all good, healthy, intimate relationships. Your child's age and developmental stage will influence how she communicates with you; at any age, however, communication is how children build healthy self-esteem, obtain what they need for physical and emotional growth, and express their ideas and opinions. Communication is crucial to children's intellectual, social, emotional, and linguistic development.

Gaining Awareness of Communication

To complicate matters, you will invariably face difficult communication tasks as you cope with these issues. These tasks will change as your kids grow and develop. At the start of parenthood, your baby can't talk; you must communicate by both verbal and nonverbal means. During your child's toddlerhood, you must deal with the remarkable but complex stages of her efforts to acquire language. Other stages and tasks soon follow. Even the parents of highly verbal children must cope with many parent–child communication issues over the years. Parents must contend with their own communications issues, too — quirks, habits, and preferences that influence the parent–child dialogue as the parenting years go by.

Monitor the Nature of Parent–Child Communication

The nature of communication may not be solely what it seems. When you hear yourself criticizing or berating your child, for instance, you may be repeating words that your parents spoke when you were young. (One of the most common remarks I hear from mothers and fathers in therapy is "I can't believe how much I sound like my parents!") If you find yourself in this situation, stall for time. Give yourself a "time out" to calm down and gather your thoughts. Once you're calmer, return to the discussion and listen to your child without interruption or judgmental behavior. This detachment is hard to maintain, but it's valuable and productive in the long run.

Don't Overgeneralize from Specific Conversations

Try to separate your child's *behavior* from her *being*. Labeling a child in categorical ways can be destructive. (I'm referring to statements like, "You're so lazy," "Don't be such a troublemaker," "You're a real pain today," and so forth.) Even frustrating behaviors may not justify an across-the-board accusation. Instead of asking "Why are you always so fussy?" ask "I've noticed you're fussy this afternoon—what's bothering you?"

Stay Open-Minded about Your Own Communication Style

You may not be communicating as effectively as you think. Listen more closely to your conversations as a way of perceiving how you really communicate with your children. Hearing yourself as others hear you may become the first step in relearning how to communicate with them.

Communication with Teens

As noted earlier in this chapter, teenagers present special communication opportunities and challenges. On the one hand, teens have rapidly developing intellects and verbal skills, and these skills allow you the option of more complex, detailed discussions about many issues. On the other hand, teens can be arrogant, stubborn, testy, and insecure, which complicates the parent–child dialogue. How should you proceed?

First of all, try to maintain your composure during intense discussions. Don't take your child's emotional ups and downs too personally. Don't overreact to her accusations, declarations, threats, and demands. When you're communicating with her, try to separate her behavior from her person or character. Don't blame her or accuse her in ways that suggest there's a fundamental flaw in her character. Blanket accusations ("You never clean up your room," "You don't listen to me," "You're a real slob," etc.) will backfire, as your teen may interpret your statements to mean "You're no good" or "We don't love you." Instead of attacking her character, focus on the specific problem. How can you resolve the conflict you're facing? When will she do the task, and how does she plan to accomplish it? Accept the emotions involved, but do so without accusation. "I felt frustrated when I came in and saw your room a mess, 'cause I asked you yesterday but you haven't gotten around to cleaning it yet. I'm really tired and stressed out. I need you to help me out. Tell me when you're going to get this done and how you're going to do it."

Here are some specific tips:

- Keep your emotions as neutral as possible.

- Don't attack your teen with a lot of criticism or blame.

- Don't tear down your child's self-esteem.

- Do provide constructive feedback, though without lecturing.

- Do communicate with your teen as a young adult, but remember that she may be emotionally less developed than her intellect would suggest.

- Don't be syrupy sweet or overly emphatic—just straightforward, candid, and level-headed.

Seven Steps to Good Communication

Here are seven steps that can foster good parent–child communication when dealing with kids of most ages. You may not be able to follow all seven in sequence all the time—or at all—but even being aware of them can prove helpful.

STEP 1: Listen to your child without interrupting.

STEP 2: After listening, paraphrase out loud what your child has just said to you.

STEP 3: Empathize or validate your child's feelings. Say things like "It sounds like you were really feeling sad and angry." Or, "I sense that I've hurt your feelings." Or, "I'm sure the situation has been frustrating."

STEP 4: Ask for clarifying statements. "Tell me again—what did Sue say to you?" Or, "Help me to understand this better." Do so without judging or offering opinions; just be curious and ask questions to clarify.

STEP 5: Start the negotiating process. Ask your child what options she sees. If she could do things over again, what could she do differently?

STEP 6: Offer suggestions and gentle guidance. "What would you think about talking with him again?" Or, "Would X [or Y or Z] have been a good solution?"

STEP 7: Working together, choose an option that might work to solve a problem or to resolve an issue next time.

In addition to these steps, here are three tips that can ease the stress of communicating with your child.

Tip 1: Use "I"-Messages.

When you speak with your child about some aspect of her behavior that's bothering you, state your observation, not a sweeping statement about her character. Examples of a sweeping statement are

"You're such a spoiled brat," or "You're so self-centered." Instead, use statements that simply state how you feel.

- "I'm feeling angry."

- "I'm feeling hurt [frazzled, stressed, tired]."

- "I worry when you don't show up on time."

- "I feel very tired, so when your room is a mess I feel even more exhausted and frustrated."

These "I"-messages are an effective way to get the message across without burdening your child with hurtful feelings. Using "I"-messages instead of accusations, judgmental statements, or blame-casting can help start a dialogue about solving the problem at hand. Rather than putting your child on the defensive, "I"-messages identify your frustration and its source, which in turn can lead to productive questions:

- "How can we figure out a better homework routine?"

- "How can we keep your room in better shape?"

- "What's a better way to make sure you get home on time?"

- "What's a good way to help you do your chores?"

Tip 2: Empathize with Your Child.

When you speak with your child, make sure that you're truly empathizing with her. Typical validating comments are:

- "I can see this is very tough for you."

- "I noticed that the situation must have made you feel very bad."

- "I understand that it must have been difficult for you not to get selected for the play."

- "I'm sure you felt very sad when Liz didn't let you play the game."

- "You must have felt disappointed not to get the part in the play."

Tip 3: Set Realistic Goals, Then Help Your Child Meet Them.

When negotiating about an issue, keep in mind that communication is more than simply words. For younger children, a timer may be useful. For older children, a checklist or chart may be preferable. Consistent, calm actions will reinforce the verbal statements you've made.

COMMUNICATION BETWEEN CHILDREN

Like parent–child communication, kid-to-kid communication is complex and often problematic. Some of the complexities are probably inevitable—the side effects of children learning to sort out issues as they grow and change. Other problems crop up in response to certain aspects of American culture, which often emphasizes confrontation over compromise and individualism over collaboration. Kids often learn to force their preferences on others rather than to work together. An abrasive, me-first communication style is a common result of this situation. Following are ways that you can help foster more creative communication among your kids.

- Teach your child that when she communicates with other kids, she's not dealing with a win–lose situation. It's possible to cooperate in ways that leave everyone a winner.

- During family discussions, encourage each member to listen to others' points of view. Don't prejudge other people. Keep their minds open.

- Try to be open-minded and flexible. By learning to compromise, family members will gain far more than they give up. Come up with options that satisfy as many people as possible.

- Try to foster the idea that situations aren't always right/wrong, good/bad; people and events are complex and ambiguous. There are many gray areas in people's personalities and circumstances.

In short, help your child see all sides of the situation—or at least as many sides as possible. This task is easier said than done, and it will be influenced by your own attitudes toward communication. What will make the most difference in how your kids communicate is whether you're a flexible or an inflexible parent. At any stage of childhood, you are the most important role model for good, open communication. If you're a flexible parent, you'll negotiate with your children; you'll include them in the process of compromise, you'll talk with them, you'll allow them to be heard, you'll validate their feelings, and you'll empathize with them and help them to come up with possible options and solutions. Taking this approach—being open to your children's feelings—will go a long way in helping them learn the subtle arts of respect and patience when communicating with others.

Chapter 7

THE SUPERPARENT SYNDROME

Tricia, the mother of two sons and a daughter, wants her children to have the best of everything. She aspires to give them the close attention that her own mother provided Tricia as a girl. That's difficult, however, given Tricia's full-time work as a lawyer—so difficult that she feels she's falling short as a parent. She compensates by spending lots of time with the kids each evening and on weekends. Her husband, Jerry, is a devoted father but is often absent because of his job as a regional sales manager. Luckily, the couple is affluent enough to afford good childcare. They also try to "make it up to the children" by giving them frequent gifts and special outings. Overall, parenthood is going well for Tricia and her husband.

"But it's hard," she confides. "There's always something I need to be doing for them. I help them with their homework. I try to read to the youngest when I can. I do the usual domestic stuff—cooking for them, bathing them, getting their lunches ready for school. I pitch in at their schools. I like being a mom, but I feel I'm not doing all I ought to be doing." Tricia's frustration isn't limited to family life.

"There's also the work situation. I need my clients—I run a one-woman legal practice, so I can't delegate to a partner. We need the money. But I resent the time it takes, since my kids are always asking why I'm not home more. Well, I just can't do more than I'm already doing. I'm always dashing about, and I feel I'm letting everyone down. I get testy, which makes the kids irritable, and we all get on each others' nerves."

FASTER THAN A SPEEDING BULLET . . .

Let's face it: parenthood is hard work. Having kids in the house guarantees that there's always more to do each day than any parent can accomplish. Maybe that's just the reality of raising children. Part of being a parent is putting the kids first and doing whatever is necessary. What concerns me, though, is how many parents are developing such high standards and such grand expectations that they inflate their parental role to the bursting point. They want to accomplish everything to perfection. They want to meet their children's every need. They want to avoid letting their kids down even in the most trivial ways. They aren't satisfied with being Mom and Dad— they want to be Supermom and Superdad.

Unfortunately, this attitude doesn't only generate a lot of frustration; it can also seriously undermine your parental authority. Why? Because no matter how hard you try, you can't be truly superhuman. It's true that parents make mistakes—in fact, parenthood guarantees that you'll make one mistake after another—but attempting to exceed normal, human limitations simply isn't productive. If you try to be Supermom or Superdad, you'll add tremendous stress to your life, and probably to your child's life as well. Doing more than what's feasible isn't altogether healthy. You run the risk of becoming overindulgent and overinvolved, which exerts great pressure on your child in its own way. What you regard as being attentive may seem to your child as demanding, even suffocating behavior. You may also raise her expectations as well, encouraging her to be demanding, self-indulgent, and self-important. Far from fostering your child's growth, being a superparent may complicate her development. All of these superparent behaviors run the risk of diminishing rather than strengthening your authority.

My hunch is that the superparent syndrome is mostly a response to guilt—guilt that parents feel over being absent long hours from the home, guilt over becoming irritable and stressed, guilt over any number of real or imagined parental shortcomings. This response is understandable, but it complicates family dynamics and often leads mothers and fathers to overindulge their kids. This overindulgence in turn becomes another source of guilt. In short, guilt becomes a vicious cycle that damages family life.

Here's a typical scenario. Jake and Marie both work full time. Their work obligations involve long office hours and frequent business trips. Jake and Marie attempt to limit the consequences of their schedules on their two daughters, but the task is difficult. As a result, they try to compensate for their intense work life by providing Kim and Lisette with all kinds of opportunities and activities— frequent playdates, trips to the movies and to amusement parks, and installation of a home entertainment center. However, all of these expensive, time-intensive activities limit the amount of relaxed time that the Hermansons can spend with their children. The results include feelings of disconnectedness, irritability, and mutual anger among Jake and Marie and their kids. Jake and Marie cope with the resulting domestic tensions by indulging their children further— buying them expensive toys and gadgets, "rewarding" them with lavish outings and trips, and escalating ordinary events (birthday parties, holidays) into extravaganzas. But Kim and Lisette often resent being bought off, or else they respond with greater and greater demands, which raise the tension levels higher. This reaction prompts Jake and Marie to feel more parental guilt, completing the cycle.

If you feel that you've fallen into this superparent syndrome, you need to make sense of the situation and regain control of it. Understanding the dynamics of your behavior and its effects on your children won't solve all these problems instantly, but it can provide a sense of perspective and increase your parental authority.

GUILT—A DOUBLE-EDGED SWORD

Perhaps the most crucial step you can take is to get a grip on guilt. Guilt isn't the only feature of the superparent syndrome, but it's central, so it's a good place to start. I'm of two minds about guilt. On the one hand, certain kinds of guilt can, in moderation, serve a purpose. Guilt can be an early warning system that alerts you to situations in which you're misdirecting your efforts or falling short. You may inadvertently be ignoring some aspect of your child's needs. You may be focusing on some aspect of life at the expense of one that's more crucial at the moment. You may be indulging yourself at a time when you ought to focus on some other member of the family. Guilt can tip you off about one or more of these tendencies.

If you feel guilty about these or other situations, it doesn't necessarily mean that you're being "bad"; I'm not advocating guilt in that moralistic sense. Rather, guilt can be a useful signal on issues such as setting limits, indulging your children, and being available to them. It can also motivate you to perceive your family's circumstances more clearly and address issues that you may have been ignoring.

On the other hand, guilt can be burdensome and disruptive. Guilt can complicate your life and disrupt your efforts to solve problems by keeping you immobilized. If you merely obsess about a situation rather than take action or cope with the issues, guilt can limit your options and energy. Guilt of this sort isn't useful; in fact, it can become an avoidance issue that compounds your problem.

Here's an example: Eileen's work obligations have required her to place her son, Eli, in a childcare center. This decision wasn't by any means a matter of self-indulgence—Eileen is a single mom and has to earn a living. However, she tends to overrely on daycare when she could be available to her son. During many of Eileen's days off, for instance, Eli goes to daycare. Eileen feels guilty about the situation but hasn't changed her behavior. She could make herself more available to her son, but she hasn't. Rather than using her guilt as a signal—as an inducement to make decisions and take action—she has just bogged down in guilt. Eileen feels bad because she hasn't been spending enough time with Eli, yet she can't get past the guilt to redress the imbalance in her family life.

THE LIMITS OF GUILT

During the parenting years, guilt comes with the turf. Children have almost infinite needs; parents have finite energy to do what needs to be done. Luckily, most parents do at least an adequate job of raising kids, and many excel at the task. The catch is that we often feel that we ought to be doing more. The result: lots of guilt.

But guilt is limited in its utility. It doesn't really solve any problems; it merely bogs you down in feeling bad. This isn't to say that you shouldn't acknowledge your mistakes or limitations; but you should focus primarily on present tasks rather than on regretting errors or lost opportunities. Parenthood is a messy, imperfect process. Despite the messiness, you're probably doing a better job of it than you think.

How can you cope effectively with guilt? One important step is to maintain good boundaries. Keep your work at work and your family life at home. Carve out no-work times each day when your children are certain to need your attention. Put on the answering machine. You'll have to acknowledge the world's demands soon enough, but don't apologize for the importance you place on parenthood. In my opinion, you can't do anything more meaningful than raise children.

DISENGAGE FROM THE GUILT TRAP

You have a great deal of power over your child's life. You have responsibilities and duties. At the same time, you aren't so powerful that you truly determine everything about how your child thinks, feels, and acts, how she will behave, or who she will become. Forces far beyond your influence have power and input too: peers, schools, and the rest of society. In addition, your child's unique genetic makeup will influence her personality, temperament, and physiology.

How should you respond? First of all, it's appropriate to take responsibility. Control as many circumstances as you can. Do whatever is possible for your child. At the same time, grasp the difference between the things that truly lie within your control and those that don't. You should make every possible effort on your child's behalf, but you can't determine the ultimate outcome. Don't complicate your life by carrying a load of guilt that will only complicate your parental tasks and possibly confound your best efforts. Don't take all events personally. In short, disengage from the guilt trap. It's good to reach insights and figure out what you can do better, but there's a big difference between pushing yourself harder and having unrealistic expectations. By all means be the best parent possible—be a good role model for your children, live your dreams, and reach for your goals. At the same time, be flexible. Take it easy not only on your kids, but on yourself.

Deal with Feelings of Guilt

Because guilt is common, even inevitable, you may as well face it and cope with it rather than simply shoving it under the carpet.

- *Weigh the pluses and minuses.* Suppose you're worried about a job-related issue, such as balancing work and family. Instead of wallowing in guilt, evaluate the situation. What will happen if you decrease your hours at work? If you increase your time at home, what are the consequences? Sketch out the alternatives. Base your decisions on assessments of your options, not free-floating guilt.

- *Change your state of mind.* If you can't solve a problem you face, can you change your *response* to it? Sometimes our emotional reactions to problems exhaust and debilitate us more than the problems themselves do. It's possible that the guilt you feel is disproportionate to what inspires it. Children are amazingly resilient. Your child may be nagging you for your time and attention, but she may be quite capable of tolerating occasional, well-planned absences. Diminishing your guilt may do your child far more good than worrying and obsessing about your problems.

- *Limit your complaining.* You have choices in how you handle negative feelings. Some people deplete their family members' patience with constant complaining. Negative attitudes may prove toxic both to you and to the people around you. Everyone grows weary of hearing endless negativity. If you end up obsessing about the same old issues, try to size up the situation. Are you really so powerless? Is the situation so awful? Are there no alternatives before you? You may well have genuine problems; however, endless complaints will almost certainly compound them, not solve them.

Prioritize

Many otherwise creative parents bog down because they let family life grow too complex. Everything becomes an ordeal; nothing goes according to plan. Many aspects of this situation are avoidable. The key is to change your attitude about what needs to be done.

- *Limit the number of activities in any given day.* Kids today are often just too busy. Many parents feel that they should make sure that their children are constantly occupied, but this strategy can backfire. Kids need downtime—time to play, time to daydream, and time simply to goof off. Try to cut the sheer number of obligations that you and your child have to meet.

- *Simplify your schedule.* Beyond the issue of *limiting* the number of commitments, it's also important to *reorganize* how you deal with them. Cluster errands. Use downtime to your advantage, such as shopping when your child is at a music lesson.

- *Pad in extra time.* Give yourself more time for the transitions from one activity to another. Avoid pressuring your child to rush-rush-rush. Allow extra time for decompression following stressful or exhausting activities.

REJOINING THE HUMAN RACE

What I've described is a common situation these days, and it's understandable—a response that many parents make to the heavy pressures they face. Still, it's a worrisome state of affairs. Parenthood is challenging enough already; add to it work-related stress, cultural expectations, kids' own demands, and a constant barrage of media messages ("If you want the best for your kids . . .") and what do you get? A strong temptation to push the envelope. It's no wonder that many parents feel they have to be Supermom and Superdad.

Given the risks involved, what's a sensible response? I'll put it bluntly: you should reject the superparent syndrome. Rejoin the human race. Be a parent, not a superparent. Do the best you can, but don't expect to do everything.

Avoid Perfectionism

Many parents today have such high expectations, both for themselves and for their kids, that their efforts border on perfectionism. This attitude stems partly from cultural inclinations; we Americans tend to push ourselves toward tangible accomplishments, whether in work, play, or parenthood. The superparent syndrome also contains elements of the guilt we've already discussed, which prompts some parents to compensate by trying to do more, buy more, and give more to their kids. Other parents may make similar efforts because they're going through a divorce. Still others make excessive efforts to compensate for feelings of deprivation in the past. (As one friend told me, "I didn't get much from my own parents, so I'm going to make sure my kids have every advantage I can provide.") In short, people have many different reasons for striving to attain parenting perfection.

However, the results often backfire. Perfectionism can cause great tension, disappointment, and stress for parents and kids alike. If you believe that things should be done only in a certain way, or only to a certain degree of excellence, your expectations can become burdensome. If you hold your kids to perfectionistic standards, you'll make it difficult for them to experiment with possibilities, to explore their imaginations and aspirations, and simply to try out what interests them. Perfectionism can also push you toward a certain parental rigidity. By expecting perfection, you're not as capable of living "in the moment"—spontaneous, playful, relaxed, flexible, and ready to enjoy the unpredictable aspects of being alive.

Both you and your child will learn as much from your failures as from your successes. Moreover, a tolerant, easygoing atmosphere generally helps children to thrive. An atmosphere in which everything has to reach some preconceived standard isn't conducive to children achieving their greatest potential; it increases pressure and it may thwart your child's efforts to perform well and enjoy life.

By contrast, rejecting perfectionism opens you to the moment and to everything that's possible within it. You're more likely to accept yourself for who you are; in turn, you're more likely to accept your child in her own right. You won't have as many expectations or arbitrary rules. You'll be more easygoing, adaptable, and open to life's surprises. Rejecting perfectionism does *not* mean that you don't have high standards; instead, it means that your standards are more realistic and flexible.

Accept Your Own Flaws

One corollary of rejecting perfectionism is that you accept your own flaws. In my clinical practice, I see many perfectionistic parents who are struggling with inner pain or with a sense of emptiness—a feeling that they're somehow "not good enough" and must therefore make up for their shortcomings by striving to be flawless. This attitude is unfortunate. The people I'm describing are often wonderful, bright, giving parents; there's nothing fundamentally wrong with them. But their rigorous, even compulsive striving isn't good for their own mental health, much less for their children's. If they could only accept their own flaws, they would relax and be easier on everyone.

We're all imperfect; we all make mistakes. If you can readily admit to your shortcomings—if you can even laugh at your quirks and foibles—then you'll give your children a much better role model than you will as a perfectionist. In striving for perfection, you set yourself on a pedestal, which isn't a safe place for anyone: it's hard to get up there and easy to fall off. It's much better to present an image of yourself as merely human—loving and intent on serving your children's best interests, to be sure, but also flawed and aware of being flawed, and therefore accepting of others' flaws and capable of compromise and forgiveness. If you can help your kids see you as a complex, contradictory, and fallible human being, you've granted them more leeway to be human, too.

Part of accepting your flaws is having realistic expectations. Consider what you can and can't do. Don't set preposterously high goals for yourself, as overreaching can easily lead to disappointment and resentment. (This suggestion is particularly important if you're a single parent, a working parent, or a parent who's also caring for elderly or infirm parents.)

- Be gentle with yourself.

- Find help where you can.

- Don't promise to do things that exceed your reach.

- Keep volunteerism (at school, at church or temple, in your community) in proportion to your time or energy.

- Take shortcuts (cooking, cleaning, shopping) when it's sensible to do so.

- Set priorities for family time.

- Simplify family logistics.

- Allow kids unstructured downtime.

- Avoid excessive scheduled activities.

- Keep special events (parties, vacations, sleepovers, etc.) as simple as possible.

- Ignore or thwart kids' manipulative or extortionate behavior, but always try to identify and address the root causes.

Focus on What You've Done Right

Avoid dwelling on the negative. Yes, you've probably fallen short in various ways, but who hasn't? Overall you'll muddle through—we all do! You don't always have time and energy to read the right story, say the right things, or buy the right gift for your child; even so, you're likely to receive their love and approval. If you focus on what you've done right, you'll be more relaxed and accepting, thus more capable of attending to your children's needs.

Seek a Sense of Balance

Strive for moderation. If you can attain balance in your life—a good mix of work, play, and family activities—you've won half the battle. You won't drive yourself or your kids crazy by expecting to do everything; you'll avoid making everyone feel tense and irritable. I'm not saying that you shouldn't be ambitious. It's good to have dreams and good to work hard to attain them. But you should strive to attain a balance between aiming for your dreams and simply accepting what life gives you.

If you don't have dreams, you may feel adrift and purposeless, but the obsessive pursuit of a dream can blind you to unanticipated satisfactions. Many of the delights of family life are subtle, unpredictable, and fleeting. Your child suddenly smiles. She gives you an unexpected gift. She understands something that reassures her. She tells you a joke. None of these moments can be planned; if you're lucky, you'll be alert to them and will rejoice in them when they occur. So, yes, pursue your dream, but not at any cost—especially not the cost of losing your sense of balance and ignoring the unexpected delights of parenthood.

Reach Out for Help and Support

In many families, one parent—usually the mother—has a primary childcare role. This arrangement may be a matter of choice or a matter of necessity. Either way, however, it's easy for mothers to become overwhelmed by the magnitude of their parenting responsibilities; it's difficult for one parent to assume all the tasks of raising children and not become exhausted.

There's no easy answer to this situation, but I believe that two issues lie at the heart of the dilemma.

First, fathers need to get more involved. This doesn't mean that dads should strive to be superdads, only that it's crucial to be present, involved, and committed. I'm aware that roles are changing, and that many American dads spend far more time with their children than fathers did in the past. It's wonderful that more and more American men are tackling a larger, fuller parenting role. Still, there's a long way to go. Many Americans, men and women alike, continue to see fathers as secondary parents. Some men who claim to want more involvement don't follow through and actually do the work. The result is a continuing burden on women's shoulders. A major solution to this dilemma is for men to take on still more child-care duties.

Second, American women should be more flexible in accommodating their husbands' contributions to the cause. I hear from many fathers that although they want to be involved in their children's day-to-day care, they find their wives reluctant to cede control over this traditionally female role. Some of these wives are the same women who have asked their husbands to get more involved! I'm aware that even mothers who want more domestic parity struggle with issues of sex-role identity. Fair enough—but while they are sorting through these legitimate issues, women shouldn't undercut their husbands' willingness to contribute their time and effort. If parenthood is going to be a true partnership, mothers have to relinquish some of the territory.

Tolerate Disorder

Raising children is a messy business. Even once you're past the stages when kids throw food on the floor, pull the books off the shelves, and scatter toys everywhere, family life involves all sorts of clutter and upheaval. It's fair enough to insist on a certain level of hygiene and safety, and every parent has a basic comfort level in tolerating messiness. Still, it's easy to go too far. If you can't tolerate a modicum of benign disorder, parenthood will drive you nuts. You'll probably drive your kids nuts, too. I'd suggest relaxing your standards a bit. Clean up to the degree possible, but don't sweat the details.

Dress your kids for comfort, not fashion. Encourage them to tackle art and cooking projects even if they make a mess (though it's fine to insist that they help clean up afterward!). Allow them to get dirty in appropriate situations, such as when they are playing outside. Untidiness goes along with childhood creativity.

Delegate

Many moms and dads stress themselves unnecessarily by believing that they alone can accomplish every parenting task. Whether because of perfectionism, a controlling personality, or a habitual belief that they alone must do everything, contemporary parents often hesitate or refuse to delegate responsibility. The result is more tension, more fatigue. It's an unfortunate situation, especially because tired parents often make avoidable mistakes or grow irritable with their children.

A better response is to assign tasks to carefully chosen helpers. Such helpers may be your own parents, in-laws, and other relatives, or they may be hired assistants such as childcare persons, "mother's helpers," or housekeepers. Many people complain that they can't afford such help. That may be so; on the other hand, some partial solutions (such as hiring a local middle school student to read to your kids or help you put away groceries) aren't expensive, and the benefits far outweigh the costs.

Make Time for Your Marriage

The foundation of family life is the parents' marriage. If this foundation is shaky, its instability can jeopardize the children's well-being. This situation leads to a conundrum: on the one hand, the parents need to focus on their children, but focusing on them *to the detriment of the marriage* can undercut everyone's best efforts. The level of intimacy, cooperation, love, and respect that the partners share will greatly influence their satisfaction with family life. The relative stability and warmth of your marriage will also influence how your children establish intimate relationships in the future. In short, nurturing yourselves as husband and wife will also help you nurture your children.

Focus on Simple Pleasures

Superparents often feel that they must provide their children with extravagant satisfactions—gifts, vacations, summer camps, birthday parties, and so forth. All of these things are expensive. The cost involved pressures parents to spend more, which means earning more, which means working more, which means being away from the family more. The result: extravagance often takes away something more valuable than what it provides. American children are notoriously covetous—often feeling entitled to every latest gadget, garment, and gewgaw—but they don't really need all this stuff. In many ways, the kids know it, too. They also may feel "bought off" if they believe that their moms and dads are compensating them for parental absence from the home.

Skip the fancy goods. Aim for simpler pleasures. Don't worry about buying the perfect present, baking the perfect cake, cooking the perfect meal, or having the perfect vacation. Spend time together. Do activities with your kids. Listen to their stories and concerns. Work on projects as a family. Adjusting to a slower pace and lower expectations may take some time and practice, but it's beneficial for everyone in the long run.

GIVE YOURSELF A BREAK

Whatever else, be gentle with yourself. If you find that you tend to be perfectionistic, ask yourself what would happen if you released your high expectations and self-criticisms. Would your children really suffer? Would they reject you and run you out of town? Or would they welcome you for who you really are, only more relaxed, accepting, and accessible? My hunch is that no one in your family would be worse off if you ceased being Supermom or Superdad and simply choose to be Mom or Dad instead.

Parenting is strenuous, demanding, and full of endless tasks. Most of the parents I've spoken with will admit that it's difficult to be a mother or father. Who among us doesn't fall short some of the time? Accept the reality of your imperfection. Do the best you can. Work hard to bolster your efforts. Get enough rest, treat yourself well, and arrange a little time off. Find other parents who can provide insight and solidarity as you raise your children. Take care of yourself as fully as possible. Don't blame yourself for what you can't control. Try to live in the moment. Look after your kids, enjoy them, and take the tasks of parenthood as they come.

Chapter 8

THE IMPORTANCE OF CIVILITY

While eating at a local restaurant some months ago, I watched a remarkable scene unfold. A large group of preteen boys and a handful of adults entered the facility. Dressed in athletic sweats and stoked up in high spirits, these guys had just finished either a game or a major practice session; now their coach and three of the team members' parents were taking the boys out to dinner. The hostess seated this loud, raucous party at a couple of big tables that the waiters pushed together; she handed out menus; she gave them her best wishes for a happy dinner. So far so good. This was a family restaurant, and nobody present would hold anything against a group of teens having a boisterous time.

Unfortunately, the situation soon degenerated. The boys' behavior wasn't just rowdy; it quickly became obnoxious. They shouted. They made disgusting noises. They tossed wadded-up napkins and straws at each other, sometimes missing altogether and striking other patrons instead. Some of them got up, shoved and hassled each other, and ran up and down the aisles. The noise they created soon overwhelmed every other party in the restaurant. What began as goofiness deteriorated into an oppressive, chaotic atmosphere that no one present could ignore.

Boyish high jinks? Mere venting of postgame energy? Well-intentioned horsing around? It's true that nothing these teenagers did was overtly destructive or menacing to other people. If they'd still been outside on the playing field, their behavior wouldn't have been a problem. Their actions *were* a problem, however, because the situation was inappropriate. It simply wasn't fair to use a restaurant as the venue for their private romp. In addition to disrupting the conversations all around them, these kids alarmed some of the elderly patrons and agitated or intimidated some of the younger children present. The crescendo of their rowdiness probably caused many people to wonder, as I did, whether the noise and dashing about would increase till someone got hurt.

What appalled me most about this situation, however, wasn't the boys' own behavior. It was the behavior of their adult chaperones. After all, these guys weren't acting up for lack of supervision. Four adults sat with the team members at their tables. One of those adults was the boys' coach. Yet not one of these grownups made any effort to calm the preteens, quiet them down, or restrain their more annoying actions. The adults watched and spoke among themselves. They looked more and more uncomfortable. But they didn't intervene.

As this situation evolved, I felt increasingly concerned about it but unsure how to respond. It wasn't really my responsibility to step in, especially given the presence of the other adults. I worried about triggering a hostile response from one or more of the boys. I felt a growing temptation simply to leave. At the same time, I felt an intensifying anger about the kids' antisocial behavior and their adult chaperones' unwillingness to respond. I resented having this incident ruin the outing I'd arranged with my sister and her child, as the boys' rowdiness was distracting us and drowning out our conversation. My frustration soon got the best of me. I turned, leaned over toward the nearby table, and spoke to the kids there as politely as I could: "Excuse me, but I think you guys are disrupting a lot of the other folks here. You think you might use your indoor voices instead of your outdoor voices?"

The response amazed me. The boys I'd spoken to reacted calmly, almost contritely. One of them apologized. A few of them laughed at my request but immediately quieted down. A couple of them told some of their pals to cool it. The rowdiness eased almost at once.

Another reaction surprised me: the boys' chaperones thanked me for intervening. *Thanked* me! Which was appropriate in some ways but almost comical otherwise—as if they couldn't have taken action themselves! I should mention that restaurant patrons at nearby tables thanked me as well. Of course they too could have stepped in, but that's not my point. Nothing I did was heroic or even diffi-cult. I'd just pointed out to these boys that their behavior was inap-propriate in a public place. Why their own adult chaperones couldn't have done so, I have no idea. All I know is that they didn't. Perhaps they wouldn't have, either, even if the kids they'd been supervising had started dancing on the tables or swinging from the chandeliers.

A NATION OF BOORS?

I wish I could report that this kind of incident is uncommon. Unfor-tunately, it's anything but rare. American kids are becoming more and more impatient, inconsiderate, and even chaotic, both at home and in public. Many children are increasingly insolent, demanding, or hostile toward parents, teachers, adults in general, and other chil-dren. Even relatively well-behaved kids can be remarkably impolite, self-centered, and rude. In short, there's a visible decline in civility among American kids, both in relations with each other and with adults. At times I worry that we're becoming a nation of boors.

Here are some of the common situations I frequently observe or hear about from teachers, school officials, merchants, parents, and people in general:

- Children increasingly misuse, mistreat, meddle with, or damage public property, such as street signs, park benches, and trees and shrubbery.

- Children speak to each other and to parents and other adults in hostile, abusive, threatening, or litigious language ("Shut up!" "Go stuff it!" "You can't make me!" "You can't tell me what to do!" "Get off my back or I'll sue you!" "Leave me alone or you're asking for it!"). Profanity is also more and more common in public.

- Children overreact, taking offense at the slightest requests or statements and interpreting others' comments or questions as "dissing" that warrants revenge.

- Children act like parents and treat their own parents like misbehaving children.

- Children make demands rather than requests, ignoring the most basic aspects of politeness such as saying "please" and "thank you."

- Children seem incapable of waiting even brief periods of time to obtain what they want, and instead react with impatience, frustration, and even rage toward any delay of gratification.

I realize that these concerns have a familiar ring. People have been complaining about the decline of civility for thousands of years; you may feel that my complaints are simply another instance of inventing the wheel. I'm aware that this issue isn't new. I'm also aware that some people have ideas about civility that make the whole issue an easy target for mockery. However, the fine points of etiquette aren't what I'm talking about. What concerns me is the basic ability and willingness *to see others as worthy of respect and to treat them as warranting the same rights and privileges that one claims for oneself.* It's this basic ability that I see deteriorating throughout American culture.

THE ORIGINS OF INCIVILITY

Assuming that American children have become increasingly rude, impatient, arrogant, and uncivil—and I don't think there's really much doubt in that regard—where is this behavior coming from?

Adult Behavior—And Misbehavior

The most obvious source is the community of adults. Inconsiderate, demanding, aggressive, and obnoxious behavior among children shouldn't come as a shock when similar (or far more extreme) attitudes and actions are common among adults throughout the country. Americans are becoming habitually more impolite, self-centered, and rude. Simply watch people at airline ticket counters, in supermarket checkout lines, in parking lots, at restaurants, and almost anywhere else in public these days and you'll frequently see grown-ups act in selfish, impatient, irritable ways that would seem funny if they weren't so appalling. Expectations about politeness and considerate behavior have diminished; instead, many otherwise sensible folks are demanding and self-centered in public. Given this sort of behavior—not to mention the tone it sets and the example it offers—is it any surprise that children also manifest more and more uncivil, antisocial behavior?

Parental Wimpiness toward Kids' Behavior

To complicate matters, many American parents foster incivility in their children by responding with excessive toleration, even accommodation, toward rude behavior. The chaotic scene I observed in the restaurant was an extreme case, but this sort of public rowdiness isn't unusual. I've seen many incidents in which parents failed to intervene, or even to respond *at all*, when their kids acted rudely or inconsiderately toward other people. Faced with such behavior, many parents just look the other way.

One of the most common situations I see is parents allowing children to run amok in public settings. Many moms and dads let their kids race around in stores, remove merchandise from shelves, take packages apart, strew things around, and generally act as if they're playing at a public playground. Merchants I've spoken with speak despairingly about this sort of behavior, it's become so commonplace. Worse yet, many parents take offense when merchants request that they rein in their kids. "You'd think I'd physically attacked their little darlings, they get so furious," one shopkeeper told me. If children learn at an early age that chaotic, self-centered behavior is acceptable, why should they adjust to a more considerate attitude as they grow older? They've already learned that they're the center of the universe.

Willful Overindulgence

Other parents overindulge their children, allowing the kids to make excessive demands, or else they apologize to the kids for having expectations for acceptable behavior, as if the parents have committed an infraction by setting standards. I've heard many dads and moms apologize to their kids when the kids have, in fact, behaved inappropriately. "Oh, I'm sorry—did I hurt your feelings?" one mother asked her eight-year-old daughter when the girl, having thrown a tantrum in public, responded angrily to a scolding. A father I observed berated himself for the audacity of criticizing his son's surly attitude: "That was stupid of me. I won't talk to you like that again." Far from shaping their children's behavior and setting appropriate standards, such abdication of parental responsibilities only reinforces the children's perceptions that their own desires, beliefs, and attitudes are what matter most.

Parentifying Children

One of the most damaging mistakes that some parents make is to switch roles with their children. This switcheroo—what child development experts call *parentification*—puts children in the parents' role and parents in the children's role. In short, the parents abdicate their responsibilities and put the kids in charge.

Here's an example. While shopping at the local supermarket, I observed a mother and her eight-year-old son as they preceded me up and down the aisles. The boy set the agenda both for the purchases and for the meals his family would eat. The mom let him pick out almost every item he wanted. Predictably, the cart ended up full of sugary cereals, fruit snacks, fast foods, and desserts. When the mother suggested other possibilities, her son snapped at her irritably: "That's bad stuff!" he'd announce, or "I hate that!" Even when he wasn't rude to her—treating his mom as a tired parent might treat a naughty child—he still made it clear who was in charge. It was, in fact, the mother's willingness to relinquish her authority that troubled me even more than the boy's irritability. A better response might have been to allow the boy a few (but limited) choices. He could pick out *one* kind of cereal, or he could choose between either of two items that the mom needed to purchase anyway, such as cinnamon applesauce *or* regular applesauce.

Giving a child a larger role in decisions may appear to boost his or her self-esteem and foster the child's growth, but it usually has the opposite effect. Children *need* structure. They benefit from age-appropriate limits and boundaries. It's true that kids want more freedom and responsibility as they grow older and more competent, but even high school students need a clear sense of what's acceptable and unacceptable, and younger children thrive in response to openly stated expectations for appropriate behavior. Putting kids in a position of excessive authority is actually stressful for most children and destructive for many. Kids may protest their parents' efforts to guide them and set limits; regardless, they need limits and guidance.

Parental Excesses and Inappropriate Modeling

Some parents overreact in ways that jeopardize or even counteract any efforts to foster civility. Admittedly, every parent loses his or her temper from time to time—that's not what I'm talking about. Rather, I'm referring to repeated, excessive outbursts that create a tense background to family life. Shouting or screaming at children, berating them in public, calling them names, and swatting or spanking them all give a message that civility doesn't matter, that the way to get things done is through angry, hostile, abrasive language or even physical force.

A family I've observed in a neighboring town provides a depressing example of this kind of interaction. Both parents (I'll call them Pete and Maggie) are well-intentioned toward their kids, and I have no doubt that all the family members love each other. Unfortunately, the Jensens' style of behavior contradicts their affectionate feelings. Maggie and Pete have set a tone that's abrasive, confrontational, and irritable. They never ask their kids to do anything; they simply order them about. "Go get the groceries from the car." "Pick up your room." "Stop making that noise." Worse yet, the parents express themselves by means of a weary sarcasm that spreads ill feeling throughout the whole family. "*Now* what is it?" "I suppose what I fixed for dinner doesn't meet your standards." "Can't you do *anything* independently?" I have reason to believe that their attitude is a result of emotional fatigue rather than anger or contempt, but the consequences are the same. The three kids—currently ages eight, nine, and twelve—unwittingly imitate their parents, treating each other with impatience, putting each other down, and ordering each other around like household servants.

The Wider Culture

Conservative social critics often complain that over the past several decades American culture has deteriorated in many ways, becoming less civil and more abrasive. William Bennett, for example, has written with concern about the general coarsening of public discourse. George Will, David Brooks, and other commentators have criticized or mocked the selfishness that characterizes much of daily life in early twenty-first-century America. Although I am by no means a conservative, I agree on some points with these critics. I share their belief that civility has declined throughout our nation, and that the entertainment media and other cultural forces share part of the blame.

Here are some instances of what prompts my concerns about American culture—including the influence of the mass media and its effects on civility:

- Cartoons such as *Rugrats* model abrasive, rude behavior for preschool and school-age children.

- TV shows like *South Park* and *The Simpsons* stress the coolness of scattershot mockery, rudeness, racial insults, and contempt for parents.

- Even relatively benign shows (*Malcolm in the Middle* comes to mind) stress the notion that adults are clueless, and only kids know the score.

- Sitcoms and movies emphasize the importance of an "edgy" conversational style and a reliance on put-downs and "zingers" to score points in interpersonal interactions.

- Many rap and rock music stars celebrate racism, sexism, anti-Semitism, homophobia, and xenophobia.

- Politicians and other public figures routinely make their points by ridiculing opponents and relying on innuendo and half-truths rather than engaging in rational discussion and debate.

I want to emphasize, however, that the societal coarseness that Bennett and others deplore isn't a right/left issue. Some of the most abrasive people I encounter are conservatives. Right-wing talk-show hosts, among them Rush Limbaugh, Don Imus, and their many imitators, fill the radio airwaves with contempt, hostility, and invective. If there's any evidence that social coarseness is primarily a liberal problem, I fail to see it. The sad truth is that incivility and rudeness are equal-opportunity problems.

For our purposes, the issue concerning me most is that American culture, influenced by the entertainment media, exerts a huge influence on our children. Almost anyone who spends time with kids can see the effects on a day-to-day basis. Even young children are often caught in the spell of their favorite TV shows and movies. The effects aren't entirely negative; I know a number of kids whose mania for the Pokémon craze, for instance, has prompted a rich fantasy life. Still, it's troubling that so many shows promote values that diminish rather than advance kids' ability to participate agreeably with other human beings. Worse yet, any parent who has listened to teenagers reviling each other in the language of rock and rap lyrics can't help but worry about the wider culture's influence on children.

HOW TO FOSTER CIVILITY

One of the major tasks facing parents is to foster civility within the family and, ideally, within the wider community. Doing so isn't a matter of simply learning to use the proper fork or of addressing every man as "Sir" and every woman as "Ma'am." Rather, civility is a more pervasive, fundamental issue: a basic ability to be considerate toward others and to avoid a self-centered approach to the world. In reality, you can't make the whole world behave in a thoughtful, considerate manner; you can, however, teach your children to be polite, to be thoughtful in dealing with other people, and to respect others' needs, abilities, and feelings. That said, I don't suggest that you pressure your children into becoming passive, syrupy sweet, overly compliant toward all authority, or incapable of independent thinking. Taking a balanced approach toward civility will reduce stress within your family and between yourself and your kids. You can then help spread these values beyond the confines of your own household.

I'm amazed by how often people confuse etiquette with civility. Etiquette—the specific rules for decorum—is a subset of civility, which is the more fundamental issue of consideration toward other people and ability to get along with them. Ideally, etiquette and civility reinforce one another. In practice, they may scarcely coexist in the same person. I know some people (adults as well as children) who, despite knowing little about the rules of etiquette, are wonderfully civil human beings. They are attentive to others. They avoid self-centered behavior. They are habitually polite. By contrast, I know other people who pride themselves on knowing all the fine points of etiquette—how to set a perfect table, for instance—yet are selfish, inconsiderate, impatient, demanding, and rude.

Ultimately what matters most, etiquette or civility? My belief is that civility is the chief goal we're discussing because it is the bedrock of our ability to get along with others.

Following are some ways to nurture civility in your children.

Start Early

Young children are self-centered. The behavior that results from their focus on themselves isn't naughty; in fact, it's developmentally appropriate. As kids grow and mature, however, they need to learn consideration and respect for others. Even toddlers gradually acquire social skills. Thus, part of your parental role is to teach your child what's appropriate for getting along with others. Doing so is easier and less stressful for everyone if you start at the right time for each set of skills. If you tolerate selfishness and impulsiveness in your kids' early years, they'll find it that much more difficult to shift to more considerate behavior at a later stage.

Set Age-Appropriate Guidelines

Raise the bar as your children mature. Don't let kids "plateau" just because it's easier for you to deal with the status quo rather than to keep challenging them. Kids need a sense of freedom and autonomy to thrive, but they also need limits and boundaries. Don't mistake your kids' demands (to do or not do one thing or another) for a clear indication of what they need. As the parent, you are the person who must ultimately evaluate and decide on what the expectations are regarding your children's behavior.

Avoid Extreme Parenting Styles

Once again I need to invoke the issue of flexible rather than inflexible or permissive parenting. If you boss your kids around—if you argue with them, shout at them, and order rather than request that they do certain tasks—you will reveal a kind of incivility that undercuts all your efforts to teach them by other means. If you're physically absent or emotionally distant, you'll leave them adrift and unable to calibrate their own behavioral and moral compass. Be present and clear-cut in your expectations, but don't go overboard. Finding this middle ground assumes that at least one parent will be around enough to monitor, shape, and modify the situation on an ongoing basis. You can't really guide your children on issues of civility (or any others) if you're not around much.

Model Civility Yourself

Civility starts at home. Don't expect children to behave in a civil manner if you and your spouse are selfish, demanding, rude, abusive, impatient, or arrogant toward each other and toward other people. The core aspect of your behavior will be how you act toward your kids. They will mimic and absorb the behavior you manifest. Although they'll have other influences as well—peers, teachers, the media, and so forth—you are still their number-one role model.

Here are some issues to monitor:

- *How do you and your spouse treat one another?* Are you respectful, curious, supportive, and considerate as marriage partners? Or are you disrespectful, indifferent, dismissive, and inconsiderate?

- *How do you treat your children?* Again, are you capable of respecting them, taking their interests to heart, listening to them closely, and valuing their thoughts and feelings? Or are you impatient, rude, bossy, and emotionally disengaged from them?

- *How do you speak about other people?* Do you express respect and interest to people's faces but speak of them with hostility or contempt behind their backs?

- *What sorts of interactions do you encourage between your children, or between your children and their friends as acquaintances?* Do you set standards for verbal and nonverbal interactions? Do you point out when your kids are impolite, rude, or aggressive toward others? Do you encourage them to mediate disputes rather than take a competitive stance toward conflicts?

- *How do you perceive issues of civility and incivility in the wider culture?* Do your family members discuss what they observe among members of your community, or in the media? Do you talk about the "in your face" attitudes that have become common, even predominant, throughout American culture?

Maintain High but Sensible Standards

There's nothing wrong with expecting your kids to behave well. If they're civil, relatively patient, and kind to others, your family life will be less stressful and more congenial for everyone in the household. Your children will also receive a warmer response from many people in the outside world. Having reasonably high expectations will boost your kids' opinions of themselves in the long run, too. That said, you don't have to expect your children to behave perfectly. Doing so will be stressful for the kids and jeopardize their confidence in the future. Let them make mistakes and learn from them. Give them the leeway to experiment with behavior in non-harmful ways and, if necessary, to take the consequences for their choices. Playacting, charades, and other role-playing games can be a safe setting for exploration among family members and close friends. Real-life rudeness and self-centered behavior, however, should warrant apologies and, if necessary, follow-up discussion.

Keep Your Cool

Teaching your children about civility can try your patience and tempt you to overreact in ways that ultimately backfire. The most obvious example is coping with toddlers, who often test the limits that parents set and, if thwarted, respond with rage and frustration. It's hard to stay patient when a screaming two-year-old is pummeling you. However, toddlerhood is just the start of what you'll face in fostering a child's abilities to get along with others. Here are some of the other difficult stages ahead:

- *Dealing with "lippy" middle-grade children.* At around age seven to nine, many children start to display an arrogant, know-it-all tone that complicates social interactions within the family and elsewhere. Kids frequently demand more detailed reasons for parental requests ("But *why* do I have to clean my room?"); they invoke outside authority during arguments ("Janice's parents don't make *her* clean *her* room!"); or they rebuff parents outright ("You're not my boss!"). The result: a much more complex task in fostering civility and gaining compliance.

- *Coping with preteens.* During pubescence and adolescence, children usually feel less bonded to their parents, which often leads to disagreements over behavior; to complicate matters, they feel a growing gravitational pull from their peers. One consequence of these changes is an increased resistance to parental authority. In itself this resistance may include annoying, cocky behavior. Social pressures to imitate arrogant attitudes can intensify parent–child conflicts over issues of cooperation and civility.

- *Staying patient with teens.* Precisely because teenagers often experiment with arrogant, hostile, even disgusting language and behaviors, adolescence is a minefield for parents. It's easy to under- or overreact. On the one hand, it's appropriate for you to expect reasonably civil behavior from your teen; on the other hand, you should avoid being too picky about the style of how teenagers go about their business. An example is the use of "in your face" language. Teenage friends often speak to each other in slang terms or even profanity that would infuriate adults. If you repeatedly scold or punish your teen for interacting with other teens in this way, you may squander your parental "capital" and have fewer resources available for other situations. Your fundamental goal: maintain your standards for what matters most, but don't get caught up in less crucial power struggles. One advantage you gain during this developmental state is teenagers' progressively more sophisticated communication skills, which can provide opportunities to discuss many concerns openly and in detail.

Reward Good Behavior as Well as Punishing Misbehavior

In fostering civility, you may be tempted to focus on your children's shortcomings rather than their progress. A better approach is to reward good behavior whenever possible, punishing misbehavior only when absolutely necessary. This rule of thumb holds true at every stage of child development. Rewarding a toddler for sharing toys with a play-mate, for instance, will increase the likelihood of future generosity far more than if you scold the child for refusing to share. Similarly, com-plimenting a middle-grade child for politeness or considerate acts toward others will boost the child's confidence and, in turn, raise the odds of a repeat performance. Stress the positive.

Be Consistent

Although it's important to have high standards, it's equally crucial to keep them consistent. You have to apply your expectations more or less evenly across the board, both within and outside the family. Some parents I know have double standards about civility. They may expect their children to treat outsiders with consideration, for instance, while allowing their kids to be rude, even abusive, toward one another. Other parents have an unwitting agenda about "special occasions": civility isn't important on a day-to-day basis—only when eating out, visiting other people, or during holidays. In these and other situations that include skewed standards, parents unintentionally undercut their own authority, as children almost invariably spot hypocrisy and erratic standards. A better tactic: try to maintain a higher degree of consis-tency. Be flexible, but stay steady in what you expect.

Don't Expect to Change the World

Does teaching civility to our own kids have a major impact on the surrounding culture? It's tempting to think so. If enough parents pressed the issue, the results would certainly be more positive than what we have now, which often approaches a frenzy of selfishness. The attitude I'm suggesting, however, probably expects too much. Even if your own kids behave in a thoughtful, civil manner toward others, many other parents will let their own children run rampant. How should you respond?

I'll admit there's a real dilemma here. It's possible to have standards so high that your kids feel constrained or burdened by your expectations. That said, children often feel proud, not ashamed, of behaving better than chaotic kids around them. (As a nine-year-old I know said while watching some other kids misbehave in a hotel lobby: "Those kids are acting like real jerks. They'd know they're jerks, too, if they could see themselves like I see them.") In some cases, it's possible that your own kids' good behavior may hold other kids in check. Finding the happy medium is something that will be unique to yourself and your family.

CIVILITY IN AN UNCIVIL WORLD

I believe in the benefits of taking the long view. In an age when almost anything goes, I'm still convinced that children are happier when they learn to get along with other people, to respect others' rights as well as their own, and to behave generously and thoughtfully. Doing so isn't always easy, but the alternative isn't satisfactory for kids or for parents. There are trade-offs as well as advantages for coexisting with society.

Civility, like so many other aspects of life, is a process. Your kids won't learn it all at once, especially in a world that's increasingly uncivil. Yet I believe that if you yourself set a good example, and if you maintain high but not unreasonable standards for your kids' behavior, your family life will be happier, less stressful, and more interesting in the long run.

Chapter 9

SOLVING THE LATCHKEY DILEMMA

If you saw Jessie in action at school, you'd assume that she was like most other thirteen-year-old girls. She's attentive in classes but a bit sassy; her teachers regard her as a thoughtful, conscientious student, though sometimes rather driven to achieve. She enjoys hanging out with friends when time permits. She's interested in movies, popular music, and teen fashions. She's somewhat self-conscious, but no more so than most other teenagers. Nothing about Jessie would suggest that she's unusual or troubled.

Her home life tells a different story. Far from living the carefree life that many adults imagine as American teens' birthright, Jessie shoulders a remarkable burden. After school each day she runs over to the local daycare center to pick up Alex, her four-year-old brother, and she walks him home. She then looks after Alex all afternoon and throughout the early evening. Jessie also straightens up the house, feeds Alex supper, bathes him, and gets him ready for bed. During the course of these childcare duties, she hustles to prepare a full dinner in anticipation of her parents' arrival. Jeb and Sally reach home separately around eight. The parents spend about an hour with Alex

before the boy goes to bed. Jessie focuses on homework until her own
bedtime around ten. In the morning the whole process starts over
again, with Jeb and Sally leaving for work around six-thirty, which
leaves Jessie responsible for waking, feeding, and getting Alex off to
the daycare center before her own classes start at the middle school.

It's easy to imagine that Jessie would resent the weight of responsibility she carries. Perhaps she does; after all, her parents have put her
in a position that's close to being her brother's primary caregiver.
Oddly, though, Jessie doesn't seem visibly resentful of this situation.
Quite the contrary: she has assimilated this domestic role and taken it
on with a vengeance. She runs a tight ship. The house is remarkably
clean. She cooks well, producing excellent meals day after day. Jessie
is also attentive to her brother's needs, protective of him, and punctual
in getting him where he needs to be and in doing whatever has to be
done. A number of outside observers—relatives, friends, and neigh-
bors alike—have noted that this girl equals or exceeds many adults in
managing the domestic scene. As a family friend once exclaimed to
Sally, "Good Lord—she's a better housewife and mom than *you* are!"

Jessie has ample cause for pride in her accomplishments. Among
other things, she manages to run her family's household without
jeopardizing her academic efforts, which routinely earn a near-A
average at school. But is this situation such a good idea? It's true that
Jessie manages the domestic juggling act with great aplomb, but at
what cost? Is it really fair to have a thirteen-year-old attending to a
preschooler during most of her afterschool hours?

A closer look at the situation reveals some of its accumulated
stresses. Jessie copes with all the demands facing her, but she often
seems driven, even frantic, as she cleans the house, fixes the meals,
and looks after Alex. Not surprisingly, she has virtually no social life
beyond her own family. She gets together with school friends now
and then on weekends, but she doesn't have time for extracurricular
activities of any kind. She's often busy on Saturdays and Sundays
too, because she needs to catch up on homework. What's more worrisome is that Jessie often seems overly engrossed in her quasi

parental duties. Even her parents—who have, after all, set up most of this arrangement—notice their daughter's near-obsession with her domestic role. "She's a little too into it," as Sally commented recently. Far from resenting the demands placed on her, Jessie sometimes resents any efforts to *reduce* those demands. She's good at running the show, and she knows it. At times she criticizes her parents for not living up to her own high standards: they aren't as tidy as Jessie; their meals aren't as tasty; they forget to buy certain groceries or make certain arrangements. Jessie has been known to scold her mom and dad for lapses in their parenting skills.

This situation might be comical—a clever sitcom scenario—if it weren't so fraught with destructive potential. It has put Jessie in a position that could limit her psychological development in some respects. It has transformed Jessie into a pseudoparent with excessive responsibilities for raising a young child. It has risked disrupting, or at least complicating, Jessie's academic career. Increasingly, it has created tensions between Jessie and her parents over who's in charge of the domestic sphere. Any one of these issues would be cause for concern; combined, they create a set of circumstances that's more and more troubling. For all practical purposes, Sally and Jeb have appointed their daughter to be their surrogate in raising both herself and her brother, and in so doing they have relinquished their parental authority and placed the burden of that authority on a girl who isn't (and by all measures shouldn't be) ready to carry it.

THE LATCHKEY DILEMMA

An awkward situation ensues when parents, facing work-related pressures or other demands, choose to leave their children unattended at home. Most parents take this path reluctantly. Employers often set schedules that conflict with childcare needs; the school day starts after and ends long before the workday. Childcare surrogates are expensive, hard to find, and sometimes entirely unavailable. How are parents to fill the gaps? Many must rely on their children to look after themselves and hold down the fort. I can understand that some-times parents have no alternative to a latchkey arrangement. At the same time, I believe that many mothers and fathers underestimate the consequences of these arrangements, most notably emotional stress for the kids and an erosion of authority for the parents. It's important to size up this situation and, if possible, limit any negative side effects. This chapter provides some suggestions for how parents can resolve—or at least minimize—the latchkey dilemma.

My story about Jessie and her pseudoparental role in raising Alex may be an extreme case, but it's by no means unusual. More and more American mothers and fathers are attempting to "solve" the latchkey dilemma by relinquishing parental authority to one or more of their children.

Here are some other instances:

- Dylan, age fifteen, is on his own between the time school lets out and about seven each evening. His parents consider him old enough to look after himself until they get back from work; they don't consider it unreasonable to expect a boy Dylan's age to come home, start his homework, and fix himself dinner. Unlike Jessie's parents, Adele and Robert don't expect their son to play housekeeper while they're gone, and Dylan has no sibling to look after. But what looks good in theory isn't so great in prac-tice. Dylan often leaves the house during his four hours flying solo; he leaves the neighborhood, wanders around, loiters at the local mini-mall, and sometimes hangs out with other unsuper-vised teenagers.

- Scarcely ten years old, Janice spends several hours alone in her family's apartment after school. Her mother, Lily, is a single mother who can't afford childcare, so she feels she has no alter-native to leaving her daughter unattended. Janice tolerates this situation but finds it stressful. She complains that she feels lonely, but her mother rightly insists that Janice not leave the house or invite guests to come and visit. The result is that Janice has no one around who can offer companionship, ask about her day, or provide help in doing homework. Janice often leaves the TV on to give her an illusion of company, but she often finds her solitude frustrating and sometimes scary.

- Peter and Emma, ages eleven and eight respectively, return home after school without knowing whether their mother will be present. Their mom, Betty, runs a small catering business out of the house and often has to make deliveries in the middle or late afternoon. Given the uncertainties of her schedule, she has trained her kids to let themselves in, get a snack, and start homework if she's still out running errands. The timing of Betty's absences isn't a problem in its own right; the difficulty is Peter's reaction to it. For many years, Peter has acted in bossy, almost abusive ways toward his younger sister. Emma dreads being alone in the house with Peter because the boy teases and hassles Emma whenever he's unattended. When nudged toward the possibility of telling her mother about Peter's behavior, Emma declines, stating that "Mom needs all her work time. That's why she's leaving us alone in the first place."

These stories are the result of parents facing genuine work–family conflicts and, in response, attempting to resolve them as creatively as possible. None of the moms or dads I'm describing is willfully negligent; they're muddling through as best they can. However, the dilemmas they face put their families in a difficult situation—a situation that a latchkey arrangement may not fully solve.

One of the trickiest logistical problems facing all parents is childcare. During a child's early years, there's no way around some kind of adult supervision, whether by means of the parents' presence, a babysitter or nanny, home care with another family, or institutional daycare. For older school-age children, however, many parents set up a latchkey arrangement for their kids: children come home from school and look after themselves until the parents return from work. Such arrangements can be relatively safe and stable from a practical standpoint. They are often *psychologically* problematic, though, for several reasons. One reason is that latchkey arrangements often put children in a position of exercising premature authority. Kids rule the roost not just figuratively, but literally; they go about their business largely unsupervised. Are they truly prepared for this level of independence? Many children are not; they experience stress, loneliness, anxiety, and sometimes fear when left on their own for long periods of time. In addition, latchkey arrangements often undercut parents' authority: when Mom and Dad return home and expect to be in charge, kids resent their "intrusion" and resist routine parental decision-making.

As a result, parents must think through their decisions about childcare situations and, if possible, they should avoid premature or extended latchkey arrangements. Doing so doesn't necessarily mean employing an expensive nanny or *au pair*; rather, satisfactory alternatives include signing up for afterschool programs, hiring a local teenager or college student for part-time baby-sitting, or employing a senior citizen for a similar purpose. Your long-term goal is to avoid putting your child in a position of contradictory roles that ultimately jeopardize family dynamics and the child's psychological well-being.

When You Can't Avoid a Latchkey Arrangement

From the standpoints of child development, parent–child interaction, and safety, I believe that whenever possible, you shouldn't leave your preteenage child without adult supervision at all. Most children younger than age twelve aren't emotionally prepared to look after themselves unattended. They can muddle through brief periods of time alone, but not without feeling at least some degree of loneliness and anxiety. Kids twelve and under have difficulty structuring their time; younger than age ten or so, they are also unpredictable in their responses to emergencies, sometimes with potentially calamitous effects on their own and others' safety.

But what if your circumstances dictate that your children *must* spend at least brief periods of time alone, or your boss isn't flexible enough to let you leave work in time for your kids' arrival after school? In short, what if there's no way around some sort of latchkey arrangement? There are some steps you can take to solve this problem.

Minimize Your Children's Time Alone

It's one thing to leave preteens and teens alone for an hour or so; it's another to expect them to manage hours and hours of solo time. The fact that your kids can manage adequately for brief periods of time shouldn't tempt you to push the envelope until they're well into their midteens—and even then only with great caution.

Make Sure You're Accessible

Although your children may be flying solo, they need—they *must have*—easy access to you. Such access most often means direct contact with you through your normal work phone number. Other options include access through a cell phone or a beeper. Cell phones are an easy solution to this issue; however, they aren't always reliable and can create a false sense of connectedness. Beepers are more consistently reliable but obviously require a second phase (calling back) to communicate. Whatever arrangements you make, you should either insist on hearing from your kids once they arrive home, or you should call them yourself to verify that they're back in the house.

Arrange for Backup Help

Make sure your kids have access to adult assistance whenever they're alone. The ideal arrangement involves a trusted neighbor who lives on your block or in your building—someone your children know, trust, and can rely upon as a resource and authority figure to intervene as needed. Other options include a friend, neighbor, or relative who may or may not live in the immediate area but is close enough to visit your house on short notice. The issue here isn't only acute emergencies, such as accidents or illness; this kind of backup help can also keep minor hitches (such as your child misplacing the house keys) from escalating into a major problem.

In addition, you should investigate whatever programs your community has instituted to protect children as they walk to or from school. These programs—variously known as Safe House, Helping Hand, and so on—ensure that kids can seek refuge among reliable members of the community if they end up hassled by other children or strangers. All of these Safe House–type programs involve the use of a symbol posted in the doors or windows of houses in the area; children who feel they're in danger can spot the symbol, go to the house, and ask for help. (See your local PTA or fire department for further information.)

Clarify the Rules for Kids at Home

Before your children start staying at home unsupervised, think through their situation from the standpoint of preventive action. Assess what will be the greatest risks to your kids' safety, happiness, and peace of mind. Decide what will contribute most to minimizing these risks. Discuss with them your expectations for behavior. State these expectations in the form of clear, age-appropriate rules. Focus on safety and emotional well-being, but add any other rules that are crucial. Here are some typical rules to emphasize:

- *Visitors.* Do not allow your children to have visitors (whether adults or children) who aren't members of the family's most trusted circle unless you have given advance permission for them to visit. Tell your children not to open the door for strangers under any circumstances. Do not let your children entertain other kids while unattended.

- *Phone calls.* If strangers call, your kids should state "My mom [dad] is busy" rather than "My mom [dad] isn't home."

- *Medical and other emergencies.* Make sure your kids understand the 911 system or its equivalent in your community. Clarify which situations warrant seeking emergency help and which warrant calling you at work (e.g., a bad cut, fall, or burn justifies calling 911; a headache means they phone the office).

- *Police.* Here again, make sure that your children know how to call 911 or the equivalent number in your community. Emergency numbers should be posted clearly.

- *Fire.* Practice fire drills. Stress the urgency of getting out of the house, *not* attempting to fight the fire.

- *Food.* Organize meals well in advance. Make sure the children have access to enough food and beverages without resorting to errands. For most preteens and younger teenagers, cooking is usually too hazardous to allow without supervision. Make sure that older kids have sufficient skills before you allow them to cook their own meals. Whenever possible, emphasize use of pre-prepared meals.

THE RISKS OF "PARENTIFYING" YOUR CHILD

Despite all these preparations and precautions, however, even a well-planned latchkey arrangement can cause stress and strain within your family. It's not just that kids need adult company and often suffer from its absence. There's another issue, too—what I call *parentification*. Parentifying your child means that you've created circumstances in which she acquires a quasi parental role. She's still a kid, but she has to act like a parent. Parentification can be problematic in its own right: even middle school children aren't ready to assume the responsibilities of adult roles, nor should they be. In addition, parentification can create a kind of dissonance between you and your child, because you're expecting her to act like an adult when you're out of the house, then revert to being a child again once you return. This repetitive changing of roles can confuse kids, create resentment toward parents for having two contradictory sets of expectations, and greatly diminish parental authority.

In extreme cases, parentification can lead to what I call the King of the Castle syndrome. Some kids, such as Jessie (whose story opens this chapter), gain so much power and responsibility that they view themselves as thoroughly in charge of the entire household. I've met several children who relish this role and grow accustomed to it. Even under the best of circumstances, this situation isn't fair to kids. There's too much power involved, and power can corrupt children as well as adults. In certain troubling family situations, the King of the Castle can grow arrogant or abusive toward others. I've seen a few of these situations in which the child bosses around his parents and siblings like servants. This sort of arrangement is damaging to everyone.

How can you limit the risks of parentification? Here as in many other aspects of parenthood, there are no easy answers, but these suggestions may help:

- *Limit your time away from home.* If you have to rely on a latchkey arrangement some of the time, keep it short.

- *Find alternatives whenever possible.* Afterschool programs— sports activities, clubs, study halls—are ideal. If organized activities aren't available in your community, consider hiring a local high school or college student to supervise your child after school. Swapping childcare services with a neighbor is another possibility.

- *Clarify expectations in advance.* Make sure that your child knows what you're expecting of her—which behaviors are permissible and which aren't. Indicate the daily routine, and make sure upon your arrival home each evening that her actions have been consistent with the routine. Don't let her role, duties, or assumptions expand without your knowledge and permission.

- *Refuse to allow off-site "hanging out."* Even in stable, safe communities, preteens and teens often congregate in packs whose behavior can degenerate as a result of peer pressure and "group think." What often starts as harmless socializing can lead to rowdy, disruptive behavior. Don't let your child seek this kind of unsupervised peer group during her latchkey hours.

- *Avoid using your child as a primary housekeeper.* Although some parents feel that their children should do household chores while home alone, I discourage this practice. It's fine for kids to take on some housekeeping duties, but they should perform only light tasks while unsupervised. Using your kids as housekeepers or cooks can be demoralizing; ironically, it can also lead them to feel an excessive sense of control over the domestic sphere—as if they're truly in charge of the house. This arrangement also risks depriving your kids of the short, precious time they have during childhood when someone else meets *their* needs, cares for them, and nurtures them. These side effects are regrettable.

- *Don't use your older child as a babysitter for extended periods.* It's especially tempting to rely on an older child to look after younger children, and this arrangement is customary in many cultures. The catch is that it's often a setup for especially acute parentification. Extended, routine baby-sitting of this sort can create tensions among your kids; in addition, the situation grants your older child a quasi parental role that can threaten your own long-term authority. As much as possible, find alternatives to this kind of arrangement.

The Special Dilemma for Single Parents

Finally, there's the quandary that single parents face. This is basically the same problem that we've discussed so far, only worse. Single parents must juggle every aspect of family life alone. There's no spouse to trade tasks with—you're the whole show. Under these circumstances, how do you deal with the latchkey dilemma?

My recommendation is essentially to do what I've already suggested, only more so. Your plans must be precise; your backup arrangements must be failsafe. Precisely because you don't have anyone as a built-in partner, you have to rely more fully on yourself, and you must simultaneously make sure that you've created multilayered safety nets to catch you in a bind. Don't take anything for granted.

There's another aspect to the situation, however, one that deserves special attention. Single parents run especially great risks of parentifying their children. By definition, being a single parent means flying solo. It's a lonely, strenuous journey even when it's satisfying overall. What's the risk, then? The risk is that you may rely too heavily on your child for companionship. You may share your worries too openly, you may expect too much of your child, or you may treat her as a little pseudopartner rather than as your child. This is an understandable reaction, but it carries great risks for your child's long-term well-being. Your kid needs to be a kid. She shouldn't shoulder the weight of adult responsibilities. She shouldn't have to be your partner—only your child. And if your work responsibilities require that you set up some kind of latchkey arrangement, you may feel a great temptation as a single parent to expect your child to take on adult roles and responsibilities. Do anything you can to avoid placing that burden on your child, thus diminishing her childhood while simultaneously diminishing your authority.

Chapter 10

COPING WITH THE
SIDE EFFECTS OF DIVORCE

- When Jed and Kay decided to end their marriage, they agreed to work carefully to ease the impact of the divorce on their daughters, Samantha, age twelve, and Ariel, age ten. The couple managed to remain civil throughout the divorce proceedings. They did everything possible to meet their children's needs throughout the process of splitting up. Even so, the divorce couldn't help but powerfully affect everyone in the family. Both Kay and Jed felt depressed and demoralized by the collapse of their fifteen-year marriage, and their low moods made it difficult to respond to the girls' own emotional reactions to this event. In addition, setting up two separate households created problems that the parents hadn't anticipated, such as having somewhat different routines and, in the longer run, slightly different rules. The result of this situation was that Jed and Kay sometimes felt disorganized or confused about the tasks of raising their daughters; Samantha and Ariel in turn often felt baffled about who was in charge and what their parents expected of them.

- By contrast, Ada and Robert's divorce was acrimonious from the start, quickly erupting into a custody battle over the couple's eight-year-old son, Alan. Ada won custody over the boy, but the war continued afterward. Not satisfied to be the custodial parent, Ada tried to alienate Alan from his father: she openly criticized and mocked Robert; she complicated Robert's efforts to spend time with Alan during his visitation days; and she asked her son to report back to her regarding his father's activities and attitudes. Meanwhile, Robert tried to counteract his ex-wife's efforts by waging a campaign to capture the boy's loyalty and affection. He bestowed many expensive gifts—toys, gadgets, sports gear, and computer games—to prove his love. He took Alan out to movies, ball games, and restaurants to make sure that they had special times together. He arranged major trips, including a long visit to Disney World, each summer. In short, both parents engaged in a protracted tug-of-war, with their son as the rope between them. What they didn't realize was that Alan, quickly weary and demoralized, held both of his parents in contempt for yanking him back and forth.

- Marcy, who divorced her husband, Lou, six years ago, is intensely close to her fourteen-year-old son, Zachary. Although cordial with Lou and comfortable with a variety of friendships and dating relationships, Marcy finds her greatest solace and companionship in her close bond with her son. She and Zachary both enjoy outdoor sports, swimming, and skating. They also have a great time going to the movies and to hockey and baseball games. In fact, Marcy feels so close to Zachary that she refers to him as "my Number One Man" and confides in him on many aspects of her life, including her concerns about money matters and her ambivalence about finding another husband. Marcy's only concern is that as her son matures, he's likely to pull away from her, and even now she feels that

Zachary has started to resent her reliance on him and distance himself from her emotionally.

THE QUANDARY OF DIVORCE AND PARENTAL AUTHORITY

Even relatively amicable divorces change life circumstances for the couple's children in many ways. Custody battles and altered living arrangements are only two of the most dramatic effects of how divorce affects kids. However, a less obvious but common and powerful consequence is a crisis of parental authority.

First of all, the parents themselves will almost certainly have experienced great upheaval, both at the time of the divorce and afterward, which leaves them vulnerable, exhausted, and confused; these states of mind often reduce the quality of parental decision-making and also limit the amount of emotional energy available to the children.

In addition, the crisis of divorce (as well as its aftermath) inevitably disrupts communication between the parents. Even fairly cooperative ex-spouses will have less frequent interaction with one another on a day-to-day basis: they won't be living together, and they won't have continuous contact with their kids. More contentious couples will have even fewer occasions to discuss the kids and to coordinate decisions, plans, and activities. The result is a greatly increased likelihood for misunderstandings, hard feelings, and even willful disruption of family life (for instance, by using the kids as pawns), all of which jeopardize parental authority and its potential for fostering the children's well-being.

If you're in this situation, you should not only focus on your kids' best interests but also concentrate on maintaining a thoughtful, age-appropriate level of authority as you parent your kids.

How Divorce Affects Children

If you're getting divorced, or if you're adjusting to the aftermath of a divorce, both you and your ex-spouse are probably distracted, self-absorbed, and stressed. This state of mind is a common, understandable reaction to a traumatic life event. It's a huge task to rebuild your life during and following a divorce. You may find that, despite your best efforts, you're not as available emotionally to your children as you'd like to be. You may put your children and their needs "on hold" as you attend to your marital problems. You may not be as readily available to your children for their day-to-day needs. You may not supervise them as consistently as usual, or you may hesitate to set limits on their behavior in the hope of easing the stress on them. You may not be able to provide the same level of emotional and physical care that you'd like. All of these responses are understandable, but they're also risky. Focusing on your own problems may leave your children feeling lonely, confused, fearful, and stressed. Divorce has probably hit you hard and may even have diminished your capacity to parent effectively.

Your challenge is to deal with the stresses of parenthood during a difficult transition and to provide a sense of structure and age-appropriate authority when your own life feels unstable, even chaotic. How do you keep your child's life emotionally stable when you yourself are coping with loneliness, grief, anger, and other emotions? Parenting is difficult enough under the best of circumstances; during the turmoil of divorce and in its aftermath, parenthood is almost invariably harder still. But the truth remains: you'll be going through the divorce process while still maintaining your parental responsibilities and obligations.

Kids' Responses to Divorce at Different Stages

One of the first steps in dealing with the effects of divorce on parental authority is to understand how divorce affects kids at each of the various developmental stages. Here's an overview, including a summary of the chief issues they face during and after a parents' divorce.

Ages One to Two

Your most important goal at this stage is to meet consistently your child's needs for food, rest, play, and comfort. Toddlers will also need clear, simple information about what has happened, such as when the other parent will be around. Ideally, keep all routines as simple as possible in both households. It's important at this stage to communicate with your ex about the details of your toddler's day so that there's a high level of continuity of care. Even very young children respond intensely to changes resulting from a divorce, so it's critical that you monitor their behavior for signs of tension, fear, or anxiety. Be alert to emotional changes, such as clinginess and moodiness, and be as supportive as possible.

Ages Three to Five

A preschooler's most intense reactions to his parents' divorce may include a sense of abandonment. He may experience separation anxiety during and after the divorce. He may worry that one or both parents will leave and never return. In response to these emotional reactions, be clear and reassuring about your presence in his life. Children at this developmental stage often resort to magical thinking, so they need a sense of constancy and reassurance that they're not responsible for the divorce and not in jeopardy of losing the parents' love. Although often unable to articulate their thoughts, many kids struggle with self-blame — if only they'd behaved better, if only they'd not thrown that tantrum — as they struggle to comprehend what caused the separation and divorce.

If your child will be living with one parent and visiting the other, be straightforward about the arrangements. Assure him that he'll see both parents if that is, in fact, the case. If, on the other hand, one parent won't be coming back, tell the truth about what's happening. Don't dissimulate or assume he won't be affected. The other parent's absence will create a deep sense of loss, but you can't avoid that response by shoving your child's emotional reaction under the carpet. Help him grieve the loss of the absent parent. If necessary, find professional help to ease the burden.

Children at this stage need regular contact with the noncustodial parent. Transitional objects such as photos of that parent or a gift from that parent, such as a teddy bear or other comfort object, can provide a sense of connection and constancy.

Ages Five to Eight

Following their parents' divorce, school-age kids often feel preoccupied with a deep sense of loss. They are prone to feel guilty, rejected, and angry. They may experience conflicts in their loyalties toward their parents. Like younger children, some kids of this age group may feel responsible for the parents' divorce or a duty to "fix" the problem. Others experience a sense of duty I mentioned earlier— *parentification*, a tendency to assume the parent's role and undertake the parent's needs. Children ages five to eight often have intense needs for continuity and stability in domestic routines and contact with their parents.

Ages Nine to Twelve

During the later school years, children depend tremendously on parents for a sense of stability. They may feel angry about the loss they've suffered, with especially intense anger at the parent whom they blame for the divorce. They're most likely to perceive the situation in black and white; they'll blame one parent or the other. They can experience deep grief and strong anxiety as well. They may feel an acute sense of loneliness or powerlessness. They may feel a desire to reunite the parents. They may act out to gain attention, but they are also more inclined to become caregivers and feel responsible for their parents' happiness. They may complain of psychosomatic symptoms, headaches, or stomachaches. If one or both parents start dating, pre-adolescents and adolescents may be overstimulated by an awareness of the parents' new love life. For this reason, avoid exposing your child to unpredictable relationships when they already feel so sensitive to abandonment; you don't want them to have to relive getting close to someone only to experience another separation and loss. Keep your dating life separate from your kids unless your new partner is capable of making a long-term commitment to you.

Ages Thirteen to Nineteen

Although they come across as mature, teenagers can be extremely fearful about the consequences of their parents' divorce. They need strong role models, especially for gender roles. The loss of a parent—especially the same-sex parent—can be disruptive, even devastating, to their sense of self. Teenagers also need a strong sense of family structure to set limits for their own aggressive, sexual, and impulsive behaviors at this age. The lack of family structure can disorient or even terrify them. Many fear that they'll repeat their parents' failures. They may become egocentric, self-absorbed, and angry at their parents. These emotions can show up as judgmental, critical attitudes toward the mother, the father, or both. Some girls experience what psychologist Judith Wallerstein calls the "sleeper effect"—acting out the loss of their father by becoming promiscuous during the teen years. Some worry about their future or develop an inability to make long-term commitments or form intimate relationships. They may feel angry about the abandonment, they may act out angrily, or they may assume a greater burden of responsibilities than they're ready to handle. They may even feel personally responsible for the parents' happiness, thus increasing the stress on themselves and potentially complicating your life as well.

PARENTING TASKS DURING AND FOLLOWING A DIVORCE

In addition to understanding the developmental issues for children, it's important to address certain parenting tasks during and following a divorce. The following recommendations won't address all of your postdivorce problems; they may, however, help you avoid decisions and actions that could diminish your parental authority both in the short and longer term. For resources relevant to divorce and parental authority, see Appendix B.

Keep Your Child Out of It

One of your most important tasks is to separate your child from your divorce experience. In short, don't put your child in the middle. Kids need to feel that they're allowed to love both their parents; they shouldn't have to choose one over the other. Putting your child in the crossfire of your divorce is detrimental to her development and growth. Here are some specific suggestions:

- *Don't bad-mouth your ex-spouse.* Doing so puts your child in an emotional bind: if she agrees with your criticism, she may feel she's betraying her other parent; if she rebuffs your criticism, she may feel she's betraying you.

- *Don't burden your child with unnecessary information about the divorce process.* Young children won't be able to follow legal or financial aspects of what's happening, and it's not fair to weigh them down with details; for that matter, even older children don't need more than generalities. Don't expect your child to be your lawyer, accountant, psychotherapist, or confidant.

- *Keep your sense of balance about parenthood and divorce.* Even if your divorce is acrimonious, remind yourself that you love your child more than you resent your ex.

- *Don't ask your child for information about your ex.* Requests of this sort put the child in a position of serving as a spy or messenger, which violates her bond with her other parent.

- *Try to minimize the fallout as much as possible.* Keep your cool. Keep your frustrations in context; your child needs you to stay level-headed.

- *Don't alienate your child against the other parent.* No matter how angry you feel toward your ex, don't make him or her your child's enemy.

- *Whatever else, do what's in the best interest of your child.* Doing the right thing for your child is an enormous act of love and maturity, and it's difficult, but it will pay off in the long run.

Remember the Impact on Your Child

Regardless of how the divorce has affected you, keep in mind that your child will be affected, too. Do whatever you can to stay tuned in to her. Listen to her without judging what she says. Validate what she's going through. Acknowledge her feelings. If she expresses anger or resentment toward you—even rage—don't take these outbursts personally. Reassure her that even though you're divorcing the other parent, you'll never divorce *her*. Lavish love and attention on her. Remind her constantly that you won't abandon her; you'll be available to her no matter what.

Provide a Stable Home Life

Following the separation, do what you can to provide your child with a stable home life. Limit constant back-and-forth travel between households. Research shows that it's better for children to have one primary home rather than being constantly shuttled around. That doesn't mean that your child shouldn't see the noncustodial parent, only that you should evaluate the situation to determine the best arrangement for her specific situation. Again, the central issue is your child's best interests. Sometimes that means that the child lives primarily with the mother, sometimes with the father. Whatever else, make a mature, adult decision to separate your own needs from what's best for your child and to devise a situation that's optimal for your child's emotional, physical, and spiritual growth.

Here are some specific suggestions:

- *Keep both parents involved with the children.* Ideally, both parents should continue to interact with the kids on a frequent, consistent basis. Both parents' presence is crucial for kids' cognitive development, academic success, sex-role modeling, and overall self-esteem.

- *A corollary to the above: keep Dad in close touch with the kids.* Children need their fathers. Dads should take their responsibilities seriously and do everything possible to help their children. Moms should avoid trying to take over all parental responsibilities, if possible, because this may alienate kids from their father.

- *Try to maintain similar values and routines in both households.* The more similarities there are, the less instability there will be in routines, discipline, goals, and procedures. Consistency eases the stress on kids.

- *If you feel that you're floundering, or if you just need help, find assistance as soon as possible.* Going it alone will make your own life—and probably your child's life as well—much more difficult.

Protect Your Child from Crossfire

Many divorcing spouses feel angry, hostile, and jealous toward one another. If possible, protect your child from the marital crossfire.

This task is much easier said than done. Your child may well get caught in the crossfire anyway, particularly while you and your ex go through the divorce process. Still, I urge you to spare your child as much as possible. This includes not speaking in a hostile way about your ex. Be honest about what's going on and why the separation is occurring, but don't overreact or use derogatory, inflammatory language, as doing so can force your child into a position of having to choose one parent over the other. You don't want to contaminate her self-esteem or have her grow up distrusting the other parent. That would put a lot of pressure on your child to reject that parent—which, given children's close ties to their parents, would essentially be asking the child to reject a part of herself.

Make Your Happiness Your Own Responsibility

Avoid making your child feel responsible for your happiness. Parentifying her or otherwise reversing parent–child roles isn't good for your child's growth. Don't put her in a position of being your psychotherapist, marriage counselor, or lawyer. Find adults who can serve these roles, and let your kid be a kid. Doing otherwise puts too much pressure and responsibility on her at a time when your child needs *you* to be the parent.

Clarify What Happened to the Marriage

Many children feel a sense of responsibility for their parents' divorce. They exaggerate their own sense of power, and they struggle with feelings of guilt. They take responsibility for events that in fact have nothing to do with them. They berate themselves with an endless game of "if only." If only they'd behaved better . . . If only they'd paid more attention to their parents . . . If only they'd "fixed things" between Mom and Dad . . . Whenever you detect such feelings of responsibility and guilt, you should clarify what really happened between you and your ex. ("Mommy and Daddy have decided not to live together now, but it's not because of anything you've done or not done.") Reinforce that the divorce isn't your child's fault. Stress the three Cs: you didn't cause it, you can't control it, and you can't cure it.

A related issue is that many children attempt to undo the divorce. Some will try to solve the problems that they perceive as being the source of their parents' decision to end the marriage; others will act out in an effort to bring parents back together. If your child takes actions along these lines, let her know that she isn't responsible for the divorce, and she isn't able to reverse it.

Don't Muddle the Issue with Mixed Messages

Despite the divorce, you may feel ambivalent too about whether this change reflects a permanent reality. Some couples waver in their belief that the divorce is truly the end of the marriage. Such ambivalence is understandable. The problem with it, however, is that your uncertainties may painfully confuse your child. How should you respond? Try to keep interactions with your ex-spouse polite but businesslike. Unless reconciliation seems certain, don't foster illusions that you and your ex might someday get back together. Keep the boundaries clear.

OTHER ISSUES AFFECTING PARENTAL AUTHORITY

In addition, here are some recommendations about issues that have direct, often dramatic impact on how parents either maintain or damage their sense of parental authority during and after a divorce.

Prevent Your Child from Manipulating You and Your Ex

As we've noted, communication often suffers during and after a divorce. It's difficult for you and your ex to share the abundance or depth of information about family matters you took for granted while married. The level of difficulty is partly a consequence of tensions and animosities between you and your ex, but it's also simply a result of spending less time together. One side effect of this communication breakdown is that it's possible for your child to manipulate either or both parents, which can erode parental authority.

In referring to manipulation, I don't necessarily mean that your child will use you and your ex in a conscious, willful, or malicious game. Most children who engage in manipulative behavior following their parents' divorce aren't even aware of what they're doing. Rather, what's more likely is that your child will "play the system," though unaware of doing so.

Here's an example. Heather, eight years old, lives with her mother, Mandy, following Mandy's divorce from Jeff; the girl spends every other weekend with her dad. Overall, this custody arrangement has worked out fairly well, and both ex-spouses are cooperative about meeting their parental obligations. Heather seems to have adjusted to the postdivorce situation. In some ways, though, Heather takes advantage of the less frequent, less consistent communication between her parents. For instance, she convinced each parent that the other allows her to stay up later than is really true, and she persuaded Jeff that Mandy lets her postpone her weekend homework assignments till Sunday night, which isn't true. Neither of these manipulations has created any permanent or drastic problems. Each is probably a reflection of Heather's insecurity following the divorce. They are cause for concern, however, because they suggest that the child is exploiting the lack of communication between her parents.

Other signs of manipulative behavior that can diminish parental authority occur when the child:

- Uses the postdivorce arrangement as an excuse for acquiring more material goods (toys, games, clothes, computer equipment)

- Demands, extorts, or wheedles more privileges (later bedtimes, more lenient playtime hours, special outings)

- Attempts to avoid responsibilities (doing chores, finishing homework, cooperating with terms of custody arrangements)

- Engages in emotional "games" (tantrums, whining, stalling, fussing, threatening, extorting)

- Becomes disrespectful or uses nasty or derogatory language

- Acts out verbally or is physically abusive.

In these and other situations, letting yourself be manipulated can have negative short- and long-term consequences. The most obvious is that your child may gain a material "payoff" that she hasn't earned and that may not be beneficial in the first place. Successful manipulation may also allow your child to experiment with interpersonal skills best left unlearned. Perhaps the issue that's most central to this book, however, is that manipulation ultimately undercuts both your own and your ex-spouse's parental authority. If your child can pit each of you against the other, and if she becomes overly empowered as a result of this situation to gain what she wants, neither you nor your ex is really in control, and your child's respect for you will almost certainly diminish. This side effect isn't beneficial either for your child or for you as her parents.

If you find yourself in this situation, I recommend that you:

- *Reestablish and strengthen communication with your ex.* Ideally, communicate frequently and in detail with your ex-spouse about parenting your child. Good communication will make it less likely that you'll lose track of issues and create misunderstandings and manipulation. There's no way around the specific tasks of frequent communication. Although good communication may not be possible in every situation—especially if one or both spouses are emotionally distant, unstable, or hostile—this goal is still a high priority.

- *Avoid undercutting each other.* Regardless of the hostility, contempt, or anger you may feel toward your ex, don't make arbitrary decisions that undercut his or her parental authority. The two of you may still be struggling with long-term post-marital conflicts, but you should do everything possible to take the long view for your child's sake. Decisions about matters such as bedtime, meals, school issues, outings, finances, and so forth are all best made calmly and away from the children. If you have to make child-related choices on the spur of the moment, stall for time as much as possible, then consult with your ex to make a joint decision; if stalling isn't feasible, make the best decision possible on your own, then tell your child that this decision is provisional and subject to change when both parents can discuss it further. These approaches will help minimize the risk of manipulation and erosion of authority.

- *If possible, coordinate planning of family routines, responsibilities, privileges, and chores.* Responding to these first two recommendations may involve coordinated efforts. Before the divorce, you and your ex could probably accomplish a lot of planning on the fly, with decisions made over breakfast, while running errands, or while getting ready for bed; after the divorce, however, you'll have to be better organized just to stay aware of developments. Ideally, each household should try to maintain consistent values, beliefs, routines, privileges, and chores. I'm aware that for many divorced spouses, this arrangement isn't feasible. It's essential, however, that you at least *attempt* to coordinate schedules and routines. Fine tuning is a good goal, but don't berate yourself if you can't work out a detailed system.

▪ *Avoid falling into the Disneyland Dad/Mom syndrome.* There's a tendency following a divorce for the noncustodial parent to use excursions and treats as a way of making limited parent–child time "special." An example is the father who, seeing his child only once or twice a month, takes her on amusement park outings or other trips in the belief that concentrated entertainment will compensate for his absence from the child's day-to-day life. I call this tendency the Disneyland Dad syndrome. Mind you, there's nothing wrong with special outings as such. However, some risks emerge if you rely too much on this sort of occasion.

—They set up a pattern in which expensive outings replace ordinary good times together.
—They raise the stakes, so that only special occasions seem to matter.
—They tempt children to manipulate circumstances so that most or all get-togethers involve outings of this sort.

Instead, I recommend focusing simply on being together and enjoying the simple pleasures of normal, day-to-day activities. Examples include playing indoor games, participating in sports, cooking, doing art projects, reading books out loud, watching movies together, and so forth.

▪ *Resist letting your child play one parent against the other.* One of the biggest risks in what we've been discussing is that your child will learn to pit each parent against the other. If divorced parents have inconsistent expectations of their child, and if the parents' communication is erratic or nonexistent, the child will tend to see family life as a chess game that she can play primarily for her own advantage. Avoid becoming a pawn. For that matter, avoid getting pulled into a chess-game scenario of any sort. Rather, communicate openly with your ex, if at all possible; explain each situation in an age-appropriate way for your child; and act thoughtfully in keeping with your parental authority.

- *Avoid using material goods as a way of communicating affection and approval.* Out of guilt, some parents may be manipulated because they use material goods too abundantly as rewards for their child. This is a risk for all parents, but especially so for parents after a divorce. I've seen many instances in which either or both parents express their affection and approval by giving gifts, money, outings, and other payoffs to their children. For instance, Roger—a divorced father with two school-age sons—frequently gives the boys gifts of sports equipment, computer games, and other consumer goods as a way of showing how much he loves them. His love is genuine, and his intentions are good. But by showering his sons with nifty gadgets to compensate for his absence from their daily lives, Roger demeans his affection (which is, in fact, the greatest gift he can offer them) and sets up a system that encourages the boys to wheedle more stuff from their dad. Express your love by spending time with your child, showing interest in her, and being a steadfast presence in her life rather than merely a source for goodies.

Don't "Spousify" Your Child

In several chapters of this book, I've described the risks of *parentification*—the process by which mothers and fathers sometimes put their children into pseudoparental roles. The risks of parentifying a child in a latchkey role most often involve ways in which an older child ends up pressured into acting as a surrogate dad or mom toward a sibling, often when the actual parent is away at work. A similar risk can occur after a divorce—something that, for lack of a better word, I'd like to call *spousification*. This is the tendency of a divorced parent to put his or her child in a pseudospousal role.

Here's an example. Lisa, age thirty-eight, has recently gone through a divorce from Howard, who she married at age twenty-four. Lisa and Howard have a son, Bennett, now fourteen. As the custodial parent, Lisa lives with Bennett and has grown close to him during and after the rancorous divorce proceedings. Howard has visitation rights with the boy every other weekend and during some vacations. Overall, the ex-spouses and their child seem to be settling into a new routine. So far so good. My concern is that in her postdivorce grief and anger, Lisa uses her son as a sounding board in ways that can be burdensome and intrusive. In long discussions with Bennett, she expresses her rage toward Howard and her sadness over the divorce, she asks the boy's opinions about how she should proceed with her life, and she expects a level of emotional closeness with him that exceeds what Bennett finds comfortable. In short, Lisa tends to put her son in a variety of situations that aren't really comfortable or appropriate for a parent–child relationship. There's an ongoing risk that she'll drive Bennett away by expecting him to violate the loyalty he feels toward his father. She's also relying on him as a confidant in ways that aren't fair to someone who's so close both to her and to her ex-husband. Many of her behaviors toward Bennett would be more typical of those we could expect between spouses than between a mother and her son.

Spousification can take other forms as well. Here are some of the most troubling:

- *Using a child as an avenger.* For example, a father might tell his daughter stories about his ex-wife—berating and demeaning her in the child's eyes—as a way of getting back at her. The likely result is that by demeaning your ex, you'll shame your child, alter his perception of himself, and damage his relationships with both parents.

- *Switching parent–child roles with the child.* Some people regress following a divorce; reacting to the collapse of the marriage, they behave immaturely, even childishly. At times such regression can prompt a father or mother to relinquish his or her parental role almost completely. One woman I know put her teenage daughters in charge of running the household while she herself partied, played, and repeatedly set off on trips to "find herself."

- *Employing a child as a lawyer, financial advisor, or psychotherapist.* It's understandable that following a divorce, a man or woman would crave reassurance, information, and advice. Most people need good counsel of many different types in the aftermath of divorce. To put your own daughter or son in a position of providing legal, financial, or psychotherapeutic insights, however, is burdensome to the child. This sort of role switch can be damaging to everyone concerned.

If you sense that you've spousified your child:

- *Work hard to keep the parent–child relationship just that.* As distraught as you may feel following the divorce, don't use your child as a surrogate for other people in your life. Your child shouldn't have to be your confidant, sounding board, or life raft. Maintain and focus on the relationship you have as parent and child rather than transforming or distorting that relationship into something else.

- *Find emotional solace among friends, family, and other adults.* It's normal and understandable that the divorce would leave you feeling emotionally wounded, and it's normal for you to crave reassurance and comfort from other people. Don't expect your child to soothe those wounds directly. Seek the company of your friends, supportive family members, and professional colleagues. When the time is right, look for the companionship of other adults who may be appropriate future lovers or mates. But don't put your child in a role that's equivalent or even approximate to what these adults can provide.

- *Seek advice from appropriate professionals.* Divorce changes most aspects of life, practical as well as emotional. It's possible, even likely, that you'll need thoughtful help from one or more professional advisors as you restructure and reorganize yourself following the divorce. Under these circumstances, many people benefit from legal counsel, financial advice, or psychotherapy. I recommend that if you feel the need for these services, do whatever is possible to obtain them. I strongly urge you *not* to use your child to provide the equivalent.

- *Let your kid be a kid.* Whatever your child's age when you end your marriage, the divorce will affect her in many ways. Some children regress dramatically following their parents' divorce; others seem to take the situation in stride but still experience some side effects. Either way, your child is still a child. Let her be what she is, not someone who's older or younger. Do whatever is possible to nurture and sustain her during the difficult aftermath of the divorce. Always keep her best interests in mind.

- *Find emotional support for your child, if necessary.* If you feel that your child is suffering severe consequences from the divorce, find her psychological help as quickly as possible. There's nothing shameful in doing so; on the contrary, therapeutic intervention often makes a tremendous long-term difference in helping children adjust to their new reality when parents divorce. Just as your child can't be your psychotherapist, you can't be your child's either, because you don't have the training or objectivity to perform that role. Don't fall prey to the misguided belief that, if your child feels troubled or depressed, you've somehow failed her. You are your child's strongest, steadiest anchor in the world, but that doesn't mean that you can provide every kind of reassurance or insight that she needs.

DIVORCE AND YOUR NEW SENSE OF AUTHORITY

In the aftermath of divorce, you may struggle with complex issues of authority. Some of these issues are the result of your losing your "co-parent"—the person who (at least theoretically) has been backing you and helping you with the tasks of raising your children. (You may, in fact, have received far less parenting assistance than what seemed necessary, which may have contributed significantly to the divorce.) In addition, custody disputes often undermine parental authority. A common example is when one parent gains full custody of the children while the other ends up in a noncustodial—and clearly subordinate—role. These are difficult situations, so difficult that they will challenge your patience and creativity to the utmost.

What I urge you to do, above all, is to take the long view. Although the emotional and practical hardships involved in ending your marriage may seem to go on forever, they won't. Your life will eventually stabilize after the divorce. If you can focus on your child and attend to his best interests, you'll maintain your parental authority in ways that will dramatically pay off for him—and for you—in the future you're rebuilding together.

Chapter 11

DEALING WITH MASS MEDIA

Not long ago, I invited two families over to my house for lunch. I've known one of the families—I'll call them the Jacksons—for a long time. I greatly enjoy my relationship with both Mick and Nancy Jackson and with their two-year-old twins, Mindy and Alyssa. The other family, who I'll call the Bedells, are acquaintances of mine but close friends of the Jacksons. The Bedells have a nine-year-old son, Keith. The gathering seemed a casual way to spend a Sunday afternoon.

Nothing about this occasion was overly problematic. Everyone got along well enough. The twins indulged themselves in a little toddlerish mischief but otherwise played congenially with one another. All the grown-ups got along. Everyone enjoyed the food. Overall, we had a good time together.

What surprised me and concerned me was Keith's behavior. During the get-together, he never interacted with anyone. Although his own parents tried to include him in our activities, which included casual backyard sports, the boy never even acknowledged what went on around him. He didn't seem angry or depressed, just completely disengaged. During the entire time he spent with us, Keith played games on his Game Boy computer toy and tuned out everyone and everything around him. Even while eating, he never once set down the gadget to speak with anyone. At one point his mother, Jacqueline, offered him some food, yet without so much as a glance Keith announced, "I'm busy!" and brushed her off. He rebuffed or ignored any of the other adults' efforts to engage with him, even when they asked about the Game Boy as a way of showing interest in his private world.

"Well, what can you do?" Jacqueline Bedell lamented later, in the kitchen, as some of us were discussing parenthood and work issues. "At this age kids are off somewhere in the Twilight Zone. There's no point in trying to connect with him. He's got his TV shows, his computer, and his Game Boy, and that's where he lives. That's his reality. It's the day-to-day world that Keith finds unreal."

This was a touchy subject; despite her oh-well attitude, Jacqueline spoke with audible concern and hurt. Her worries seemed appropriate. During the several hours of our family visit, I never once saw any sign of Keith responding to anyone—not to me, not to my husband, not to my teenage son, not to our other guests, not to his own parents—as if we were human beings worthy of acknowledgment, much less of curiosity or enthusiasm. His own interactions took place only with his beloved Game Boy and, briefly, with a TV set he turned on without permission. No wonder his mother felt concerned. Yet I didn't know Jacqueline well enough to express my own worries—worries that her son had retreated almost totally from human company and had isolated himself in a world of bits and bytes and media images. If I had, she might have taken offense. Even my few questions prompted a barrage of excuses: "I'm sure he'll come back to earth eventually, but right now he's off on his own planet, isn't he? The Planet of the Preteens!" she joked. "Except they think *we're* the aliens! Kids Keith's age don't even want to *see* us grown-ups, much less *deal* with us. All they want is to interact with each other—and their gizmos."

To Jacqueline's credit, she has identified a phenomenon that's more and more common. I don't fault her for that. What worries me, however, is that she and her husband, like many parents, are identifying a problem but refusing to address it. Yes, American children often retreat into a world that consists almost entirely of gadgets, TV shows, movies, and computers. Yes, they often withdraw from human interaction, especially with adults. Yes, they seem in many respects to be a species all their own. These patterns are widespread and, if anything, they're spreading farther all the time. But I refuse to believe that what I observed in Keith (and what his mother described about him) can be considered an inevitable, age-appropriate form of social segregation. Rather, I feel that the behavior I witnessed that afternoon is part of a phenomenon that we American parents allow to happen, or even encourage. I worry most of all that this phenomenon is largely a consequence of our having abdicated our parental authority to the various mass media—especially TV, movies, and computer-related pastimes—which influence and often dominate so many aspects of modern life.

THE QUANDARY OF MEDIA INFLUENCE

Is it really so bad if kids "zone out," submerging themselves in a harmless alternate reality? Isn't this just a stage they're going through? Haven't kids always created their own subcultures—especially during the preteen and teen years—and marked them as their own turf? Isn't it better for parents to go with the flow under these circumstances rather than demand that children engage with people despite their frequent preference for interacting with computers, TVs, and other gadgets?

First of all, I need to clarify what I find problematic. I'm not objecting to kids creating an alternate reality. Children have always constructed fantasy worlds—worlds in which pirates, dragons, knights and princesses, cowboys, bandits, space aliens, or other denizens of their imaginations seem more real and persuasive than the inhabitants (especially parents!) of everyday reality. Part of what makes childhood powerful and magical is kids' ability to move back and forth between the realms of the imaginary and the real. I have no objection to kids spending some time in these alternate realities.

Rather, what concerns me is, first, that many American children now spend much of their time disengaged from the everyday world. Although there appears to be a decline in the overall number of hours that kids spend watching TV, I'm not convinced that they're making up the difference by playing with toys, reading, doing art projects, or engaging in other low-tech, hands-on activities; on the contrary, it's likely that for many kids, less time watching TV means more time playing computers games or other high-tech forms of entertainment. I observe many boys, especially, spending long hours in front of computer terminals. Face-to-face interaction with other human beings during free time is sporadic and, in some instances, reluctant.

Second, what concerns me even more is that *these alternate worlds aren't what children themselves have created.* They are, instead, worlds that corporations have designed, manufactured, and marketed, leaving little room for kids themselves to put their own imaginations into play. Ultimately, what I'm objecting to is the world of the mass media. This isn't really a children's world at all. It's a world that *adults* have created, often based not on what kids need or want, but on profit-oriented marketing plans. *Adults* then sell these creations aggressively to children primarily to make money. This is the world of network TV, of heavily advertised movies, of corporate rock 'n' roll, and of electronic toys and computer games.

Finally, what concerns me most of all is that these media products often encourage passive rather than active participation; they do little to prompt children to play imaginatively, to exercise their bodies or minds, or to interact openly with other people. They often promote values that are aggressive, selfish, prejudicial, or in other ways dismissive of other people.

Am I sounding too alarmist? Too strident? Too conservative? Too liberal? Some people may object to my objections—may regard them as reflecting an excessive degree of anxiety. What difference does it make (these people may ask) if kids watch a little TV, listen to a little music, or play a few computer games? Surely children take all this media input in stride. They'll develop just fine. Well, maybe so. But I'm still concerned. I spend a lot of time with kids—as a mother, as a therapist, and as a member of my community—and I feel strong reservations about how mass media affect children, especially considering how these media affect children's attitudes toward parents and parental authority.

WHY ARE THE MEDIA A PROBLEM?

The issues we're discussing are complex. I realize that many people have strong opinions about the mass media, and that some observers have expressed rather extreme statements about how television, computer games, and other media affect children. Certain social critics, for example, have claimed a nearly direct connection between media violence and outbursts of violence among children. I'm not making such claims. Personally, I don't believe that there's a clear-cut, direct correlation between media influence and kids' misbehavior. Neither do I believe that exposure to one TV show, movie, or computer game is destructive in its own right. Rather, what concerns me is that contemporary children grow up bombarded by media images, messages, and propaganda; as a result, mass media exert a disproportionate sway over kids' ideas, feelings, beliefs, and behavior. It's even possible to argue that, past the age of five or so, some children are more thoroughly influenced by the media than by their parents, and this influence increases as kids move into their teens.

Media Messages

The upshot? Although I can't offer definitive proof, I feel that, as a result of these influences on children, the media:

- Disrupt the teaching of humane values

- Encourage racist, sexist, anti-Semitic, xenophobic, and homophobic attitudes

- Model generally negative behavior

- Desensitize children to suffering

- Foster hostile or dismissive attitudes between kids, and between parents and children

- Undercut parental authority.

Because the last item on this list falls most fully within my book's scope, I'll focus on it to the partial exclusion of the others; I should add, however, that many of the other issues can contribute to tension between parents and children. For this and other reasons, they can intensify friction over issues relevant to parental authority.

Some relatively harmless shows and movies can be damaging in these regards. For instance, the TV show *Malcolm in the Middle*, though benign and even sentimental in many respects, contains many thinly veiled messages that undercut parents' authority. Even the well-meaning parents in this show come off as thick-headed and hopelessly tuned out; by comparison, kids are savvy, insightful, quick thinking, and infinitely more cool. Similarly, popular movies such as *Home Alone* build their stories on the premise that parents are so incompetent, if not in fact so acutely negligent, that they leave a boy in a quandary that he solves only by his own wits—which, for the most part, means defeating other incompetent (and often malicious) adults by violent means.

Here are some of the messages that children acquire (or have reinforced) through the media:

- Parents are inept and incompetent when not downright selfish or ill-intentioned (*The Simpsons*).

- When the going gets tough, kids will save the day (*Free Willy, The Great Panda Adventure, Spy Kids*).

- Life can get complicated, but taking control—by violent means, if necessary—will solve all problems.

- Members of different generations can't get along; at best, kids can barely tolerate parents and other old people.

- The worse your attitude, the cooler you are.

The Consumption of Mass Media as a Process

In addition to the issue of these negative messages, however, what concerns me is that kids' consumption of media products is problematic as a *process*. Watching shows and movies, listening to music, and playing computer games are, to a greater or lesser degree, all passive activities. They don't involve much interaction with other people, parents included, from whom kids might learn practical, social, or emotional skills. These games often encourage a high degree of disengagement from everyday reality. Many forms of electronic media function to some degree as high-tech pacifiers. In addition, they sometimes foster a form of emotional desensitization, as when children play violent computer games that can diminish their responses to pain and suffering. Such games can also have effects that are lulling, even hypnotic—a quick fix that kids use for dealing with stress and anxiety.

Some parents I've spoken with defend their children's consumption of media products by stressing that kids, too, need downtime. Children lead such intense lives these days, with scheduled lessons, organized sports, and participation in clubs or other extracurricular activities, that they have only limited time to rest or engage in low-stress pastimes. Isn't it possible that kids, like adults, need opportunities to kick back and simply take it easy? Just like adults, don't children deserve a chance to decompress by watching a movie or playing a computer game? To these objections I can only respond with a qualified but enthusiastic "Yes". Children *are* overscheduled and stressed out. They *do* need opportunities to kick back. They do need chances to decompress. And I'll hasten to add that, in moderation, TV, movies, and computer games are legitimate ways to reach these goals. I don't have any across-the-board objection to them. Rather, what concerns me is an overreliance on mass media as a way of easing kids' stress and anxiety levels. Many American kids (perhaps most) consume mass media products in a steady diet that limits the children's experience with more direct forms of play, such as sports, art projects, music, make-believe, board games, role playing, and so forth.

There's another worrisome aspect to this situation. Far too many parents use the media as childcare surrogates, which isn't necessarily good for the kids themselves and which moreover undercuts the parents' authority. The classic example of this situation is parents who use television as a babysitter. Granted, many moms and dads have no choice but to let their child watch TV to keep them occupied while the parents accomplish important tasks, such as fixing dinner. I have no objection to that sort of occasional use of TV. Sometimes there's just no way around it, and resorting to this ploy now and then shouldn't be harmful. What I'm concerned about, however, isn't occasional or intermittent, and it's not limited to kids watching TV. Rather, what I'm referring to is the constant, often unsupervised use of mass media—not just TV but also videos, computer games, and handheld gadgets—to keep kids busy on a routine basis. Under these circumstances, these media aren't one of a variety of experiences that children encounter; rather, they are the bedrock on which kids build their sense of the world and their habitual ways of interacting with it. Relying on mass media becomes the fundamental process by which children experience the world. Like Keith, whose Game Boy–centered world I described at the start of this chapter, such children often find interactions with computers and other gadgetry more appealing and compelling than interactions with the complex, mysterious world around them. I find this scenario chilling in its own right. From the standpoint of our discussion, though, it's also disturbing: a child whose parents allow him or her such an unlimited diet of media experiences is unlikely to pay much attention to the parents' insights, opinions, or preferences.

How to Limit Media Influence on Your Kids

If you believe that mass media should have only a partial role in your child's life, the task facing you is how to limit the media's influence. Limiting does not mean outright prohibition. First of all, excluding mass media altogether would be almost impossible to achieve. In addition, total exclusion would prevent your children from learning to cope with the influence of television, movies, the Internet, and even more innovative forms of communication that heavily influence contemporary life. The goal, then, is to help children to become savvy observers and consumers of the media.

Size Up the Media "Turf"

It should be obvious that different families have different tastes and standards about what's acceptable entertainment at specific ages. What may seem sensible in some households (such as allowing kids to watch any TV show they want) will be totally out of the question in others. As a result, your first step is to determine what you'll allow your children to watch or participate in. Doing so assumes a willingness to explore what's available. This task in itself isn't easy, and it requires some time and effort to accomplish. You will need to "surf" the channels, zero in on shows that may interest your kids, and watch for long enough to size up their level of appropriateness. The situation with computer games is more difficult; you'll have to borrow the games, learn enough about them to operate them, and explore them yourself. Alternatively, you can seek the opinion of someone who's knowledgeable and trustworthy about these forms of entertainment. (This person might be an older child in your own family, a niece or nephew, a friend of the family, or someone else who's both reliable and media-savvy.) The same holds true regarding the Web and other Internet-based activities. Don't get me wrong—my recommendation will require a lot of legwork. I can't see any easy way around it, however, if you really want an overview of what your children may be using as their pastimes.

Exert Your Authority about What's Age-Appropriate

Once you have a sense of what's available, make clear-headed decisions about what you regard as acceptable and unacceptable. You can make these decisions outright for preschool-age children. Kids aged five through eight can be part of the decision-making process, but feel free to follow your own hunches without letting a child sway you by pleading, fussing, or throwing tantrums. Most children simply aren't able to assess the issues that many forms of entertainment involve. Your five-year-old may object to your prohibition of scary movies, for instance, yet may feel traumatized if he watches horror, suspense, or science fiction films. Similarly, you shouldn't capitulate to your child's entreaties based on the claim that "all the other kids are seeing it." Make it clear that you have your own values and that you feel an obligation to stand by them; "going with the crowd" isn't what you'll do. Make it clear, too, that you're the ultimate decision-maker about what's acceptable.

Check in with Other Parents

Precisely because assumptions vary from one family to another regarding what sorts of pastimes are acceptable, you should ask outright before your children watch movies or play computer games with friends. Some relevant questions to ask include:

- "What sorts of games [or movies] will they be playing [or watching]?"

- "Have you played these games [or watched these movies] yourself?"

- "What's the content like [such as violence, sexual themes, and profane language]?"

- "What other pastimes are the kids likely to be doing in addition to computer [or video] activities?"

If you have any doubts about what your child will be seeing or doing in another household, find out. Most parents will appreciate your concern. Many will be willing to compromise if you're hesitant about one or another activity. If they don't appreciate your concerns—or if they're dismissive about them—it's a red flag. Moreover, some parents won't even *know* what their own kids are watching or doing, so they may doubly value your interest. The bottom line is that you have a right to know what sorts of entertainment your child will participate in. It's not inappropriate to suggest alternatives if what's scheduled seems out of line with your own guidelines. The key, as always, is to be thoughtful and polite rather than aggressive when you make your inquiry.

Discuss the Media with Your Kids

Whatever your kids see and do, talk with them about their media experiences. Let them express their concerns about TV and movie violence, images of sexuality and gender, and other issues. Ask them questions about shows, movies, music videos, and computers games. Help them understand what seems to be going on in the media, as compared to what's really happening.

For instance, one girl I know remarked that she enjoyed rock music because it was so antiestablishment; in the ensuing discussion, she was surprised to learn that entertainment corporations manage almost every aspect of music production—they hire the composers, assemble market-oriented rock bands, record the songs, then distribute the CDs and promote the concerts in keeping with carefully designed marketing strategies. What seems anti-establishment is, in fact, a highly calculated product of the media establishment itself. Similarly, many children are intrigued, even outraged, by learning how corporations manipulate consumers into purchasing their products.

Seek Alternatives to the Mass Media

For millennia, most families provided their own entertainment. Family members played musical instruments, sang songs, worked on arts and crafts projects, cooked, baked, and told stories as means of enjoying specific activities and each others' company. Even special forms of entertainment—plays, concerts, fairs, and so forth—were highly social occasions. It has only been during the past several decades that people have felt a need for constant outside entertainment. One of the ways that you can respond to the barrage of media pressure on your children is to return to more family-oriented forms of entertainment.

Here are some strategies:

- *Ease up on structured, scheduled activities.* Many parents tell me that they resort to electronic media because their kids seem stressed out. The diagnosis of the problem is accurate even if the "cure" is ill-considered. In fact, lots of American kids are overscheduled. If you feel that your children are suffering from overload, do what you can to ease the pressure, but don't rely on the media as the safety valve. Cutting back on high-stress activities (lessons, competitive sports, extracurricular clubs, and so forth) may take some of the burden off your children's shoulders. Let your kids "go into neutral" now and then. Non-media alternatives include playing alone, playing with friends, reading, building things, playing musical instruments, or doing projects at home.

- *Find family-related pastimes.* A remarkable number of families I know have few or no shared activities. Individual family members entertain themselves in private, each watching his or her own TV set or playing games at his or her own computer. I realize that from the teen years on, many kids don't really want to participate in family activities; however, that sort of standoffishness needn't exclude *all* group pastimes, especially if there's a long-standing tradition of parents and children doing some activities together. Inviting kids' friends to be part of the action can help increase the options. Possibilities include casual outdoor sports (such as Frisbee, touch football, volleyball, softball, swimming), hiking, art projects, cooking projects, and so forth.

- *Disengage from compulsive consumerism.* Despite the constant barrage of advertisements suggesting that you don't own enough consumer goods, you probably don't need more gadgets, goodies, and belongings. It's likely that your kids have too many, not too few, possessions. In fact, most children who complain about feeling bored are swamped in toys and amusements; what they lack is experience in entertaining themselves and in exercising their imaginations. In addition, consumerism may well prompt you to spend so much money that you'll work harder and harder, resulting in less and less time with your children. This situation creates more stress both for you and your kids, more friction between parents and children, and a likely diminishment of parental authority.

- *Allow measured use of the media.* You probably can't exile the media from your life altogether. Even if you could, doing so might create a backlash among your kids—a sense of deprivation intense enough to cause even greater craving for media products. Moreover, mass media have the potential to offer genuine benefits; although most TV shows, movies, CDs, computer games, and other media products are shallow and often inane, there are exceptions, including works of great artistic merit and educational value. Stepping carefully, you can use the media responsibly, thoughtfully, and creatively.

You—Not the Media—Are the Parent

I hope it's clear from this discussion that I don't advocate banning the media from family life. Even if that goal were desirable, it wouldn't be feasible. The mass media have such power and such a central place within American culture that eliminating them altogether just isn't in the cards. What's more, banishing them would require giving up some crucial advantages: the modern media have made some great works of art possible, as well as a communications network that has to some extent connected almost every corner of the world. It's important for us to help our children understand what's beneficial about the media and to take thoughtful advantage of those benefits.

Concerning the media and their effects on parenthood, the crux of the matter is to avoid letting gadgets, games, mass-market entertainment, and advertisements replace you as your children grow and change. This warning may sound odd, even silly, but it's one that many parents would do well to heed. The Bedells—the parents whose son Keith interacts primarily with his Game Boy— are an example of what concerns me. There's a risk of American parents ceding their authority to the media, thus allowing movies, TV shows, and computer games a disproportionate, even dominant role in shaping their children's tastes, insights, values, and behaviors. This issue is what concerns me most in any discussion of the media.

What's the alternative? Simply this: don't eliminate mass media from your home, but diminish their influence on your children. Give the media products their due, but don't let them supplant you as your children's guide. Keep things in proportion. Doing so will not only be salutary in its own right; it'll also help preserve and augment your authority as a parent.

Conclusion

THE COMPASS OF PARENTAL AUTHORITY

Parenthood is the ultimate in on-the-job training. No matter how much time you've spent around children before you have your own kids, you can understand the depth and breadth of parenting only through day-to-day interactions with your own kids. I'm not talking just about the many practical tasks that go with the turf: feeding them, dressing them, and all the minutiae of family life. I'm referring also—especially—to the countless decisions that affect children's well-being and development. Those decisions are, after all, what add up to create both the greatest burdens and the greatest satisfactions of parenthood.

It's a pity that, as parents, we can't know what we need to know *before* we start the incredibly complex project of raising children. Unfortunately, life just doesn't work that way. This holds true for me as much as for anyone else. Despite years of training and many more years of experience as a teacher and family counselor, I've struggled like any other mother or father to keep "ahead of the curve" as I parent my children. (I was a single parent during most of the time I've raised my son, Jason. I remarried a few years ago, and my wonderful husband and I are now raising our baby daughter together.) I love being a mother. To be honest, though, I wish I knew back at the beginning of parenthood what I've learned over the years. It's one of nature's great ironies that mothers and fathers gain knowledge and wisdom about parenthood precisely by learning throughout the parenting process as they love and nurture their children.

I believe that parents' most complex and important role is to be a compass for their children. Kids have a powerful, inborn drive to grow and develop. Much of what parents do (or ought to do) is simply to avoid obstructing children's innate drive toward development. In this sense, kids already have the engines that power them on their journey through the early years of life. However, children need more than just power to drive them forth. They also need direction. And this need for direction is what parents must somehow provide. Serving this purpose is parental authority—parental authority as a compass.

The goal of everything we've discussed throughout *Who's the Boss?* is essentially to help you recalibrate (or, in some cases, to acquire for the first time) the compass of parental authority. Too many contemporary parents expect children to find their own way through the complexities of modern life. This is neither fair nor possible: children simply don't know enough to understand the changes taking place inside them or the events taking place around them. At the same time, the ancient verities—infallible codes of Right and Wrong—don't always function well in a complex multicultural world. What I urge you to do, then, is to establish your authority thoughtfully and wield it flexibly, at once guiding and teaching your children carefully yet learning constantly yourself as your kids develop. My hope is that *Who's the Boss?* can contribute to your efforts to achieve that purpose.

Here are some final thoughts to help you deal with these issues.

ACCEPT THAT PARENTING ISN'T INNATE

Most parenting skills are learned, not instinctual. In traditional cultures, these skills are passed systematically from one generation to the next. In our mobile, fragmented society, new mothers and fathers can learn from their own parents but also from nontraditional sources—parenting classes, support groups, books, videos, even the Internet. (See Appendix B for further suggestions.) Broadening your knowledge of child development and parenthood will help you in many ways, including your insights into issues of parental authority.

PAY YOUR DUES EARLY

If you can establish a warm, confident sense of authority with your kids during their early years, you'll do them and yourself a great favor. You can't avoid or sidestep this issue; parental authority is an inevitable aspect of family life. You may as well face the whole matter head on, make thoughtful decisions about it, and ensure that your sense of authority (or its absence) is a creative, loving source of energy rather than a limiting, debilitating, or even destructive force. Attempting to ignore the issue of authority will simply postpone dealing with it till later, when your children may be less receptive to a cooperative relationship with you. (As the saying goes, "Little kids, little problems; big kids, big problems.")

ACCEPT THAT PARENTING IS HARD WORK

It's no secret that parents' work never ends. Family life throws one challenge after another at you. This is as true concerning authority as any other aspect of parenthood. I wish I could offer a magic solution to the problem, but I can't; it doesn't exist. The truth is that as your kids grow and change the developmental tasks will change too, and the changes will include shifts in which issues of authority are relevant. They'll test the limits you've set. They'll question your decisions. They'll experiment with behaviors that try your patience. I don't mean to sound negative about these challenges; some of them will be delightful or fascinating rather than difficult in any negative sense. They are all part of the adventure of raising children. But at the end of the day, when you're frazzled and exhausted, remember that these ups and downs serve a purpose. Focus on the moment but keep your eye on the road ahead.

REMEMBER YOUR ORIGINS

Each of us has been influenced by our own upbringing. Most of us benefited greatly from our parents' efforts on our behalf. That said, it's also true that our mothers and fathers inevitably made mistakes. They were fallible human beings. They sometimes chose courses of action that may, in retrospect, seem regrettable. Among other things, the ways in which they expressed their parental authority may have been too strict, too lax, too confused, or too disorganized. And your parents' own manner of authority may affect you in ways that differ from how you wish to interact with your own children. My point is simply to remind you that your own origins—what you experienced during your own childhood—will almost certainly influence the decisions you make about your own children. Does this influence mean that you're locked in the past? Not at all. But being aware of the influence can help you make decisions more insightfully than if you pretend that the influence doesn't exist. Pick and choose from what your parents taught you. Stay open to new ideas. Above all, pay close attention to what your children need.

DON'T FORGET THAT KIDS' NEEDS CHANGE CONSTANTLY

Keep in mind that because children change constantly, their needs for authority change as they do. This changeability is, in fact, one of the trickiest and most challenging aspects of parental authority. Just when you think you've figured out what suits your kids best, they enter a new developmental phase and transform themselves. Here again, a good understanding of child development will serve you well. At times, kids need more freedom, more leeway to explore; at other times, they need more structure and clearer limits and boundaries. How will you know *what* they need? Only by knowing the overall developmental context, observing your children carefully, and making flexible, insightful decisions as you go. The key is to create a safe, loving environment in which your kids can explore the world.

ACCEPT YOUR OWN IMPERFECTIONS

The psychologist D. W. Winnicott invented a memorable, useful concept: the "good-enough mother." By this phrase he referred to the mother who is attentive to her children's needs but isn't *too* attentive, which can tend to make kids overly dependent, thus limiting their development. Amplifying Winnicott's concept to include fathers as well, I'd urge you to be a good-enough parent. By all means be a good, caring, loving parent, but don't expect to be flawless. The very nature of parenthood guarantees that you'll make one mistake after another. How can you do otherwise? The tasks of parenthood don't lend themselves to precision, and most of what happens in family life is ambiguous, messy, and unpredictable. Mistakes go with the territory. As with so many other aspects of raising children, dealing with parental authority will require you to guess about what your kids need, make decisions on a wing and a prayer, experiment, and learn from your errors.

ACCEPT YOUR CHILD'S INDIVIDUALITY

One of the most difficult aspects of parental authority is a consequence of each child being different from every other child. Even if you're able to "get it right" with your firstborn, you'll face another slightly different set of issues with any other children you raise. Precisely because every human being is unique, each child will have individual needs, interests, capabilities, tastes, and shortcomings that influence his development. You, too, are unique, with specific talents, experiences, personal history, abilities, flaws, and virtues. The combination of your child's individuality with your own guarantees a complex, unpredictable interaction. What does this mean about parental authority? Among other things, it means you'll always be learning as you go. Yes, you'll grow more confident and experienced, but family life (like life in general) will always be full of surprises. Once again the key is flexibility.

PERCEIVE PARENTHOOD AS A DANCE

Although I've used the image of parental authority as a compass, I'd like to switch metaphors for a moment and suggest that parenthood is also fundamentally a dance. Dancing isn't linear, yet every style of dance has its own order, its own rules and rhythms. Not only that: dancing is a partnership. Dance partners work together, yet each has a different role. The dance can be smooth and graceful, with parent and child in harmony. The dance can also be awkward—the partners out of step, stumbling over one another's feet—and that's frustrating but normal. Even the most accomplished dancers can't always be graceful or harmonious. How should you respond? Just enjoy the process. You'll be in tune most of the time, and you'll learn the steps as you go.

BE PREPARED TO CHANGE

If you're like most parents, you will significantly, even radically change throughout the course of the parenting years. I believe that such change is usually positive: men and women often become kinder, more generous, more thoughtful, more flexible, and more imaginative as a result of being parents. Sometimes the consequences are negative; parenthood can be exhausting, confusing, and frustrating at times. That said, I'd still wager that you'll probably end up a wiser and more substantial human being as a result of raising children.

One of the changes that many parents undergo is a deeper realization of their own creativity. Of course, as parents you literally create a child; in addition, though, you experience creativity in the years that follow your child's birth. Parental authority is part of that creativity. By working hard to foster your child's best interests, by seeking a gentle but firm style in which to express your authority, and by guiding your child as wisely as possible, you'll assist your child's development and simultaneously become more than you were before.

DON'T BE AFRAID TO BE THE PARENT

You are in charge. You are the boss. This doesn't free you to behave impulsively or selfishly as you go about the tasks of parenthood; on the contrary, parental authority confers a huge responsibility to see clearly, act wisely, and treat your child with great sensitivity. But the fact remains that until your child's late teens, you have the legal, moral, and psychological responsibility to guide your son or daughter through the many stages of his or her development. I'd be the first to say that this is a daunting task. But there's no way around it; relinquishing your authority won't benefit your child and may, in fact, do him or her great damage. Not only that: establishing and maintaining a thoughtful, creative manner of parental authority will prove to be positive both for you and your child. As Ellen Galinsky puts this issue in *The Six Stages of Parenthood*:

[T]he parent has the major task of accepting this new dimension of responsibility, accepting his or her authority over the child. This entails determining the scope of authority, communicating, then enforcing what has been established . . . It is a transforming experience to understand that the negative impulses which exist in everyone—the well-meaning parent as well as the most innocent child—can be put into the service of nurturing and care.

Don't be afraid to be the parent. Do everything you do "in the service of nurturing and care," make the best decisions you can, and attend to your children as if parenting is the most important and meaningful role in the world.

Appendix A

CHILD DEVELOPMENT AND AGE-APPROPRIATE BEHAVIOR

What is appropriate behavior at each stage of childhood? This question has complex answers—so complex that psychologists and pediatricians have written scores of books on the subject. No brief summary can describe it in detail. For this reason, what follows is just an *outline* of predictable milestones and how they affect children's behavior. It is a sketch, not a detailed analysis, of developmental issues that affect many issues, including parental authority.

NORMS—NOT TIMETABLES

Developmental milestones are useful but deceptive—useful, because they provide you with an overview of how children change and grow over the years; deceptive, because the overview doesn't predict a specific child's behavior. In short, developmental milestones refer to *norms* within a group of children. They aren't timetables for what your own child will experience. Each child will develop in her own way at her own rate. Her development will vary in relation to other children's; in addition, her development in particular areas (such as verbal or motor skills) will also vary in relation to other areas (such as intellectual growth).

NEWBORN TO AGE ONE

The first year of a child's life presents you with the most dramatic changes you'll see during the parenting years. From a state of almost total helplessness, the child develops into a still-dependent but remarkably expressive creature capable of complex motion, perception, and communication. Parental authority during your child's babyhood means protecting her, anticipating her physical and emotional needs, and providing her with enough freedom to explore safe surroundings but not enough freedom to risk injury or other hazards to her well-being. Babies feel whatever they feel; "appropriate behavior" is not a useful concept at this stage. The only exception: monitoring your child for signs of sensory, motor, cognitive, or emotional disability. If you have concerns about whether your child's behavior falls within the normal range, consult with your pediatrician. Disciplining a baby is not appropriate.

AGES ONE TO TWO

At age one, the child has generally started to walk and talk but hasn't yet mastered these skills. By the age of two, she is exploring the world with constantly growing physical and verbal sophistication. She is also beginning to exert her will. Rather than tolerate what her parents demand, she now insists on a greater and greater degree of independence.

Emotional Development

- Manifests separation anxiety if parents leave

- Shows "magical thinking"—fear that perceiving something (such as parents' departure) makes it happen permanently

- Continues to exhibit oral behavior—puts everything in mouth

- Shows initial venturing away from parents for short periods of time

- Delights in transitional love objects—blankets, plush animals, etc.

- Shows initial capacity for independence—experiments with evading parents as a game, etc.

- Says "no" more often; starts to throw tantrums

- May show fear of thunder and lightning, big animals, and the dark

- Struggles to distinguish between fantasy and reality

Verbal Development

- Enjoys vocalizing for its own sake

- Responds verbally to other people

- Responds accurately to many simple commands ("Up," "Come here," etc.)

- Gradually acquires a greater and greater vocabulary

- Gradually uses questions like "What's that?" and "Why?"

- Combines words ("All gone," "Want mama," etc.)

- Uses "no" or "not" in understandable phrases or sentences

- Employs about ten different phrases or sentences regularly

Motor (Physical Skill) Development

- Creeps and crawls

- Gets into things—cabinets, bookcases, drawers, etc.

- Stands alone competently

- "Cruises" alongside walls, furniture, etc.

- Starts walking with assistance

- Starts to pile blocks

- Stoops to pick up objects

- Puts small objects into larger ones

- Touches and handles many objects

- Turns knobs on appliances

Appropriate Behavior

- Shows a need (early on) for holding, cuddling, and rocking

- Responds to praise and verbal interaction as well as eye contact, smiles, and other nonverbal cues

- Responds to parental consistency and warmth

- Starts (at about eighteen months) to manifest egocentric "it's mine" behavior—rearranging furniture, dumping toys, and generally "pushing the envelope" in exploratory activities

- Starts (at about the same time) to express willful naysaying

- Shows a growing need for autonomy

AGES TWO TO THREE

Between the second and third years, the child consolidates the skills that she has acquired in the year before. Energetic, willful, and demanding, she is a force of nature—at once delightful and exasperating to her parents.

Emotional Development

- Sees the world almost entirely through the lens of her own needs

- Manifests frequent mood swings

- Expresses sadness or stress

- Throws frequent temper tantrums

- Pouts or sulks when frustrated

- Struggles to distinguish between fantasy and reality

Verbal Development

- Rapidly increases vocabulary

- Mimics adults' verbal inflections

- Grasps simple commands

- Starts combining nouns with verbs to form sentences

- Begins to use pronouns such as "I" and "me"

- Asks frequent "Why?" questions

- Starts to understand a few prepositions ("on," "under," "with")

- Uses three- and four-word sentences

- Begins to refer to future events

- Uses regular plurals (such as those formed by adding s to a word)

Appropriate Behavior

- Continues to venture out and explore the environment

- Alternates clinginess toward and pushing away from parents

- Exhibits emotional volatility

- Shows possessiveness toward belongings (both her own and others')

AGES THREE TO FOUR

A three-year-old can seem much more settled than when she was even a few months younger; she may be relaxed, content, and comfortable with herself and with the people around her. By three and a half, however, the situation often changes, with growing restlessness and demanding attitudes toward others.

Emotional Development

- Begins to grasp what's acceptable and what's not

- Grows increasingly aware of others' feelings

- May show empathy toward familiar people

- Shows frustration when sharing

- Tends to be egocentric and self-obsessed, with the world viewed almost entirely through the child's own viewpoint

Verbal Development

- Increasingly fluid use of language

- May ask for help or clarification on tasks

- Asks questions rhetorically

- Expresses refusals in complex ways ("I don't want to" rather than "No")

- Is able to talk on the telephone

- Introduces questions with "where," "what," and "why"

- Understands the gender contrast of pronouns such as "he" and "she" or "him" and "her"

- By age four, tells stories that mix fantasy and reality

- By age four, can carry on elaborate conversations

- By age four, develops a more elaborate sense of humor

Appropriate Behavior

- Shows an intensifying need for autonomy

- Manifests more sensitivity toward parental admonishments

- Imitates parents' behavior

- Shapes emotions after what she sees modeled around her

- Engages mostly in parallel play

AGES FOUR TO FIVE

Physically capable, the four-year-old can be emotionally unpredictable. Many children are secure at this age, but they have entered a period of willful confidence. Boasting, bragging, and exaggeration are common, and many children test adults' patience by outbursts of wild activity and language.

Emotional Development

- Attains greater (if still sporadic) emotional equilibrium

- Acquires an increased ability to compromise

- Gains an increased sense of emotional cause–effect relationships (such as "If you hit your sister, she'll be angry and might hit back.")

Verbal Development

- Tells elaborate stories, both realistic and fanciful

- Demands detailed answers to questions

- Exhibits a tendency toward self-praise ("I'm smart," "I have good ideas," etc.)

- Understands the concept of opposites

- Rhymes words

- Uses articles ("a" and "the") consistently

- Can define some words

- Bosses and criticizes others

- Elicits attention of adults

- Hesitates to admit inability

Appropriate Behavior

- Manifests growing independence concerning attire, diet, play, and routines

- Starts to show more autonomy in doing chores and homework

- Shows greater interactivity in play with others

- Tests limits with backtalk

- Experiments (sometimes) with the truth through "white lies" and tall tales

AGES FIVE TO SIX

By age five, the child probably "settles down" to some degree. She can be conformist in attitude and eager to please her parents and other adults. She is capable of many activities but probably more conservative in attitude and behavior than she was at four years old. Then, by the time of the child's sixth birthday, the situation may grow more complicated: while generally cooperative, enthusiastic, and warm, the six-year-old can be impatient, demanding, and difficult.

Emotional Development

- Starts to identify with the same-sex parent in learning about gender roles and relationships

- Imitates and mirrors others through role-modeling

- Feels a great need to be cherished for intrinsic worth, not just accomplishments

- Continues to have an egocentric, self-absorbed worldview

- Manifests a worldview that's a mixture of fantasy and reality

- Struggles with the complexity of information and issues

- May continue to struggle to distinguish between fantasy and reality

Verbal Development

- Can tell a long story accurately

- "Embroiders" stories to make them more fantastic

- Is capable of politeness and tact in speech

- Asks many questions about how things work, what things are for, and what words mean

Appropriate Behavior

- Engages in a wider social circle

- Shows more industry and autonomy in doing homework, assignments, and chores

- "Tests the limits" with parents

- May show some inconsistency in following through, yet is eager to please

- Responds more consistently to setting of limits

AGES SEVEN TO TEN

During the three-year span between ages seven and ten, the child consolidates many skills but also acquires a host of new ones. These years are a time of less dramatic physical change than during preceding stages, but they are revolutionary in another way, because children start to focus less totally on their own perceptions and begin to perceive and learn about the complex world around them.

Emotional Development

- Manifests increased self-confidence and self-worth

- Starts to focus on the peer group as central to the child's social experience

- Develops more resourcefulness, greater self-reliance, and more self-awareness

- Manifests an increasing ability to think critically about ethical issues such as integrity, character, and individual versus community rights

- Manifests a tendency toward stereotypic gender behavior

Verbal Development

- Acquires a significantly larger vocabulary

- Perfects many aspects of spoken language

- Masters many skills relevant to reading and writing

Appropriate Behavior

- Advances in many aspects of self-care

- Focuses more consistently on social relationships outside the family

- Experiments with "lippy" language and defiant attitudes

- Tolerates more responsibility in doing chores

THE PRETEEN YEARS

The years preceding the onset of puberty have tended to be a period of relative stability in a child's overall development. By age ten, the child has undergone many of the striking changes that take place during middle childhood, yet she hasn't yet experienced the confusion and transformation of adolescence. This period of stability continues to occur for most children. However, physiological and cultural changes are now shortening, even disrupting, what used to be a predictable calm before the storm. The average onset of puberty occurs earlier and earlier, and social pressures prompt children to imitate adolescent values, attitudes, and behavior.

Emotional Development

- Shows a heightened sensitivity to any kind of disapproval or rejection from the peer group

- Manifests a tendency toward black-and-white ethical thinking

- Tends to be judgmental and stereotypic in ethical issues

Verbal Development

- Grows increasingly sophisticated in use of language

- Acquires slang vocabulary and usage as part of peer-group bonding

- Experiments with linguistic taboos (profanity, insults, etc.)

Appropriate Behavior

- Starts to shift attention from the parent–child bond to the peer group

- Experiments more widely with social roles and attitudes

- May test limits energetically

- Experiments with language, attire, and hairstyles as expressions of identity

- Values (despite many behaviors and statements) bonds with parents and other family members

THE TEEN YEARS

Adolesence is transformative in every possible way. Physically, emotionally, and socially, children undergo changes that challenge their own patience and understanding as well as that of almost everyone around them. From the standpoint of mothers and fathers, this phase is usually more difficult than any other during the parenting years, and it provides the most complex dilemmas in making decisions about parental authority.

Emotional Development

- Shows great emotional volatility supercharged by hormonal changes

- Focuses on (or grows obsessed with) the peer group

- Explores love relationships outside the family

- May grow more nuanced in ethical thinking, though also inclined toward passionate statements of belief

- May be judgmental about ethical issues

Verbal Development

- Continues to grow more sophisticated in use of language

- Experiments further with slang vocabulary as part of peer-group bonding

- Experiments further with linguistic taboos (profanity, insults, etc.)

Appropriate Behavior

- Moves closer toward adult autonomy in activities and choices

- Experiments more widely with social roles and attitudes

- Grows more proficient in assessing cause–effect relationships

- Grows more proficient in longer term planning of activities

Appendix B

RESOURCE GUIDE

A common source of frustration throughout the parenting years is a feeling that you have to solve your problems on your own. The isolation this creates and the resulting sense of fatigue can demoralize even the most committed, competent parents. Dealing with issues of parental authority can be especially daunting. Fortunately, many resources exist to help you with the problems you face. Sometimes what you need is a specific answer to a specific question; at other times, it's a general sense of community with other parents. Finding resources takes some effort, but in many ways the task of finding information about parenthood is getting easier, not harder.

This section of *Who's the Boss?* therefore provides a sampling of resources that may be useful throughout the parenting years. I've categorized the listings carefully; however, some organizations' services overlap, so please check the whole list to make sure you aren't missing a good source of help. Also, note that some resources are clearinghouses or umbrella organizations, not direct providers of services. They can inform you of specific agencies or groups that offer resources in your community.

This guide contains three sections:

- Organizations and Associations
- Online Information
- Further Reading

ORGANIZATIONS AND ASSOCIATIONS

A large number of organizations can provide useful information on specific issues and problems that may arise during the parenting years. These organizations usually focus on a problem or cluster of problems rather than more general tasks of parenthood. Here's a sampling, presented in alphabetical order by general category:

Child Abuse

American Professional Society on the Abuse of Children
407 S. Dearborn Street, Suite 1300
Chicago, IL 60605-1111
(312)554-0166

National Committee for the Prevention of Child Abuse
P.O. Box 2866
Chicago, IL 60690
(312)663-3520

Childcare

National Association of Child Care Resource and Referral
Agencies
1319 F Street, N.W., Suite 810
Washington, DC 20004-1106
(202)393-5501

National Child Care Association
1029 Railroad Street, N.W.
Conyers, GA 30207-5275
(800)543-7161

Child Safety

National Child Passenger Safety Association
P.O. Box 841
Ardmore, PA 19003
(215)525-4610

National SAFE KIDS Campaign
111 Michigan Avenue, N.W.
Washington, DC 20010-2970
(202)939-4993

Educational Issues

Work and Family Life
Bank Street College
6211 West Howard Street
Chicago, IL 60648
(800)727-7243

Exceptional Children

Association for Children and Adults with Learning Disabilities
4156 Library Road
Pittsburgh, PA 15234
(412)341-8077

Council for Exceptional Children
1920 Association Drive
Reston, VA 22091-1589
(703)620-3660

Dyslexia Research Foundation
600 Northern Boulevard
Great Neck, NY 11021
(516)482-2888

National Center for Learning Disabilities, Inc.
99 Park Avenue, 6th Floor
New York, NY 10016
(212)687-7211

Food and Nutrition

Bulimia Anorexia Self-Help, Inc.
522 North New Ballas Road
St. Louis, MO 63141
(314)567-4080

National Association for Anorexia Nervosa and Associated
Disorders
P.O. Box 7
Highland Park, IL 60035
(708)831-3438

Health Issues

American Academy of Pediatrics
141 Northwest Point Boulevard
P.O. Box 927
Elkgrove Village, IL 60009-0927
(847)228-5005 or (800)433-9016

Loss and Bereavement

Accord Aftercare Services
1930 Bishop Lane, Suite 947
Louisville, KY 40218
(800)346-3087

Center for Death Education and Research
Department of Sociology
University of Minnesota
909 Social Science Building
267 19th Avenue South
Minneapolis, MN 55455-0412

The Compassionate Friends
P.O. Box 3696
Oak Brook, IL 60522-3696
(708)990-0010

Marriage and Relationships

Academy of Family Mediators
4 Militia Drive
Lexington, MA 02173
(617)674-2663

American Association for Marriage and Family Therapy
1133 15th Street, N.W., Suite 300
Washington, DC 20005
(202)452-0109
Association for Marriage and Family Therapy
(800)374-2638

Media

Action for Children's Television (ACT)
10 University Road
Cambridge, MA 02138
(617)876-6620

Mental Health Issues

American Association of Psychiatric Services for Children
1200-C Scottsville Road
Rochester, NY 14624
(716)236-6910

Self-Help

National Self-Help Clearinghouse
Graduate School and University Center
City University of New York
25 West 42nd Street, Suite 620
New York, NY 10036

Single Parenthood

Parents Without Partners
401 North Michigan Avenue
Chicago, IL 60611-4267
(800)637-7974

Step-Parenthood

Step Family Association for America
(800)735-0329

Stress

Parental Stress Line
(800)632-8188

ONLINE INFORMATION

The Internet has increased your options for obtaining information on a
multitude of issues. That's the good news. The bad news is that the
sources of information change often and unpredictably. Although what
follows is a list of specific online resources for parents, keep in mind
that any list of resources will change over time. In addition, the quality
of what's available varies from genuinely useful to gimmicky and shallow. I've tried to assess these resources as fully as possible, but I can't
vouch for the availability or the content of any of the sites listed here.

Specific Web Sites Regarding Parenthood

Here's a selection of Web sites that focus on parenting issues. With
the exception of the first, most general heading—general parenting
issues—I've organized these sites alphabetically by category and
within each category.

General Parenting Issues

www.abcparenting.com
Essentially a search engine for Web sites on parenting issues: pregnancy, parenting, and family life.

www.familyeducation.com
Established by the Learning Network, this site provides educational
information resources.

www.parenthoodweb.com
A compendium of resources and articles covering many issues,
including pregnancy, children's products, and expert advice.

www.parent.net
Information for parents on a wide variety of topics.

www.parents.com
Parenting information from the publishers of *Parents, Child, Family
Circle,* and *McCall's* magazines.

www.parentsoup.com
A "parents-helping-parents" community in iVillage that offers
advice, interactive tools, and firsthand wisdom from real parents;
topics include infertility, illness, and bereavement.

www.wholefamily.com
Information, advice, and interactive resources on issues of marriage,
parenting, adolescents, and seniors.

Attachment and Bonding

www.attach-bond.com
A Web site intended to "help parents and professionals learn more
about attachment parenting . . . attachment disorder, bonding problems, adoption difficulties, attachment therapy," and other related
issues.

Computers and Internet Safety

www.safesurf.com
The Web site for a group that's working to create an Internet rating
standard for browsers.

www.thelist.com
A list of Internet Service Providers (ISPs)—online "gateways" to the
Internet.

www.worldvillage.com
"Family Friendly Internet"—a list of 300 educational and multi-
media software programs, games, and Web sites.

Divorce

www.divorceinfo.com
A detailed, text-intensive Web site designed to "help you survive your divorce."

www.divorcenet.com
An extensive Web site with state-by-state resource centers, interactive bulletin boards, a "reading room," and other resources regarding divorce issues.

Fathers

www.acfc.org
The Web site for the American Coalition for Fathers and Children, a national fathers'-rights advocacy group.

www.fathers4kids.org
Multinational resources provided by the National Fathers' Resource Center, a fathers'-rights advocacy group.

www.fathersworld.com
A virtual community for men interested in fathers' issues, including balancing work and family.

www.slowlane.com
"The online resource for stay-at-home dads and their families."

Health Issues

www.docguide.com
Medical news, literature, and alerts drawn from the Web's medical resources.

www.drs4kids.com/
A pediatrician's information on topics concerning infants, children, and adolescents.

www.healthtouch.com/level1/about.htm
Information on health, wellness, and illness.

www.kidshealth.org
Tips on keeping children healthy or helping them when they're
sick.

www.menninger.edu
An educational Web site sponsored by the Menninger Child &
Family Center with intent to spread useful information about psy-
chiatric issues regarding children.

Loss and Bereavement

www.growthhouse.org
Includes detailed information on family bereavement, helping children with illness and grief, the aftermath of miscarriage and still-
birth, and resources for the bereaved.

School and Related Issues

www.factmonster.com
Reference materials, "fun facts and features," and individualized
homework help for kids.

www.funbrain.com
One of the Internet's most frequently visited sites, featuring more
than fifty interactive learning games for kids, parents, and teachers.

www.infoplease.com
An online version of the *Information Please Almanacs.*

Teenagers

http://education.indiana.edu/cas/adol/adol.html
Online support for teenagers, parents, and counselors, with a guide
to various resources for teens.

www.react.com
A teen news, sports, and entertainment e-zine.

Women's Issues

www.aauw.org
Web site for the American Association of University Women, an advocacy group for women's and girls' issues in education.

www.academic.org
Information from the Women's College Coalition for parents interested in bolstering their daughters' education.

FURTHER READING

The most traditional source of information about parenting—other than talking with other parents—is reading. Books about parenthood have been part of American culture for about a hundred years, and the number and variety have increased almost exponentially since the publication of Benjamin Spock's *Baby and Child Care* in the 1950s. Any big American bookstore now contains hundreds of titles about parenting. The catch is finding the information you need. Here's a selection of classic and current books on parenthood that covers most of the topics discussed in this book.

Attachment and Bonding

Ainsworth, M. D. S., et al. *Patterns of Attachment: A Psychological Study of the Strange Situation.* Hillsdale, N.J.: Erlbaum, 1978.
Bowlby, John. *Attachment and Loss.* Vol. 1, *Attachment.* New York: Basic Books, 1969.
———. *Attachment and Loss.* Vol. 2, *Separation.* New York: Basic Books, 1973.

Klaus, Marshall, and Phyllis Klaus. *Parent-Infant Bonding*. St. Louis: Mosby, 1982.

Behavior

Ames, Louise Bates. *Your One-Year-Old*. New York: Delacorte Press, 1982.

———. *Your Two-Year-Old*. New York: Delacorte Press, 1982.

———. *Your Three-Year-Old*. New York: Delacorte Press, 1982.

———. *Your Four-Year-Old*. New York: Delacorte Press, 1982.

———. *Your Five-Year-Old*. New York: Delacorte Press, 1982.

———. *Your Six-Year-Old*. New York: Delacorte Press, 1982.

———. *Your Seven-Year-Old*. New York: Delacorte Press, 1982.

———. *Your Eight-Year-Old*. New York: Delacorte Press, 1982.

———. *Your Nine-Year-Old*. New York: Delacorte Press, 1982.

———. *Your Ten- to Fourteen-Year-Old*. New York: Delacorte Press, 1982.

Ames, Louise Bates, et al. *The Gesell Institute's Child from One to Six: Evaluating the Behavior of the Preschool Child*. New York: Harper & Row, 1979.

Brazelton, T. Berry. *Infants and Mothers*. New York: Delacorte Press/Lawrence, 1983.

———. *Touchpoints: The Essential Reference*. New York: Addison-Wesley, 1992.

Brazelton, T. Berry, M.D., and Bertrand G. Cramer. *The Earliest Relationship*. Reading, Mass.: Addison-Wesley, 1990.

Editors of *Parents* Magazine. *The Parents Answer Book: From Birth through Age Five*. Rev. ed. New York: Griffin, 2000.

Gesell, Arnold, et al. *The Child from Five to Ten*. New York: Harper & Row, 1977.

Gesell, Arnold, et al. *Youth: The Years from Ten to Sixteen*. New York: Harper & Row, 1977.

Greenspan, Stanley, and Nancy Thorndike Greenspan. *First Feelings*. New York: Viking, 1985.

Kagan, Jerome. *The Growth of the Child: Reflections on Human Development*. New York: W.W. Norton, 1978.

——. *The Nature of the Child*. New York: Basic Books, 1984.

Klaus, Marshall, and Phyllis Klaus. *The Amazing Newborn*. Reading, Mass.: Addison-Wesley, 1985.

Leach, Penelope. *Babyhood*. New York: Alfred A. Knopf, 1976.

——. *Your Baby and Child: From Birth to Age Five*. New York: Alfred A. Knopf, 1997.

——. *Your Growing Child: From Babyhood through Adolescence*. New York: Alfred A. Knopf, 1986.

Spock, Benjamin, and Steven J. Parker. *Dr. Spock's Baby and Child Care*. New York: Pocket Books, 1998.

Boys

Abbott, Franklin, ed. *Boyhood: Growing Up Male*. Freedom, Calif.: The Crossing Press, 1993.

Bassoff, Evelyn. *Between Mothers and Sons: The Making of Vital and Loving Men*. New York: Dutton, 1994.

Blankenhorn, David. *Fatherless in America*. New York: Basic Books, 1995.

Gurian, Michael. *A Fine Young Man: What Parents, Mentors and Educators Can Do to Shape Adolescent Boys into Exceptional Men*. New York: Tarcher/Putnam, 1997.

——. *The Wonder of Boys: What Parents, Mentors and Educators Can Do to Shape Boys into Exceptional Men*. New York: Tarcher/Putnam, 1997.

Miedzian, Myriam. *Boys Will Be Boys: Breaking the Link between Masculinity and Violence*. New York: Anchor, 1991.

Moore, Sheila, and Roon Frost. *The Little Boy Book*. New York: Ballantine, 1986.

Olsen, Paul. *Sons and Mothers*. New York: M. Evans, 1981.

Phillips, Angela. *The Trouble with Boys*. New York: Basic Books, 1994.

Pollack, William S. *Real Boys: Rescuing Our Sons from the Myths of Boyhood*. New York: Random House, 1998.

Child Development

Erickson, Erik. *Childhood and Society*. New York: W. W. Norton, 1950.

——. *Identity and the Life Cycle*. New York: International Universities Press, 1959.

Piaget, Jean. *The Construction of Reality in the Child*. New York: Basic Books, 1954.

——. *Play, Dream and Imitation in the Child*. New York: W. W. Norton, 1962.

——. *The Child's Construction of the World*. Totowa, N.J.: Littlefield Adams, 1967.

Winnicott, Donald Woods. *Collected Papers*. London: Tavistock, 1958.

Communication between Parent and Kids

Alkind, David. *Parenting Your Teenager*. New York: Ballantine, 1983.

Faber, Adele, and Elaine Mazlesch. *How to Listen So Kids Will Talk*. New York: Avon, 1982.

Fraiberg, Selma. *The Magic Years: Understanding and Handling the Problems of Early Childhood*. New York: Scribner, 1959.

Ginott, Haim G. *Between Parent and Child*. New York: MacMillan, 1965.

——. *Between Parent and Teenager*. New York: MacMillan, 1969.

Communication between Spouses

Tannen, Deborah. *You Just Don't Understand: Women and Men in Conversation*. New York: Ballantine, 1990.

Wallerstein, Judith. *The Good Marriage: How and Why Love Lasts*. New York: Houghton-Mifflin, 1995.

Conflicts and Discipline

Brazelton, T. Berry. *Touchpoints: The Essential Reference*. New York: Addison-Wesley, 1992.

Crary, Elizabeth. *Without Spanking or Spoiling*. Seattle: Parenting Press, 1979.

Coles, Robert. *The Moral Life of Children*. New York: Atlantic Monthly Press, 1986.

Dodson, Fitzhugh. *How to Discipline with Love: From Crib to College*. New York: New American Library, 1982.

Dreikurs, R. *Logical Consequences: A New Approach to Discipline*. New York: Dutton, 1990.

Faber, Adele, et al. *How to Talk So Kids Will Listen*. New York: Avon, 1991.

Fraiberg, Selma H. *The Magic Years: Understanding and Handling the Problems of Early Childhood*. New York: Scribner, 1959.

Ginott, Haim G. *Between Parent and Teenager*. New York: MacMillan, 1969.

Schulman, Michael, and Eva Mekler. *Bringing Up a Moral Child*. New York: Doubleday, 1994.

Scull, Charles. *Fathers, Sons and Daughters*. Los Angeles: Jeremy Tarcher, 1992.

Winnicott, D. W. *Thinking about Children*. New York: Perseus, 1998.

Wright, Robert. *The Moral Animal*. New York: Vintage, 1994.

Divorce

Blau, Melinda. *Families Apart: Ten Keys to Successful Co-Parenting*. New York: Putnam, 1993.

Blume, Judy. *It's Not the End of the World for Teens*. New York: Yearling, 1986.

Fassel, Diane. *Growing Up Divorced*. New York: Pocket Books, Simon & Schuster, 1991.

Gardner, Richard. *Boys and Girls Book about Divorce*. New York: Bantam Young Readers, 1985.

Kaufman, Taube S. *The Combined Family: A Guide to Creating Successful Step Relationships*. New York: Plenum, 1993.

Marguilis, Sam. *Getting Divorced without Ruining Your Life*. New York: Fireside, 1992.

Neuman, M. Gary. *Helping Your Kids Cope with Divorce: The Sandcastles Way*. New York: Times Books, 1998.

Wallerstein, Judith S., and Sandra Blakeslee. *Second Chances: Men, Women and Children a Decade after Divorce*. New York: Ticknor & Fields, 1989.

Energetic Children and Hyperactivity

Feingold, Ben. *Why Your Child Is Hyperactive*. New York: Random House, 1974.

Feingold, Ben, and Helene Feingold. *The Feingold Cookbook for Hyperactive Children*. New York: Random House, 1979.

Taylor, Eric, ed. *The Overactive Child*. London: McKeith, 1986.

Exceptional Kids

Doman, Glenn. *What to Do about Your Brain-Injured Child*. Garden City Park, N.Y.: Avery, 1994.

Featherstone, Helen. *A Difference in the Family: Life with a Disabled Child*. New York: Basic Books, 1980.

Greene, Lawrence. *Learning Disabilities and Your Child*. New York: Fawcett, 1987.

Kirk, Samuel A. *Educating Exceptional Children*. Boston: Houghton-Mifflin College, 1997.

Osman, Betty. *Learning Disabilities: A Family Affair*. New York: Random House, 1979.

Pernecke, Raegene, and Sara Schreiner. *Schooling for the Learning Disabled.* Glenview, Ill.: SMS Publishing, 1983.

Takacs, Carol A. *Enjoy Your Gifted Child.* Syracuse, N.Y.: Syracuse University Press, 1986.

Turecki, Stanley. *The Difficult Child.* New York: Bantam, 1985.

Turnbull, R., et al. *Disability and Family: A Guide for Decisions for Adulthood.* Baltimore: Paul H. Brookes, 1989.

Family Life

Jones, Charles, Lauren Temperman, and Suzanne Wilson. *The Futures of the Family.* Englewood Cliffs, N.J.: Prentice Hall/Simon & Schuster, 1995.

Satir, Virginia. *The New People Making.* Mountain View, Calif.: Science & Behavioral Books, 1988.

Spock, Benjamin. *Rebuilding American Family Values.* Chicago and New York: Contemporary Books, 1994.

Fathers

Brott, Armin A. *The New Father: A Dad's Guide to the Toddler Years.* New York: Abbeville Press, 1998.

Lamb, Michael, ed. *The Role of the Father in Child Development.* New York: John Wiley & Sons, 1976.

Louv, Richard. *Father Love.* New York: Pocket Books, 1993.

Osherson, Samuel. *Finding Our Fathers: The Unfinished Business of Manhood.* New York: The Free Press, 1986.

Pruett, Kyle. *The Nurturing Father.* New York: Warner Books, 1987.

Scull, Charles. *Fathers, Sons and Daughters.* Los Angeles: Jeremy Tarcher, 1992.

Secunda, Victoria. *Women and Their Fathers: The Sexual and Romantic Impact of the First Man in Your Life.* New York: Delta, 1992.

Sullivan, S. Adams. *The Father's Almanac.* New York: Doubleday, 1992.

Williams, Gene B. *The New Father's Panic Book: Everything a Dad Needs to Know to Welcome His Bundle of Joy*. New York: Avon, 1997.

Gender Bias

Katz, Montana. *The Gender Bias Prevention Book*. Northvale, N.J.: Jason Aronson, 1996.

Girls

American Association of University Women. *Shortchanging Girls, Shortchanging America: A Call to Action*. Washington, D.C.: American Association of University Women, 1991.

Apter, Terri. *Altered Loves: Mothers and Daughters during Adolescence*. New York: Fawcett Columbine, 1990.

Bassoff, Evelyn. *Between Mothers and Sons: The Making of Vital and Loving Men*. New York: Dutton, 1994.

Brown, L. M., and Gilligan, C. *Meeting at the Crossroads: Women's Psychology and Girls' Development*. New York: Ballantine, 1992.

Gilligan, Carol. *In a Different Voice: Sex Differences in the Expression of Moral Judgment*. Cambridge, Mass.: Harvard University Press, 1982.

Kaschak, Ellyn. *Engendered Lives: A New Psychology of Women's Experience*. New York: Basic Books, 1992.

Pipher, Mary. *Reviving Ophelia: Saving the Selves of Adolescent Girls*. New York: Grosset/Putnam, 1994.

Scull, Charles. *Fathers, Sons and Daughters*. Los Angeles: Jeremy Tarcher, 1992.

Wolf, Naomi. *The Beauty Myth: How Images of Beauty Are Used against Women*. New York: William Morrow, 1991.

Health

Kunz, J. R. M., and A. J. Finkel. *American Medical Association Family Medical Guide*. New York: Random House, 1987.

Leach, Penelope. *Babyhood*. New York: Alfred A. Knopf, 1976.

———. *Your Baby and Child: From Birth to Age Five*. New York: Alfred A. Knopf, 1997.

———. *Your Growing Child: From Babyhood through Adolescence*. New York: Alfred A. Knopf, 1986.

Lovejoy, F. H., and D. Estridge, eds. *The New Child Health Encyclopedia: The Complete Guide for Parents*. New York: Delacorte Press/Lawrence, 1987.

Neifert, Marianne. *Dr. Mom: A Guide to Baby and Child Care*. New York: Signet, 1986.

Samuels, Mike, and Nancy Samuels. *The Well Baby Book*. New York: Summit, 1979.

Sears, William, and Martha Sears. *The Baby Book: Everything You Need to Know about Your Baby from Birth to Age Two*. Boston: Little, Brown & Co., 1993.

Spock, Benjamin, and Steven J. Parker. *Dr. Spock's Baby and Child Care*. New York: Pocket Books, 1998.

Juggling Work and Life

Dappen, Andy. *Shattering the Two Income Myth*. Brier, Wash.: Brier Books, 1997.

Hochschild, Arlie. *The Second Shift*. New York: Avon, 1997.

———. *The Time Bind: When Work Becomes Home and Home Becomes Work*. New York: Owl Books, 1998.

Houston, Victoria. *Making It Work*. Chicago and New York: Contemporary Books, 1990.

Middleman-Bowfin, Gene. *Mothers Who Work: Strategies for Coping*. New York: Ballantine, 1983.

Oldes, Sally. *The Working Parents' Survival Guide*. New York: Bantam, 1983.

Shreaves, Anita. *Remaking Motherhood*. New York: Ballantine, 1988.

Let Your Kid Be a Kid

Alkind, David. *The Hurried Child: Growing Up Too Fast Too Soon*. New York: Perseus, 1989.

Chopra, Deepak. *The Seven Spiritual Laws for Parents: Guiding Your Children to Success and Fulfillment*. New York: Crown, 1997.

Hendrix, Harvel. *Giving the Love That Heals*. New York: Pocket Books, 1997.

Loss

Bowlby, John. *Attachment and Loss. Vol. 3, Loss*. New York: Basic Books, 1980.

Edelman, Hope. *Motherless Daughters: The Legacy of Loss*. Reading, Mass.: Addison-Wesley, 1994.

Grollman, Earl. *Explaining Death to Children*. Boston: Beacon Press, 1964.

————. *Living When a Loved One Has Died*. Boston: Beacon Press, 1974.

Krementz, Jill. *How It Feels When a Parent Dies*. New York: Alfred A. Knopf, 1981.

Kübler-Ross, Elisabeth. *On Death and Dying*. New York: MacMillan, 1969.

LeShan, Eda. *Learning to Say Good-by*. New York: Avon, 1976.

Myers, Edward. *When Parents Die: A Guide for Adults*. New York: Penguin, 1997.

Raphael, Beverley. *The Anatomy of Bereavement*. New York: Basic Books, 1983.

The Media

Carlson, Page, and Diane Levin. *Who's Calling the Shots?—How to Respond Effectively to Children's Fascination with War Play and War Toys.* Santa Cruz, Calif.: New Society, 1990.

deGaetono, Gloria. *Television and the Lives of Our Children.* Redmond, Wash.: Train of Thought, 1993.

Mander, Jerry. *Four Arguments for the Elimination of Television.* New York: Quill, 1978.

McKibben, Bill. *The Age of Missing Information.* New York: Plume, 1993.

Winn, Marie. *The Plug-In Drug: Television, Children, and the Family.* New York: Viking, 1985.

Mothers

Bassoff, Evelyn. *Between Mothers and Sons: The Making of Vital and Loving Men.* New York: Dutton, 1994.

Bernard, Jessie. *The Future of Motherhood.* New York: Penguin, 1974.

Chodorow, Nancy. *The Reproduction of Mothering.* Berkeley: University of California Press, 1978.

Faludi, Susan. *Backlash: The Undeclared War against American Women.* New York: Crown, 1991.

Kelly, Marguerite, et al. *The Mother's Almanac.* New York: Doubleday, 1975.

Lerner, Harriet. *The Dance of Anger.* New York: Harper & Row, 1985.

———. *The Dance of Intimacy.* New York: Harper & Row, 1989.

———. *The Mother Dance: How Children Change Your Life.* New York: HarperCollins, 1998.

Towle, Alexandra. *Mothers.* New York: Simon & Schuster, 1998.

Parenting Styles

Brazelton, T. Berry. *On Becoming a Family.* New York: Delacorte Press/Seymour Lawrence, 1981.

Galinsky, Ellen. *The Six Stages of Parenthood.* Reading, Mass.: Addison-Wesley, 1987.

Satir, Virginia. *The New People Making.* Mountain View, Calif.: Science & Behavior Books, 1988.

Parents as Partners

Galinsky, Ellen. *The Six Stages of Parenthood.* New York: Addison-Wesley, 1987.

Samalin, Nancy. *Love and Anger: The Parental Dilemma.* New York: Penguin, 1992.

———. *Loving Your Child Is Not Enough.* New York: Penguin, 1989.

Satir, Virginia. *The New People Making.* Mountain View, Calif.: Science & Behavior Books, 1988.

Steinberg, Lawrence. *Crossing Paths: How Your Child's Adolescence Triggers Your Own Crises.* New York: Simon & Schuster, 1994.

Play and Learning

Axline, Virginia. *Play Therapy.* New York: Ballantine, 1974.

Bruner, Jerome, A. Jolly, and K. Sylva. *Play: Its Role in Development.* New York: Penguin, 1946.

Cherry, Claire. *Creative Art for the Developing Child.* Belmont, Calif.: Fearon, 1990.

Erikson, Erik. *Childhood in Society.* New York: W. W. Norton, 1964.

Lloyd, Janice, and Jean Marzello. *Learning through Play.* New York: Harper-Colophon, 1972.

School Issues

Alkind, David. *Miseducation: Preschoolers at Risk.* New York: Alfred A. Knopf, 1988.

Self-Esteem

Briggs, Dorothy. *Your Child's Self-Esteem.* New York: Doubleday, 1975.

Clarke, Jean Illsley. *Self-Esteem: A Family Affair.* San Francisco: Harper & Row, 1978.

Glenn, H. Steven, and Jane Nelsen. *Raising Self-Reliant Children.* Rocklin, Calif.: Prima, 1989.

Sexuality

Bourgeois, Paulette, et al. *Changes in You and Me: A Book about Puberty.* New York: Andrews & McMeel, 1994.

Coles, Robert, and Geoffrey Stokes. *Sex and the American Teenager.* New York: Harper-Colophon, 1985.

Elkind, David. *Parenting Your Teenager.* New York: Ballantine, 1993.

Gravelle, Karen. *The Period Book: Everything You Don't Want to Ask (But Need to Know).* New York: Walker & Co., 1996.

Harris, Robie H. *It's Perfectly Normal: Changing Bodies, Growing Up, Sex, and Sexual Health.* Cambridge, Mass.: Candlewick Press, 1994.

Madaras, Lynda. *My Body, My Self for Boys.* New York: New Market Press, 1995.

——. *What's Happening to My Body? A Book for Boys.* New York: New Market Press, 1987.

——. *What's Happening to My Body? A Book for Girls.* New York: New Market Press, 1987.

Sibling Rivalry

Bank, Stephen P., and Michael D. Kahn. *The Sibling Bond*. New York: Basic Books, 1982.

Cassill, Kay. *Twins: Nature's Amazing Mystery*. New York: Atheneum, 1982.

Dunn, Judy, and Robert Plomin. *Separate Lives: Why Siblings Are So Different*. New York: Basic Books, 1990.

Faber, Adele, and Elaine Mazlesch. *How to Listen So Kids Will Talk*. New York: Avon, 1982.

Leman, Kevin. *The Birth Order Book*. New York: Dell, 1985.

————. *Growing Up First Born*. New York: Dell, 1989.

Greer, Jane, with Edward Myers. *Adult Sibling Rivalry*. New York: Fawcett Crest, 1992.

Single Parenthood

Wayman, Anne. *Successful Single Parenting*. Deephaven, Minn.: Meadowbrook, 1987.

Step-Parents

Burns, Cherie. *Stepmotherhood: How to Survive without Feeling Frustrated, Left Out, or Wicked*. New York: Times Books, 1985.

Diamond, Susan. *Helping Children of Divorce*. New York: Schocken, 1985.

Eckler, James. *Step-by-Stepparenting*. While Hall, Va.: Betterway, 1988.

Kaufman, Taube S. *The Combined Family: A Guide to Creating Successful Step-Relationships*. New York: Plenum Press, 1993.

Nelsen, Jane, Cheryl Irwin, and H. Stephen Glenn. *Positive Discipline for Blended Families*. Rocklin, Calif.: Prima, 1997.

Rosen, Mark Bruce. *Stepfathering: Stepfathers' Advice on Creating a New Family*. New York: Ballantine, 1987.

Stress

Arent, Ruth. *Stress and Your Child*. Englewood Cliffs, N.J.: Prentice-Hall, 1984.

Carlson, Richard. *Don't Sweat the Small Stuff*. New York: Hyperion, 1997.

Chopra, Deepak. *The Seven Spiritual Laws for Parents: Guiding Your Children to Success and Fulfillment*. New York: Crown, 1997.

Covey, Stephen. *The Seven Habits of Highly Effective People*. New York: Fireside, Simon & Schuster, 1989.

Ginsberg, Susan. *Family Wisdom*. New York: Columbia University Press, 1996.

Houston, Victoria. *Making It Work*. Chicago and New York: Contemporary Books, 1990.

Pillsbury, Linda. *Survival Tips for Working Moms*. Los Angeles: Perspective, 1994.

Saltzman, Amy. *Downshifting*. New York: HarperCollins, 1991.

The Teen Years

Alkind, David. *All Grown Up and No Place to Go: Teenagers in Crisis*. New York: Perseus, 1997.

Ginott, Haim G. *Between Parent and Teenager*. New York: MacMillan, 1969.

Kaman, Ben. *Raising a Thoughtful Teenager*. New York: Penguin, 1996.

Pipher, Mary. *Reviving Ophelia: Saving the Selves of Adolescent Girls*. New York: Grosset/Putnam, 1994.

Powell, Douglas H. *Teenagers: When to Worry and What to Do—A Guide for Parents*. New York: Doubleday, 1987.

Wexler, David B. *The Adolescent Self*. New York: W.W. Norton, 1991.

Twenty-First Century Parenting

Chopra, Depak. *The Seven Spiritual Laws of Success: A Practical Guide to the Fulfillment of Your Dreams*. New York: New World Library, 1994.

Horney, Karen. *The Neurotic Personality of Our Time*. New York: W. W. Norton, 1994.

Jones, Charles, Lorne Tepperman, and Suzanna Wilson. *The Futures of the Family*. New York: Prentice-Hall, Simon & Schuster, 1995.

Pipher, Mary. *The Shelter of Each Other: Rebuilding Our Families*. New York: Grosset/Putnam, 1996.

Rank, Mark Robert, and Edward L. Kain. *Diversity and Change in Families: Patterns, Prospects and Policies*. New York: Prentice-Hall, 1995.

Wright-Edelman, Marion. *The Measure of Our Success: A Letter to My Children and Yours*. New York: HarperCollins, 1993.

Work-to-Home Transitions

Brazelton, T. Berry. *Working and Caring*. Reading, Mass.: Addison-Wesley, 1985.

Hewlitt, Sylvia Anne. *When the Bough Breaks: The Cost of Neglecting Our Children*. New York: Basic Books, 1991.

Hochschild, Arlie. *The Time Bind: When Work Becomes Home and Home Becomes Work*. New York: Owl Books, 1998.

Hochschild, Arlie, with Anne Machung. *The Second Shift: Working Parents and the Revolution at Home*. New York: Viking Penguin, 1989.

Notes

INTRODUCTION

Page 6: "Do Kids Have Too Much Power?" *Time*, 6 August 2001, 42–46.

Page 6: Jacob Azerrad, "Why Our Kids Are Out of Control," *Psychology Today*, October 2001, 43.

CHAPTER ONE: THE GROWING DILEMMA OF PARENTAL AUTHORITY

Page 16: Laura Schlessinger, "Parents' Neglect Leaves Too Many Kids out on a Limb," *Jewish World Review*, 12 May 2000; [http://www.jewishworldreview.com/dr/laura051200.asp].

Page 23: Ellen Galinsky, *The Six Stages of Parenthood* (Reading, Mass.: Addison-Wesley, 1987), 135.

Chapter Two: How Parenting Style Influences Authority

Page 28: Paul Veyne, ed., *From Pagan Rome to Byzantium*, vol. 1 of *A History of Private Life*, eds. Philippe Ariès and Georges Duby (Cambridge, Mass.: Belknap Press of Harvard University Press, 1987), 16–17.

Page 28: Roger Chartier, ed., *Passions of the Renaissance*, vol. 3 of *A History of Private Life*, eds. Philippe Ariès and Georges Duby (Cambridge, Mass.: Belknap Press of Harvard University Press, 1989), 607.

Pages 28–29: Michelle Perrot, ed., *From the Fires of Revolution to the Great War*, vol. 4 of *A History of Private Life*, eds. Philippe Ariès and Georges Duby (Cambridge, Mass.: Belknap Press of Harvard University Press, 1990), 167–168, 208, 211.

Page 30: Clifford Geertz, "The Visit," *The New York Review of Books*, 48, no. 16 (18 October 2001), 27–30.

Page 30: John B. Watson, *Psychological Care of Infant and Child* (New York: W. W. Norton, 1928).

Page 30: Benjamin Spock, *Common Sense Book of Baby and Child Care* (New York: Pocket Books, 1945).

Page 31: Fitzhugh Dodson, *How to Discipline with Love: From Crib to College* (New York: Rawson, 1977).

Chapter Three: Discipline and Conflicts

Page 76: Selma H. Fraiberg, *The Magic Years: Understanding and Handling the Problems of Early Childhood* (New York: Fireside, 1997).

Pages 76–77: Benjamin Spock, *Dr. Spock's Baby and Child Care*, 6th ed. (New York: Simon & Schuster, 1992).

CHAPTER FOUR: THE INFLUENCES
OF TEMPERAMENT AND GENDER

Pages 81–82: Stella Chess, Alexander Thomas, and Herbert G. Birch, quoted in Galinsky, *The Six Stages of Parenthood*, 67–68.

Pages 82–83: Galinsky, *The Six Stages of Parenthood*, 69.

Page 89: Susan Gilbert, *A Field Guide to Boys and Girls* (New York: HarperCollins, 2000).

CHAPTER TEN: COPING WITH THE
SIDE EFFECTS OF DIVORCE

Page 187: Judith S. Wallerstein and Sandra Blakeslee (contributor), *Second Chances: Men, Women, and Children a Decade After Divorce* (New York: Hyperion, 2000), 186–194.

CONCLUSION: THE COMPASS OF PARENTAL AUTHORITY

Page 221: D. W. Winnicott, "Transitional Objects and Phenomena," in *Collected Papers* (London: Tavistock, 1958), 234–238.

Pages 223–224: Galinsky, *The Six Stages of Parenthood*, 120–121.

Index

Abusive language of children, 155
"Acting out" as positive event, 52
"Affluenza" issue, 19–20
Age-appropriate
    child development, 225–37
    civility, 163
    conflict, 68–69
    consequences, 57, 59
    limit setting, 18, 61, 63–64, 120
    media, 211
    problem-solving, 43–44, 56
    responsibilities, values, 116
    rule setting, 44
*Alexander and the Terrible, Horrible, No
    Good, Very Bad Day* (Viorst), 53–54
Authoritarian parenting style, 27–29, 31,
    34, 47
Authority. *See* Parental authority
Autonomy for teenagers, 63
Awareness of communication, 129–30
Azerrad, Jacob, 6

Baby Boomer narcissism, 14
Baby-sitters (older children as), 179
"Bail-out" time, 46

Balance, 23, 147, 167–68, 188
Battles, choosing, 66, 69–71, 125
Behavior differences from gender, 86–87
Behaviorism school, 30
Bennett, William, 160
Birch, Herbert G., 81
Brain gender differences, 87–88
Brooks, David, 160

Categorical statements, 59, 72–73
Cause-effect relationships, 56–57
Chess, Stella, 81
Childcare from media, 209–10
Child development, 15, 17–18, 225–37.
    See also Age-appropriate
*Children Are People, and Ideal Parents Are
    Comrades* (Post), 30
Choosing battles, 66, 69–71, 125
Civility, 152–69
    abusive language of children, 155
    age-appropriate guidelines, 163
    balance for, 167–68
    consideration, learning early, 162
    culture of America impact, 159–61
    delay gratification impact, 155

Civility (*cont.*)
    demands vs. requests by children, 155
    etiquette vs., 162
    flexible parenting style and, 163
    fostering civility, 161–68
    incivility, origins of, 156–61
    media impact, 160, 161
    modeling civility, 159, 163–64
    need for, 120–21
    overindulgence of children, 18, 157
    overreactions of children, 155
    parental excesses impact, 159
    parentifying children, 157–58
    preteenagers and, 166
    public property, damaging, 155
    punishing misbehavior, 166–67
    restaurants, 152–54
    rewarding good behavior, 166–67
    social coarseness, 159–61
    standards for, 164–65
    teenagers and, 166
    tolerating incivility, 156–57
*Common Sense Book of Baby and Child
    Care* (Spock), 30
Common sense (lack of), 17–18
Communication between parents,
    122–28
    battles, choosing, 125
    children-related issues, 126–27
    content issues, tackling, 126–27
    divorce and, 183, 194–95, 196
    do's and don'ts for, 127–28
    fighting fairly, 124–25
    frustration sources, identifying, 124
    leveling with one another, 125
    modeling healthy relationships, 126
    problem-solving and children, 125
    respecting each other and, 123
    time for couples, 126
    See also Gender; Parenting style;
        Temperament; Values
Communication with children, 129–35
    actions of parents and, 110–11
    awareness of communication, 129–30
    between children, 134–35
    clarifying statements, asking, 132
    disparity between parents, 111
    empathizing with children, 133–34

    feelings of children, validating, 132,
        133–34
    flexible parenting style for, 135
    goals, setting realistic, 134
    "I"-statements for, 57, 132–33
    listening, 41–42, 117, 132
    negotiating, 132
    overgeneralizing, avoiding, 130
    paraphrasing, 132
    problem, focusing on, 131
    steps for good communication,
        131–32
    style of communication (parental),
        111, 130
    teenagers and communication,
        130–31
    See also Values
Compass, parental authority as, 217–18
Computer games. *See* Media influence
Conflict, 66–76
    age-appropriate choices, 68–69
    battles, choosing, 69–71
    categorical statements, 59, 72–73
    control (sense of) for children, 70
    cooperation, stressing, 70
    empathy, expressing, 68, 71–72
    expectations of parents, 74–75
    feelings of children, validating, 66–68,
        74
    frustration venting, 54, 74
    independence of children, 75
    judging children, 65, 67–68, 85
    mirroring emotions of children,
        66–67
    modeling appropriate behavior, 72
    negotiation, stressing, 70
    reactions (parental), sources, 73
    root causes for, 68
    self-respect of children, 75–76
    stress in children and, 73–76
    "winning," letting children, 70
    See also Discipline
Consequences, age-appropriate, 57, 64
Consideration, learning early, 162
Consumerism (compulsive), 214
Control (sense of) for children, 53, 70
Corpus callosum, 87–88
Culture issue, 20–21, 29–31, 87, 159–61

Delay gratification, 115, 155
Delegation and Superparent, 149
Demands vs. requests by children, 155
Depression from coping with past,
    107–8
Development of children. See Age-
    appropriate; Child development
Discipline, 48–66
    "acting out" as positive event, 52
    battles, choosing, 66
    do's and don'ts of, 64–66
    education from, 76–77
    feelings expression of children, 43, 56,
        62, 65
    issue behind misbehavior, 51–52
    judging children, 65, 67–68
    modeling, 65
    negotiation for, 65
    overreacting, avoiding, 51–52
    overscheduling children and, 65
    past influence on, 98
    positive reinforcement for, 44–45, 65
    present focus for, 64
    punishment and, 65
    rules, reasonable for, 65
    self-control for, 65, 113
    self-discipline from, 50
    standards and, 65
    See also Conflict; Discipline for child
        developmental stages
Discipline for child developmental stages,
    52–64
    background of limits, 64
    categorical statements, 59, 72–73
    cause-effect relationships, 56–57
    consequences, 57, 59, 64
    developmental issues, 60–61
    feelings expression, 54, 56, 62, 65
    frustration venting, 54, 74
    "I"-statements, 57
    lecturing, 57–58, 65, 120
    limit setting, 18, 61, 63–64, 120
    paraphrasing emotions, 56
    preschoolers, 55–59
    preventive vs. reactive attention, 61
    school-age children, 60–62
    stories for guiding toddlers, 53–54
    teenagers, 62–64

time-outs, 45, 58–59
    toddlers, 53–54
Disengaged parenting style, 38–39
Disneyland Dad/Mom syndrome, 196
Disorder, tolerating, 148–49
Divorce, 181–201
    balance and, 188
    children, separating from, 188–89
    communication between parents, 183,
        194–95, 196
    criticizing ex, 188, 189, 195, 198
    crossfire and children, 189, 190–91
    details, avoiding, 188, 199
    Disneyland Dad/Mom syndrome, 196
    expectations of parents, 196
    home life stability, 189–90
    manipulation by children, 192–97
    material goods as affection, 197
    messages (mixed), 192
    overview, 22
    parentification from, 186, 198–99
    responses to, 185–87
    responsibility for divorce, 191–92
    spousification, avoiding, 197–200
Dodson, Fitzhugh, 31
"Do Kids Have Too Much Power?," 6

Education from discipline, 76–77
Emotional gender differences, 88
Emotional literacy and gender, 94–95
Empathy for children, 42, 68, 71–72,
    133–34
Endocrine system gender differences, 87
Etiquette vs. civility, 162
Example setting for values, 119–20. See
    also Modeling appropriate behavior
Expectations of parents
    conflict, 74–75
    divorce and, 196
    gender of children, 89–90
    latchkey dilemma, 178–79
    past influence on, 98
    Superparent syndrome, 145–46
Experimentation of children, 92–93

Family communication. See
    Communication between parents;
    Communication with children; Values

FamilyEducation.com, 6
Family of origin, 33, 97–98
Family-related pastimes vs. media, 214
Farge, Arlette, 28
Father Knows Best parenting, 16, 35–36
Fathers and parenting, 27–29, 147–48
Feelings of children, validating
    communication, 132, 133–34
    conflict, 66–68, 74
    discipline, 54, 56, 62, 65
Field Guide to Boys and Girls, A
    (Gilbert), 89
Fighting fairly, 124–25
Flexible parenting style, 33–35, 39–41,
    46–47, 135, 163
Fraiberg, Selma, 76
Free Willy, 208
Friends of children and media, 211–12
Frustration of Superparent, 137
Frustration venting by children, 54, 74

Galinsky, Ellen, 23, 82–83, 223–24
Gender, 86–95
    behavior differences from, 86–87
    bias, risks of, 89–94
    brain structure differences, 87–88
    corpus callosum differences, 87–88
    cultural prejudices about, 87
    emotional differences, 88
    emotional literacy importance, 94–95
    endocrine system differences, 87
    expectations of parents and, 89–90
    experimentation of children, 92–93
    hormonal differences, 87, 88
    innate differences, 85, 87–88
    maturity differences, 88
    Nature vs. Nurture, 80, 82, 89
    parental values, examining, 91
    physiological differences, 88
    resiliency differences, 88
    serotonin differences, 88
    social issues and, 88
    stereotypes, dangers of, 89–94
    values of parents, examining, 91
    See also Temperament
Gesell, Arnold, 30
Gilbert, Susan, 89
Goals, parenting. *See* Parenting style goals

"Good-enough mother," 221
Great Panda Adventure, The, 208
Guidance from discipline, 76–77
Guilt, 139–43
    boundary maintenance and, 140
    control vs. out-of-control, 141
    disengaging from, 141–43
    disruptions from, 139–40
    limits of, 140
    misdirected efforts signal, 139
    perfectionism from, 144
    pluses and minuses, weighing,
        141–42
    prioritization and, 142–43
    schedule simplification, 143
    state of mind, changing, 142
    value teaching selective use of, 115
    See also Superparent syndrome

Healing wounds of past, 108–9
Home Alone, 207
Home stability after divorce, 189–90
Hormonal gender differences, 87, 88
Housekeepers (children as), 179

Ilg, Frances, 30
Imperfections, accepting, 145–46, 221
Imus, Don, 161
Incivility, origins of, 156–61
Independence of children, 46, 75
Individuality of children, 79–81, 221–22
Infant and Child in the Culture of Today
    (Gesell and Ilg), 30
Inflexible parenting style, 16, 35–36
Innate gender differences, 85, 87–88
Instinctual vs. learning parenting, 219
Internet, 21. *See also* Media influence
"I"-statements, 57, 132–33

Journaling (coping method), 104–5
Judging children, 65, 67–68, 85

King of the Castle Syndrome, 178

Latchkey dilemma, 169–80
    baby-sitters (children as), 179
    backup help, arranging for, 175–76
    expectation clarification, 178–79

housekeepers (children as), 179
King of the Castle Syndrome, 178
off-site hanging out, 179
parentification from, 177–80
psychological problems of, 174
rule clarification for, 176–77
Safe House-type programs, 176
single parents and, 180
stress to children of, 170–71, 172
time alone (children's), 175
time away from home (parent's), 178
Learning vs. instinctual parenting, 219
Lecturing, avoiding, 57–58, 65, 120
Letter writing (coping method), 106
Limbaugh, Rush, 161
Limit setting, 18, 61, 63–64, 120
Listening to children, 41–42, 117, 132

*Magic Years: Understanding and
    Handling the Problems of Early
    Childhood* (Fraiberg), 76
Malcolm in the Middle, 160, 207
Manipulating children, 192–97
Marriage, making time for, 149–50
Martin-Fugier, Anne, 28–29
Mass media. *See* Media influence
Maturity gender differences, 88
Media influence, 202–16
    age-appropriateness of media, 211
    alternatives to media, 213–15
    childcare from media, 209–10
    civility and, 160, 161
    consumerism (compulsive), 214
    consumption of media (process), 208–9
    family-related pastimes vs., 214
    fantasy worlds vs., 204–5
    limiting, 210–15
    negative messages from, 206–8
    overscheduled children and, 213–14
    parental authority and, 21
    passive vs. active participation, 205,
        208, 209
    world, disengaging from, 205, 208
Medical Era of parenting style, 30
Mirroring emotions of children, 66–67
Modeling appropriate behavior
    civility, 159, 163–64
    communication, 126

conflict, 72
discipline, 65
values, 118
Movies/music. *See* Media influence

Nature vs. Nurture, 80, 82, 89
Needs of children, changing, 220–21
Negative messages from media, 206–8
Negotiation, 41, 65, 70, 117–18, 132
Non-Western cultures, parenting, 29

Overgeneralizing, avoiding, 130
Overindulgence of children, 18, 157
Overintellectualization issue, 17
Overreactions of children, 155
Overreactions of parents, 51–52
Overscheduled children, 65, 213–14

Paraphrasing, 56, 132
Parental authority, 217–24
    challenges of, 219–20
    change, being prepared to, 222–23
    compass for children, 217–18
    early establishment of, 219
    "good-enough mother," 221
    imperfections, accepting, 145–46, 221
    individuality of children, 79–81,
        221–22
    learning vs. instinctual parenting, 219
    needs of children, changing, 220–21
    resources for, 239–64
    responsibility for parenting, 223–24
    See also Civility; Communication;
        Conflict; Discipline; Divorce;
        Gender; Latchkey dilemma;
        Media influence; Parental
        authority dilemma; Parenting
        style; Past influences;
        Superparent syndrome;
        Temperament; Values
Parental authority dilemma, 1–23
    "affluenza" issue, 19–20
    Baby Boomer narcissism impact, 14
    balance of authority, 23
    child development and, 15, 17–18
    common sense (lack of) impact,
        17–18
    crisis of, 3–6

Parental authority dilemma (*cont.*)
  cultural issues, 20–21
  Father Knows Best, 16, 35–36
  importance of authority, 11–13
  limit setting, 18, 61, 63–64, 120
  misbehavior, learning, 10
  origins of, 13–22
  overindulgence issue, 18, 157
  overintellectualization issue, 17
  perfectionism issue, 20, 143–45
  permissive parenting, 16–17, 31,
    36–38, 47
  relinquishing authority, 9–11
  role isolation issue, 21–22
  social trends impact, 15–17
  societal stress from, 13
  stress and, 12, 14–15
  timid parents, unruly kids, 1–7
  trends impact, 15–17
Parentcenter.com, 6
Parentification, 157–58, 177–80, 186,
  198–99
Parenting style, 24–47
  authoritarian style, 27–29, 31, 34, 47
  authoritative vs. authoritarian, 34, 47
  Behaviorism school, 30
  child's temperament influence, 32
  culture, trends within, 29–31
  disengaged style, 38–39
  family life experience and, 33, 97–98
  Father Knows Best style, 16, 35–36
  fathers, 27–29, 147–48
  flexible style, 33–35, 39–41, 46–47,
    135, 163
  history of, 27–29
  inflexible style, 16, 35–36
  Medical Era of, 30
  Non-Western cultures and, 29
  permissive style, 16–17, 31, 36–38, 47
  personal experience influence, 31–33
  synergy of temperaments (spouses), 32
  See also Gender; Parenting style goals;
    Past influences; Temperament
Parenting style goals, 41–46
  age-appropriateness, 43–44, 44
  "bail-out" time, 46
  communication, honest and open, 42
  creativity encouragement, 45

  empathy for children, 42, 68, 71–72,
    133–34
  flexible parenting style, 33–35, 39–41,
    46–47
  independence encouragement, 46, 75
  listening to children, 41–42, 117, 132
  mistakes, admitting, 45
  positive reinforcement, 44–45, 65
  problem-solving, 43–44
  reactivity, avoiding, 43
  rule setting, 44, 65, 114, 176–77
  stress, counteracting, 46
  time-outs, 45
Passive vs. active participation, 205, 208,
  209
Past influences, 96–109
  blessings of the past, 100–103
  burdens of the past, 97–100
  coping methods, 103–8
  depressed at times of the year, 99
  depression from coping with, 107–8
  discipline experiences, 98
  expectations, 98
  fallibility of parenthood, 101
  family of origin, 33, 97–98
  healing wounds of, 108–9
  journaling, 104–5
  letter writing (coping method), 106
  overview, 220
  parents (yours), 98, 99
  psychotherapy, 103–4, 107
  resentment toward children's
    responses, 99, 101
  "rut," falling into, 99
  sibling experiences, 98
  tape recorders (coping method), 105
Peer pressure, coping with, 121
Perfectionism, 20, 143–45
Permissive parenting style, 16–17, 31,
  36–38, 47
Perrot, Michelle, 28–29
Personalities and temperament, 82
Physiological gender differences, 88
Positive reinforcement, 44–45, 65
Post, Emily, 30
Preschoolers, 55–59, 185–86
Preteenagers, 166, 186–87
Preventive vs. reactive attention, 61

Prioritization, 142–43
Privacy of children, respecting, 122
Psychological Care of Infant and Child (Watson), 30
Psychotherapy, 103–4, 107
Public property, damaging, 155
Punishment, 65, 121, 166–67

Reactivity, avoiding, 43
Redirecting behavior, 114–15
Reinforcement, positive, 44–45, 65
Relinquishing authority, 9–11
Resiliency gender differences, 88
Responsibility
    divorce, clarifying, 191–92
    parenting, accepting, 223–24
    relinquishing authority vs., 11–12
    values, teaching, 118
Restaurants, incivility, 152–54
Rewarding good behavior, 166–67
Role isolation, 21–22
Role-modeling. *See* Modeling appropriate behavior
Role playing to foster insights, 117
Rugrats, 160
Rules, 44, 65, 114, 176–77
"Rut," falling into, 99

Safe House-type programs, 176
Schlessinger, Laura, 16
School-age children, 60–62, 186
Self-control of children, 65, 113
Self-discipline from discipline, 50
Self-respect of children, 75–76
Sendak, Maurice, 54
Seneca, 27–28
Serotonin gender differences, 88
Simple pleasures, focusing on, 150
Simpsons, The, 160, 207
Single parents, latchkey dilemma, 180
Six Stages of Parenthood, The (Galinsky), 23, 83, 223
Social issues, 15–17, 88, 159–61
South Park, 160
Spock, Benjamin, 30, 31, 76–77
Spouses. *See* Communication between parents; Parental authority
Spousification from divorce, 197–200

Spy Kids, 208
Standards for children, 65, 164–65
Stereotypes (gender), 89–94
Stress
    conflict of children and, 73–76
    counteracting, 46
    flexible parenting for reducing, 40
    latchkey children, 170–71, 172
    parental authority dilemma, 12, 14–15
    Superparent syndrome and, 137
Superparent syndrome, 136–51
    balance, seeking, 147
    break, giving yourself a, 150–51
    delegation and, 149
    disorder, tolerating, 148–49
    expectations of parents, 145–46
    fathers, involved more, 147–48
    flaws, accepting, 145–46
    frustration from, 137
    imperfections, accepting, 145–46, 221
    marriage, making time for, 149–50
    mothers and husbands' contributions, 148
    perfectionism, avoiding, 20, 143–45
    positive, focusing on, 146
    simple pleasures, focusing on, 150
    stress from, 137
    support, reaching out for, 147–48
    See also Guilt
Synergy of temperaments (spouses), 32

Teenagers, 62–64, 118–22, 130–31, 166, 187
Temperament, 78–86
    assessment of, 18
    authority influenced by, 83, 84–85
    changes to, 82, 83, 85, 86
    features of, 81–82
    individuality of children, 79–81, 221–22
    inherent temperamental tendencies, 85
    interactivity of, 82–83
    judging children, 65, 67–68, 85
    Nature vs. Nurture, 80, 82, 89
    parenting style and, 31–32
    parent's and children's, 82–83
    personalities and, 82
    See also Gender

Thomas, Alexander, 81
Time-outs, 45, 58–59
Timid parents, unruly kids, 1–7
Toddlers, 53–54, 185
Trends and parental authority, 15–17
TV. *See* Media influence

Unconditional love, 113–14

Validating feelings. *See* Feelings of
    children, validating
Values, 110–22
    age-appropriate responsibilities, 116
    civility, need for, 120–21
    communication, maintaining open,
        122
    conscience role, 112–13
    delay gratification, 115
    disparity between parents, 111
    example setting, 119–20
    gender and parental values, 91
    guilt, using selectively, 115
    lecturing, avoiding, 120
    limit setting, 120
    listening to children, 41–42, 117, 132
    modeling, 118
    negotiation for conflict, 117–18

peer pressure, coping with, 121
persistence, teaching, 118
privacy, respecting, 122
punishment, thoughtful, 121
redirecting behavior, 114–15
responsibility, teaching, 118
role playing to foster insights, 117
rule simplicity, 114
schedule (consistent), 116
self-control and conscience, 65, 113
teenagers and values, 118–22
unconditional love, 113–14
See also Communication between
    parents; Communication with
    children
Veyne, Paul, 28
Video games. *See* Media influence
Viorst, Judith, 53–54

Watson, John B., 30
Where the Wild Things Are (Sendak), 54
"Why Our Kids Are Out of Control"
    (Azerrad), 6
Will, George, 160
Winnicott, D. W., 221
"Winning," letting children, 70
World, disengaging from, 205, 208